Riding into History

RIDING INTO HISTORY

THE SURPRISING STORY OF
SARAH KEYS EVANS
AND THE FIGHT TO DESEGREGATE
BUS TRAVEL

Amy Nathan with Sarah Keys Evans

DUKE UNIVERSITY PRESS
Durham and London

2026

Project Editor: Lisa Lawley
Designed by A. Mattson Gallagher
Typeset in Garamond Premier Pro, National 2 Narrow, and Trade Gothic LT Std by Westchester Publishing Services

Library of Congress Cataloging-in-Publication Data
Names: Nathan, Amy author | Evans, Sarah Keys author
Title: Riding into history: the surprising story of Sarah Keys Evans and the fight to desegregate bus travel / Amy Nathan, with Sarah Keys Evans.
Other titles: Surprising story of Sarah Keys Evans and the fight to desegregate bus travel
Description: Durham: Duke University Press, 2026. | Includes bibliographical references and index.
Identifiers: LCCN 2025028054 (print)
LCCN 2025028055 (ebook)
ISBN 9781478033165 paperback
ISBN 9781478029717 hardcover
ISBN 9781478061922 ebook
Subjects: LCSH: Evans, Sarah Keys | United States. Army. Women's Army Corps—Biography | Segregation in transportation—North Carolina—History—20th century—Biography | African Americans—Civil rights—North Carolina—History—20th century—Biography | Race discrimination—United States—History—20th century | Women soldiers—United States—Biography | African American women civil rights workers—Biography | Civil rights workers, Black—Biography | LCGFT: Biographies
Classification: LCC F260.42.E93 N384 2026 (print) | LCC F260.42.E93 (ebook) | DDC 323.092 [B]—dc23/eng/20251117
LC record available at https://lccn.loc.gov/2025028054
LC ebook record available at https://lccn.loc.gov/2025028055

Cover art: Private First Class Sarah Keys in her Women's Army Corps dress uniform in the early 1950s. Courtesy Sarah Keys Evans.

publication supported by a grant from
The Community Foundation for Greater New Haven
as part of the URBAN NEW HAVEN PROJECT

To Sarah Keys Evans and her sisters, nieces,
and nephews, and their grandchildren

Contents

Author's Note

In early chapters on her childhood and civil rights efforts, the text refers to Sarah mainly as Sarah Keys. In later chapters, after her marriage, the text refers to her as Sarah Keys Evans.

Preface

I first learned about Sarah Keys Evans in 2001 when I saw a plaque about her at the Military Women's Memorial, located at the entrance to Arlington National Cemetery. I was a history major in college and was doing research at the memorial for a book for young people on the history of women in the US military, to be published by National Geographic. But I had never heard of Sarah Keys Evans or her role in civil rights history.

After the National Geographic book went into production, I asked the memorial staff if they could help me contact Sarah Keys Evans. They kindly put me in touch with her. I wrote her to ask if she would be willing to speak with me about working together to create a book that would tell young readers about her. She graciously agreed. I phoned her on January 20, 2004, for the first of many conversations we had over more than nineteen years as part of a long collaboration and friendship.

She made it clear during our first phone call that she valued accuracy. When I asked if I could record our conversation, she replied, "Yes. Would you let me in on what you type?" I promised to send her a transcript. "I would appreciate that," she said. "I have been promised tapes before but never received them." We spoke for hours that day and on several subsequent days. I sent her the interview transcripts, which met with her approval.

A reserved and private person, Sarah seemed to appreciate the chance to describe her life in detail to a willing and interested listener who agreed with her on the importance of accuracy. She gladly answered my many questions about her military service and her life growing up in Washington, North Carolina. I then interviewed members of her family, who were also gracious about describing the impact on their lives of what she had done. I did research to learn more about her civil rights experience, reading news articles and a 1983 book by Catherine Barnes, *Journey from Jim Crow*, published by Columbia University Press. I was shocked that no other major books on civil rights history mentioned her. That made it all the more important to right that wrong, at least with a book that could inspire young people. We collaborated in creating *Take a Seat—Make a Stand*, published in 2006, which was reviewed positively in the *Washington Post*. We shared equally in the book's royalties.

We continued to stay in touch, getting together a few times to have lunch in Brooklyn, New York, where she lived. That gave her a chance to tell me more about her life's journey. I attended several events in the New York area where she was honored, meeting her family members there. In two books I wrote for adults and teens on other civil rights events, I mention her briefly. She arranged for two of her young cousins to appear on the cover of my 2011 book about Baltimore civil rights history. I also wrote about her in an online teachers' forum and helped a Black history magazine publish an article about her. In addition, Sarah and I did a joint radio interview for New York's NPR station in 2011.

But it wasn't until we both received a surprising email in 2013 that we began collaborating on an account of her life story for an adult audience. That email came from a young man in Roanoke Rapids, North Carolina, where her civil rights journey began in 1952. He had just learned about her and asked for our help in finding a way for his city to honor her. That launched a series of events that led to Roanoke Rapids doing that in 2020, with Sarah and I both helping to make the recognition happen. We restarted our phone interviews to create the book you're reading now. She shared more aspects of her life, spurred no doubt by being acknowledged and appreciated by the people of Roanoke Rapids. This new book also includes extensive research to place her civil rights role in its rightful place as an important part of history that deserves to be remembered and explored, helping with the still unfinished work of putting an end to racial injustice.

Sarah Keys Evans did not live to see this book completed. But before her death in 2023 at age ninety-four, she knew it was on its way. She had read an early version of this book, which strives for accuracy and a touch of inspiration, as she would have wished.

1

Leading the Way

THREE YEARS BEFORE ROSA PARKS WAS ARRESTED for refusing to move to the back of a city bus in Alabama, another young Black woman, Sarah Keys, led the way with a similar act of courage. Shortly after midnight on a hot summer night in 1952, a bus she had boarded many hours earlier in New Jersey stopped at a lonely bus station in the small North Carolina city of Roanoke Rapids.

Just twenty-three years old, she was traveling by herself. A member of the Women's Army Corps, she was wearing its "dress uniform," a signal that this young woman had stepped up to help her country while it was engaged in a war in Korea.

A new driver took charge of the bus in Roanoke Rapids and ordered Sarah to move to the rear so a white Marine could have her seat. She told the driver she was fine sitting where she was. No one stepped up to defend her when police officers took her to jail. She spent the night locked up all alone in a filthy jail cell, not knowing what might happen next.[1]

Her bravery that night is not well known. Nor is the effort that Sarah Keys made to win justice, with help and support from her father, David Artis Keys Sr., and from a young Black woman lawyer, Dovey Johnson Roundtree, arguing her first big case.[2]

1.1 Sarah Louise Keys in the early 1950s in her Women's Army Corps dress uniform. Courtesy Sarah Keys Evans.

Before her arrest, this small-town North Carolina girl had never been part of a civil rights protest, yet she wound up making civil rights legal history. She and the lawyers who supported her played an important role in the long struggle to end transportation segregation.

This book weaves together many stories. One thread presents the courage of young Sarah Keys, who was determined to seek justice as a "matter of moral principle,"[3] as she framed it, to redress an attack on her personal integrity that also demeaned the dignity of the Women's Army Corps. Scenes from her life as she was growing up in Washington, North Carolina, show how the strength she gained from her family gave her the self-confidence to stand up for fairness. That inner strength also helped her deal with the lasting emotional impact that her brush with injustice had on her long life. Her quiet courage as a young woman, combined with the dignified way she continued on throughout her life journey, would help bring people together, including in the city where her personal fight against injustice began. A monument honoring her was installed in Roanoke Rapids, North Carolina, in 2020, signaling a significant change of heart by local officials there in the intervening decades.[4]

Not a standard biography, this book positions the story of this overlooked hero as part of the history she helped create. Historical and legal overviews from the early 1800s onward help frame her stand for fairness within the decades-long battle waged by many others against various forms of racially discriminatory segregation, known colloquially as "Jim Crow" segregation. This derogatory term sprang from the title of a song performed in nineteenth-century minstrel shows that was as insulting as the restrictions imposed on people of color by the segregation rules and laws that would come to be referred to by the song's name. Titled "Jump Jim Crow," the song depicted Black men as crude buffoons and was sung by white minstrel show performers who blackened their faces with burnt cork. Segregation—whether called Jim Crow or not—severely restricted the life of Sarah Keys Evans (her name after her marriage in 1958) both before and after she took her history-making bus ride.[5]

This book's legal overviews also describe the creative arguments and use of precedent that Sarah's lawyers marshaled as they tried to achieve a decisive victory for her, an achievement that had eluded so many others in earlier years who had also faced discrimination on public transportation. In addition, the book presents several attention-getting protest strategies used by others that helped widen the impact of Sarah's quest for justice, illustrating the slow, step-by-step path often required to achieve significant social change.[6]

The book's appendix includes brief accounts of some of the many other heroes who took stands against transportation segregation from the mid-nineteenth century onward. These warriors stood up for fairness when success was unlikely and have often been overlooked in history books, as Sarah Keys Evans was for so long.

Many foot soldiers played a role in helping to eventually put an official end to transportation injustice. One was an actual soldier, Private First Class Sarah Louise Keys.

2

A Glimmer of Hope

EARLY ON AUGUST 1, 1952, SARAH LOUISE KEYS put on her army uniform and checked herself in the mirror. "When we traveled, we always made sure we were well-groomed, well-polished," she explained, describing that historic day many years later. "You traveled in a 'dress uniform,' in heels—at least one and one-and-half-inch heels. You had a lot of pride in your dress and your uniform."[1]

Sarah had two weeks off from her job at the US Army hospital at Fort Dix, New Jersey, and was going to take a long bus ride home to visit her family in North Carolina. "I was so happy about it," recalled Sarah. This was her first trip home since joining the Women's Army Corps (WAC) in the fall of 1951.[2]

It would take all day and all night to reach her hometown, Washington, North Carolina, in the southeast part of the state. But she didn't mind. She was eager to see her parents, grandparents, younger sisters, and youngest brother. They were eager to see her, too, especially now that she was Private First Class Sarah Louise Keys.

Two of her brothers wouldn't be there to greet her because they were stationed in Korea, part of the US military effort there. One brother was in the army; the other, in the air force. Women soldiers in the army weren't allowed to fight in wartime battles yet. Sarah had joined the WAC to help in other ways. At the army hospital where she worked as a receptionist, her role was to offer support for injured soldiers and their families.[3]

But Sarah soon found herself in the middle of a significant battle on that bus ride home. It was dangerous. She had to think fast to survive. The only weapons she had to defend herself were her abilities to stay calm, remain focused, and be courageous.

Private First Class Keys wasn't thinking about playing a part in civil rights history when she boarded the bus in Trenton, New Jersey, that morning. She was planning to sleep during most of the ride home. "I could fall asleep in a jiffy," she recalled. She had taken a few long bus rides back home since she had moved away four years earlier, right after graduating from high school. She had lived first in New Jersey and then in New York City before signing up with the WAC in 1951. She had not run into any trouble on those earlier trips. She expected to have no trouble on this one either. "I found that midway on the bus was always the most comfortable," she explained. She found a window seat halfway down the aisle and soon fell asleep as the bus rolled through New Jersey and then headed south.[4]

To Sarah, there was nothing wrong or dangerous about sitting in the middle of the bus because of a new travel development that happened while she was in high school. A US Supreme Court decision in 1946—*Morgan v. Virginia*—said that on bus trips which started in one state and went to another state, Black travelers could sit anywhere they wanted. The court ruled that local state segregation legislation did not apply to interstate passengers.[5]

That 1946 court decision received enthusiastic coverage in Black newspapers. "My father had told us about that," Sarah recalled. "He had read about the *Morgan* case. My father was an ardent reader [of] all the weekly papers on weekends." He often shared stories with her as they sat together on the porch on Sunday afternoons at their North Carolina farm. Before she left home in 1948, moving north to New Jersey shortly after her high school graduation, she definitely knew about the *Morgan* case. She recalled later that her father had advised her: "'When you board a bus from the North, you can sit any place.'"[6]

Before the *Morgan* decision, Black bus passengers often had to change seats during a state-to-state bus trip, depending on the laws of the states through which the bus was traveling. In 1951, eleven states had segregation laws that stipulated where Black and white passengers could sit on buses, according to a book by North Carolina–born civil rights lawyer Pauli Murray: Oklahoma, Virginia, North Carolina, and all the other states that had been members of the Confederacy during the Civil War, except Tennessee, which had segregated seating laws only for streetcars and trains. However, a report from the historically Black Tennessee State University notes that the "customs" in Nashville in the 1950s called for separating Black and white riders on buses, too. New Jersey and other Northern states had no segregation laws for buses during the 1950s, although in earlier years segregation did occur in Northern states on buses, railroads, and streetcars, too—often not because of official laws but instead because of transportation company policies, common practice, or the whim of the driver or conductor. On trips that started in the North and were headed south, some bus companies would (as late as the 1930s) direct Black customers who boarded in Chicago or New York City to take seats in the back of the bus to avoid the hassle of changing seats once the bus rolled into a Southern state. The same often occurred on southbound train trips. Miles before the train entered states whose laws required segregated seating, Black passengers boarding in New York City, Chicago, or Los Angeles would be directed to the Jim Crow car, as the car for Black riders was called. To avoid the seating choice issue, bus drivers on some long-distance bus trips would let white passengers enter the bus first, allowing them to sit in the front, leaving seats in the rear for Black travelers. If white riders filled all the seats, Black passengers would then have to wait for the next bus.[7]

Virginia's bus-seating law was particularly complicated and could cause a lot of seat-moving during a trip. The state's transportation segregation legislation, as revised in 1942, specifically forbade Black and white travelers from sitting next to each other in "contiguous" or adjoining seats. Over the course of a trip, as a bus picked up additional passengers at each stop, Black passengers might have to keep changing seats to avoid sitting too close to a newly arrived white traveler. On an interstate trip, this seat-changing could slow down a trip and irritate travelers—white as well as Black—when Black passengers and their luggage had to move around the bus to make the required seating changes.[8]

Segregation like this on public transportation, whether on trains or buses, was an especially distressing and humiliating form of discrimination, as the scholar W. E. B. Du Bois noted in several articles, including this comment in a 1920 piece for the *New Republic*: "There is not in the world a more disgraceful denial of human brotherhood than the 'Jim-Crow' car of the southern United States." He seconded that opinion decades later in a 1948 article for *Phylon*, a journal he started at Atlanta University:

"Probably no phase of discrimination has irked the American Negro more than the so-called 'Jim Crow' cars for travel, because of its publicly insulting character." The same opinion held true for segregated seating on buses. In 1909, Du Bois helped to found a new civil rights organization, the NAACP (National Association for the Advancement of Colored People).[9]

It was the NAACP that pointed out to the US Supreme Court that letting individual states use their own state laws to require seat-changing during interstate travel violated the first section of the US Constitution—Article I, Section 8. That section contains the Commerce Clause, which says, "The Congress shall have the power to . . . regulate Commerce with foreign Nations, and among the several States."[10] Thus, only the US Congress had the right to make laws about seating requirements for companies that did business with various US states, including transportation companies engaged in state-to-state travel. The Commerce Clause would suggest that because the US Congress had not established seating requirements for state-to-state bus travel, Virginia, on its own and without congressional approval, did not have the right to impose its bus-seating law on travelers whose trips would also pass through states that didn't have such laws.

Lawyers with the NAACP made that point at the US Supreme Court in 1946. They were representing Irene Morgan, a young Black woman from Baltimore, Maryland, who worked at a defense plant that produced military aircraft. She had been arrested in 1944 during a bus trip that would have taken her back home to Maryland after a visit with family in Virginia. She knew about the Virginia bus-seating law and chose her original seat carefully. For the first part of the trip, there were no empty seats. Another young Black woman sitting at the back of the bus offered to share her seat with Irene Morgan.

At the next stop, Morgan took the seat of a passenger who got off the bus, making sure it didn't place her next to a white passenger. When additional white passengers boarded the bus, the driver ordered her to give her seat to a newly arrived white traveler. Losing that seat meant she would probably have to stand for the rest of the trip. She had recently suffered a miscarriage and thought standing for a long time would be difficult. She refused to move. An argument ensued. The driver called the local sheriff. Two deputies were dispatched and they dragged her, kicking and protesting, off the bus.

Irene Morgan was arrested and taken to jail. After her mother posted bail, Morgan pleaded guilty to a charge of disorderly conduct, but not to the charge of violating Virginia's Jim Crow seating law. She wanted to appeal that charge and contacted the local branch of the NAACP for help.

The NAACP had become increasingly concerned about the growing number of problems Black travelers were having with bus segregation in the 1930s and '40s, especially on overcrowded buses, in both the North and South. There had been a shocking series of arrests, beatings, and even killings, including of Black soldiers and sailors in uniform, who frequently traveled by bus during World War II to get to their training bases or to return home. During those years, many military bases were located in the South, and conflicts could arise over local bus segregation practices, particularly for soldiers from other parts of the country who weren't used to obeying Jim Crow rules. The NAACP didn't have the resources at that time to mount legal cases for all of those incidents. Its lawyers kept looking for a case that would be strong and clear enough in its unfairness that they could take it all the way to the US Supreme Court to try to put an end to transportation segregation altogether. They thought they'd found it with Irene Morgan's determination to challenge her 1944 arrest.

Her experience offered a clear example of the inconvenience that using different seating rules could pose for an interstate bus ride. Once the bus crossed into Washington, DC, which had no segregation seating law, she could have legally sat in any seat, both while the bus was in DC and for the rest of her journey to Maryland. Citing the Commerce Clause, NAACP lawyers appealed her arrest, first in a Virginia court, where they failed to win. Then they appealed that decision to the US Supreme Court, where they were successful.[11]

Justice Stanley Reed, in delivering the Supreme Court's opinion in *Morgan v. Virginia*, noted that "eighteen states, it appears, prohibit racial separation on public carriers." Given the complexity of Virginia's bus-seating law, he observed that, because of that law, "an interstate passenger must, if necessary, repeatedly shift seats while moving in Virginia to meet the seating requirements of the changing passenger group," an experience that he added "would be disturbing." A majority of the court's other justices agreed with the decision he issued, in which he said, "State legislation is invalid if it unduly burdens interstate commerce where uniformity is necessary. . . . Seating arrangements for the different races in interstate motor travel require a single uniform rule to promote and protect national travel."[12]

This was the first case involving transportation segregation that NAACP lawyers argued at the US Supreme Court. The *Morgan* decision affected only interstate travel and changed nothing for local bus trips. Even so, this victory gave Black travelers hope that at least state-to-state travel would go well. Unfortunately, that was not the case on the trip Sarah Keys took in the summer of 1952.[13]

Transportation Segregation: The Early Years

Buses were a relatively new form of interstate travel, having started in the 1920s, about twenty-five years before Irene Morgan's Virginia-to-Maryland trip. But seating passengers separately depending on skin color had been a central part of earlier forms of public transportation for generations, in both North and South. Mid-1800s Massachusetts may have been the first place where the words "Jim Crow" were used in connection with transportation segregation, serving as a name for the low-quality train car that Black passengers were forced to use.

The Jim Crow car was generally smaller than other cars on the train, sometimes windowless, with no plush upholstery to soften the seats. Rarely cleaned, it was a cramped, smelly space, which in addition to holding Black passengers was also a kind of "break room" for white crew members and other white men, who often smoked and spat tobacco juice on seats and floor, a detention space where sheriffs sat with white or Black convicts they were transporting, and a holding tank where white men too drunk to ride in a whites-only car were placed. Luggage from white travelers in other cars was often stored in the Jim Crow car, along with farm animals at times. The car was generally placed directly behind the engine to keep the smell of engine fumes from bothering white travelers. Jim Crow cars were made of wood, including well into the early 1900s, when other cars began to be made of metal. In crashes, the wooden Jim Crow car would crumble easily and even catch fire, resulting in deaths of Black travelers. It wasn't until the 1950s that these wooden cars were replaced with sturdier metal ones.[14]

Frederick Douglass wrote in his memoir about his first encounters with a Jim Crow car in 1841, three years after he had fled from slavery in Maryland. Twice that year he was ejected from a first-class train car in Lynn, Massachusetts, and forced to ride in the Jim Crow car, which he described as "mean, dirty, and uncomfortable."[15] On his second ejection, he grabbed his seat so tightly that the six white men who dragged him out of the train pulled out the seat along with him. He wrote from personal experience that the public humiliation of transportation segregation "has a sting for the soul hardly less severe than that which bites the flesh and draws the blood from the back of the plantation slave."[16]

A local newspaper expressed support for Douglass. Protests about others who were similarly mistreated led to the end of train segregation in Massachusetts two years later, in 1843. The state didn't succeed in passing a law to specifically outlaw train segregation, although the state's 1780 constitution stated that "all men are born free and equal." That constitution made no distinctions in rights for individuals based on color, a point that Massachusetts abolitionists cited in calling for equal rights for all. When the legislature failed to pass a law banning train segregation, abolitionist legislators threatened the railroads that they would lose their state charters unless they ended segregation. Railway companies gave in and discontinued segregated seating. However, in other states, the dirty, cramped Jim Crow cars continued to roll.[17]

Long before the railroad era, segregation had placed limits on Black travelers in other forms of transportation, such as when stagecoach drivers either refused to transport Black passengers or made them sit on the outside of the coach. A similar insult occurred on steamboats, where Black travelers had to stay outside on the boat's deck instead of in rooms indoors. On horse-drawn streetcars, Black riders were often forced to stand on the cars' dangerous outside platforms or ride only in cars designated for Black passengers.[18]

That kind of streetcar policy led to one of the first major campaigns against transportation segregation, when Elizabeth Jennings, a schoolteacher and church organist, was on her way to church on July 16, 1854. She was forcibly removed from a New York City horse-drawn streetcar for white riders when she refused to obey the conductor's order that she get off the car and wait for a car for Black riders. She had traveled on streetcars for white riders earlier with no trouble because some drivers allowed Black travelers to stay onboard if white passengers didn't object. When the conductor on this trip tried to pull her off the car, Jennings grabbed the window frame so tightly that he had to call on the car's driver to tie up his horses and help him drag her across the platform. When that too failed, the conductor hailed a police officer, who roughly threw her onto the ground "and tauntingly told me to get redress if I could," as she wrote in an account of her ordeal. That account was read aloud on Jennings's behalf during a protest at her church the next day, while she was recovering at home from her injuries.[19]

Her father, Thomas Jennings, encouraged her to sue the streetcar company, a parallel to what would happen a hundred years later with Sarah

Keys and her father. Elizabeth Jennings won a settlement of $225. The judge told the jury that streetcars are "common carriers, and as such bound to carry all respectable persons; that colored persons, if sober, well-behaved, and free from disease, had the same rights as others; and could neither be excluded by any rules of the Company, nor by force or violence."[20]

The term *common carrier* comes from common law, which is based not on specific legislation but on previous judicial decisions. The US judicial system initially used English common law because in the country's early days it didn't have many previous decisions to guide a judge. Those common-law precedents had established the principle that common carriers, such as streetcars or trains, had to carry all who paid the required fee.[21]

Although the court's decision for Elizabeth Jennings banned segregation on the streetcar line that mistreated her, it didn't affect the city's other streetcar companies. Her father helped create the Legal Rights Association to encourage other Black New Yorkers to board streetcars for white riders, with the risk of being arrested if necessary, and then file lawsuits to win a wider victory. Many participated in this early form of nonviolent civil disobedience, a strategy that would be used a century later to widen the impact of Sarah Keys's legal decision.

It took ten years, however, for that strategy to wind up ending segregation on all New York City streetcars. The 1864 victory in New York City came thanks to another courageous Black woman, Ellen Anderson, the widow of a Black soldier who had died fighting with Union forces in South Carolina during the Civil War. When she was ejected from an Eighth Avenue streetcar, her lawyer sued the police officer who arrested her, not the streetcar company. The head of the Board of Police Commissioners sided with Anderson, criticizing the arresting officer, saying he should have instead "arrested the conductor," not Anderson. Publicity about this ruling and reprimand was bad news for New York City's other streetcar companies, leading to all the city's streetcar lines dropping their segregation rules. Later, in 1873, this kind of transportation segregation became illegal in the whole state of New York when it was one of the first states to pass a law banning railroad and streetcar segregation.

News reports about Elizabeth Jennings appeared in Black newspapers around the country, sparking others to take similar action in Pennsylvania, California, Washington, DC, and elsewhere. Some of those early heroes are profiled in this book's appendix, as are others who opposed transportation injustice in later years but whose stories are also not widely remembered.[22]

A Brief Upswing

After the Civil War ended in April 1865, there was a hope-filled period when many thought racial segregation in transportation might become a thing of the past. New amendments to the US Constitution suggested a fresh beginning. The Thirteenth Amendment (1865) abolished slavery, and the Fourteenth (1868) said that people born or naturalized in the United States were citizens, which by inference would include Black people who had been denied rights before the war, whether they were enslaved or free. The Fourteenth Amendment also said no state shall "deprive any person of life, liberty, or property, without due process of law." The Fifteenth Amendment (1870) made it illegal to deny citizens the right to vote "on account of race, color, or previous condition of servitude."

Those amendments were needed because as soon as the Civil War ended, white Southerners devised ways to continue the prewar social and economic system by passing Black Codes, which, as Du Bois noted in his book on the history of that era, made Black people "slaves in everything but name." The Black Codes denied Black people the right to vote and included strict vagrancy laws that called for the arrest of any Black person who could not prove employment. The punishment could even involve being signed up to work for white employers without pay. In some states, the Black Codes also continued prewar transportation segregation rules for trains and streetcars.[23]

Outrage over the Black Codes among Republican lawmakers in the US Congress led to the passage of the Civil Rights Act of 1866, which made these Black Codes illegal. The ratification of the Fourteenth Amendment solidified the federal government's official commitment to equal rights for Black citizens. Black communities in some areas of the South then stepped up to try to personally undo a particularly demeaning everyday example of public insult and discrimination: streetcar segregation. In New Orleans, after William Nicholls was arrested in 1867 for sitting in a mule-drawn streetcar for white passengers, spontaneous examples of civil disobedience burst out around the city for several days. Other Black riders boldly took seats in whites-only streetcars, creating such a disturbance that streetcar companies decided to end their separate car policies. Similar Black sit-in type protests—along with legal action in some cases—succeeded in ending streetcar segregation in other Southern cities, including in Richmond, Virginia; Charleston, South Carolina; Mobile, Alabama; Savannah, Georgia; Nashville, Tennessee; Baltimore, Maryland; and Washington, DC. For more than thirty years streetcar segregation disappeared in some parts of the South.[24]

In the same year of Nicholls's arrest, 1867, additional avenues for change seemed possible when Congress passed the Reconstruction Act. It divided the South into five military districts, with federal troops stationed in each district to preserve order and help guarantee fairness for Black citizens. Southern states were also required to write new state constitutions to be approved by a majority of local voters. Those voters had to include Black men. As a result, some Black legislators were elected to office. Reconstruction-era constitutions in Mississippi and Louisiana called for equal access for all on public transportation. So did new laws passed by South Carolina, Georgia, Florida, Mississippi, Louisiana, Texas, and Arkansas between 1868 and 1873, according to Catherine Barnes's book *Journey from Jim Crow*. Then, in 1875, the US Congress tried to expand rights for Black citizens nationwide when it passed the Civil Rights Act of 1875. It called for equal treatment for all "citizens of every race and color" on public transportation as well as in theaters, inns, and other facilities open to the public.

Some states did a good job of enforcing their new transportation laws. Others did not, and some transportation companies did not abide by the new laws. In 1869, Louisiana passed a law making transportation segregation illegal. That same year, Oscar Dunn, a Black equal rights activist, had just been elected the state's lieutenant governor. Even so, he was unable to book a first-class seat with the local train company, which was owned by a former Confederate general. Instead, Lieutenant Governor Dunn had to sit in the train's poorly equipped Jim Crow car, with no comfortable place to sleep during the first leg of his long journey to Washington, DC, where he met with President Ulysses S. Grant and US senators to lobby for more anti-discrimination efforts.[25]

Oscar Dunn didn't lodge an official complaint against the railroad, but several Black women in other states did when they faced unfair treatment on trains. They had not intended to be equal rights activists when they paid extra for first-class tickets so they could ride in a first-class ladies car. They thought this was a reasonable thing to do because of the new constitutional amendments and equal rights laws some states had passed. Ladies cars were outfitted more comfortably than other cars, with no smoking allowed. These cars had been created for women traveling alone, or with a male escort, to protect women from dealing with male strangers. But as these Black women discovered, some train companies seemed to feel that only white women were "ladies" who deserved protection.

Legal scholar Barbara Y. Welke discovered court documents for twenty-four lawsuits filed by Black women who were denied access to ladies cars from 1865 to 1890, in Southern states and in Illinois, Ohio, and Pennsylvania as well. She also discovered five lawsuits filed by Black men who had bought first-class tickets and felt that entitled them to first-class seating. About half of the women's lawsuits resulted in positive verdicts, but there were few wins for the men. Welke suggested that a Black woman requesting to be regarded as a lady was perhaps less threatening to the system of segregation than allowing a Black man to pay for better seating and sit with white passengers.[26]

Some Black women were badly injured when they were prevented from sitting in a ladies car. That happened to Catherine (Kate) Brown in 1868. She took a day trip to Alexandria, Virginia, from Washington, DC, where she worked for the US Senate as the lead attendant for the "ladies retiring room," which most likely involved distributing towels and being helpful to white women visiting the Senate. She bought first-class tickets and sat in the ladies car from DC to Virginia. On the way back, the railroad's private police officer dragged her out of the ladies car in Alexandria, pulling her by the neck, injuring her shoulder and elbow, and also causing internal injuries because she refused to go willingly. "I had made up my mind not to leave the car, unless they brought me off dead," she said, as Kate Masur reports in her book on the history of the effort in Washington, DC, to win equal rights. A DC newspaper wrote about the "outrage" Kate Brown experienced. A Senate committee investigated. She sued the railroad company, which had an 1863 charter from the US Senate that prohibited segregation. A DC court ruled in her favor and awarded her $1,500.

The railroad company appealed the decision, noting that it had separate and identical cars for Black and white travelers. Kate Brown won at the US Supreme Court in 1873. Its decision, delivered by Justice David Davis, said that the railroad's use of the "separate but equal" argument was "an ingenious attempt to evade compliance with the obvious meaning" of the railroad's charter. Justice Davis added that Congress had issued a charter to the railroad company "in the belief that . . . discrimination must cease and the colored and white race, in the use of the cars, be placed on an equality."[27]

In a few ladies car cases, conductors questioned a Black woman's virtue when denying her access to the ladies car. That happened in Tennessee in 1879 when Sallie Robinson was traveling with her lighter-skinned nephew. The conductor blocked them from the ladies car because he thought the nephew was a white man traveling with a prostitute.

Lola Houck had an especially tragic experience trying to ride in a ladies car when, although visibly pregnant, she was prevented from entering that car on a train trip in Texas in 1886. Instead, she spent the ninety-mile trip standing on the platform between cars and later suffered a miscarriage. She sued the railroad company and in 1888 won a $7,500 settlement from a Texas circuit court, which was reduced on appeal to $2,500. The court ruled that although laws may require train segregation, Black passengers who buy first-class tickets must have cars comparable to those for white first-class passengers.[28]

The "law" that judges used to reach decisions in these ladies car cases "was not statutory or constitutional law," as Barbara Welke noted, "but the common law of carriers." A judge had made that point quite clearly in an earlier 1882 lawsuit that involved Selina Gray, who had been traveling with her husband in Ohio. A federal district court judge, D. J. Swing, ruled in her case that railroads "may have the right to make a regulation that the gentlemen shall ride in one car, and the ladies shall ride in another car" and also "perhaps have a right (which it is not now necessary to determine) that the colored people shall ride in another car." But he felt that this didn't give the railroads the right to have unequal facilities. He instructed the jury that under common law for common carriers, the train company needed "to provide for this colored woman precisely such accommodation in every respect as were provided upon their trains for white women."[29]

Other judges reached similar common law–based conclusions in these cases, which might seem like a positive step forward for supporters of equal rights. But for segregationists, those common law–focused rulings meant trouble, suggesting that in future court cases, judges might require open seating for everyone on all cars, not just in ladies cars. That prompted pro-segregation legislators to devise new legal maneuvers to guarantee a future for racially separate cars. As Welke noted, "denying respectable women of color status as ladies barred all blacks—men and women—from the world of respectability. Both processes—the denial of political and social rights to blacks—were essential to re-establishing the pre-Civil War racial and social status quo in the American South."[30]

Rise of Separate but Equal

By 1882, when the Selina Gray case was decided, Reconstruction had come to an end, federal troops having been removed from the South in 1877. Without federal oversight, the white officials who gradually took control in Southern states had the opportunity to restore the white dominance and strict racial separation that had existed before Reconstruction. They began to pass laws that would give judges something besides common law to use in deciding train segregation cases.

Instead of having a train car with the ambiguous name "ladies car," which could be interpreted as being a car for both Black and white "ladies," Southern lawmakers began to pass laws that required totally separate cars in all situations. Some cars would be only for white passengers, and others would accommodate Black passengers. Those separate car laws would claim to adhere to the basic premise cited in the Selina Gray case, that people who paid the same for their tickets should have the same "accommodation in every respect." That's the premise stated in the first of these new transportation segregation laws. Tennessee was the trendsetter with its 1881 separate car law. Tennessee had passed another law earlier, in 1875, claiming that common law no longer applied in the state in connection with public transportation and public accommodations, as a way to try to sidestep any future rulings on segregation that might cite common law.

Then, with its new 1881 train segregation law, Tennessee made sure that in any future lawsuits about segregation on trains traveling within the state, a judge would have a specific segregation law to refer to. The judge could then simply rule on whether the state's separate car law was being adhered to correctly by keeping train cars racially separate, rather than referring to common law, which might suggest other possibilities, such as requiring that Black and white passengers be seated together. The text of Tennessee's 1881 separate car law said railroads had to "furnish separate cars, or portions of cars cut off by partition walls, in which all colored passengers who shall pay first-class rates of fare, may have the privilege to enter and occupy." The law also said that the separate cars for Black passenger needed to "have the same conveniences" as the separate cars for white passengers.[31]

In 1891, Tennessee revised this separate car law to apply to racially separate train cars for all passengers, not just for those in first class. First-class train cars created and managed by railroad companies became a thing of the past. Black passengers could no longer try to escape the indignity of the Jim Crow car by paying a higher fare to ride in a railroad's first-class car or in its ladies car. From then on, all passengers in Tennessee, Black and white, would pay the same fare to travel in the railroad's racially separate train cars. White passengers would ride in what would be considered a regular train car. Black travelers would be consigned to what had long been known as Jim Crow car, and which continued to live up to its decades-long reputation as a dirty, crowded, and unpleasant space, a place often without enough seats for paying Black customers, who would then have to stand. A reporter for the *Chattanooga Observer* tried out the two types of train car options available after the 1891 Tennessee train law update, noting that one train car "is a cattle pen, the other is a car."[32]

By 1885, Alabama had also converted to a separate-but-equal train cars policy, allowing railroads to charge the same railroad fare for both Black and white train passengers to travel in racially segregated train cars, calling all its cars "first-class." In 1888, Mississippi no longer mentioned "first class" when it allowed train companies to charge the same rate for the railroad's only option: separate train cars for white and Black riders. By 1904, all Southern states' railroads were offering only segregated train cars, forcing Black travelers to pay the same fare as white riders for what was clearly an inferior travel experience. In 1905, the Niagara Movement, a precursor of the NAACP, included a protest in its Declaration of Principles criticizing Black train travelers having to "pay first-class for third-class accommodations." Other groups also protested, but none were able to force Southern states to change their new railroad policies.[33]

There was an option, however, available to very wealthy Black travelers to try to avoid the Jim Crow car. They could try to book tickets for a space on a luxurious Pullman sleeper car, owned and operated by the Pullman Palace Car Company. Since 1867, it had been providing its sleepers to railroad companies to add to the other cars that the railroad was pulling along its routes. The railroad companies had no control over the Pullman cars. To book a Pullman sleeper, a passenger would pay the basic fare the railroad charged for its other cars, along with an extra charge that would go to the Pullman company. Historian Mia Bay, in her book *Traveling Black*, estimates that the Pullman surcharge averaged from 30 to 70 percent of a railroad's base ticket price.

It was often hard, however, even for wealthy Black customers to book a Pullman reservation. From 1893 to 1907, four Southern states—Georgia, Arkansas, Texas, and Oklahoma—passed laws stating that sleeper cars could serve either Black or white customers but not both at the same time. In addition, ticket agents often claimed that the Pullman cars were already full when a Black customer tried to make a reservation, leading some to use subterfuge to book a space on a sleeper, claiming to be booking a ticket for someone else or having a white friend make the reservation. Pullman staff tried to keep Black customers who succeeded in booking Pullman tickets from interacting with white customers and would not serve Black customers in the dining area while white Pullman riders were eating. Black Pullman customers could also be forced to move to the Jim Crow car when a train entered one of the states that outlawed sleeper cars with both Black and white riders, which led to a court case that later had an impact for Sarah Keys Evans's quest for justice.[34]

Waning Federal Support

It wasn't only state governments that were curtailing Black rights. The US Supreme Court had also begun to turn its back on fair treatment for all. In 1876 and 1883, the US Supreme Court eliminated an option that many hoped could be used in equal rights cases: the Fourteenth Amendment, which had been ratified in 1868, with its call for "equal protection of the law" for all.

In 1876, the US Supreme Court noted that the Fourteenth Amendment didn't actually give the federal government the right to create laws about how individual citizens should behave. Only state governments could do that, because of the use of the word *state* in the amendment, which says, as noted earlier, that "no state shall make or enforce any law which shall abridge the privileges or immunities of citizens . . . nor shall any state deprive any person of life, liberty, or property, without due process of law." The Fourteenth Amendment didn't specifically mention a role for the federal government in making laws to protect citizens' rights.

The court showed its support for that view of the Fourteenth Amendment during its deliberations on the 1876 case *United States v. Cruikshank*. This case involved a law Congress had passed, the Enforcement Act, to prevent groups like the Ku Klux Klan from terrorizing Black communities; the court case focused on a massacre of Black citizens in Colfax, Louisiana, in 1873. The Supreme Court noted in its official discussions on the case that the federal government had no right to punish people who broke that anti-Klan law because the Fourteenth Amendment didn't give the US Congress the right to pass such a law. Only states could pass laws regulating individual citizens' behavior. The court then decided not to find the white perpetrators of the Colfax Massacre guilty, claiming that this decision resulted in part because the case materials were not well written. The perpetrators were allowed to go free.[35] Historian Eric Foner, in his book on Reconstruction, noted that decisions like this "rendered national prosecution of crimes committed against blacks virtually impossible, and gave a green light to acts of terror where local officials either could not or would not enforce the law."[36]

The Supreme Court showed a similar view of the Fourteenth Amendment a few years later in the 1883 case known as the *Civil Rights Cases*, which combined five different cases that all concerned whether the Civil Rights Law of 1875 had made it illegal for businesses to discriminate against Black people. The court concluded this time that the Fourteenth Amendment didn't give the federal government the right to have passed the Civil Rights Act of 1875 because it regulated individual citizens' behavior. The court's view was that only state governments could do that because the Fourteenth Amendment gave the federal government only the right to correct a state's actions, not individual citizens' actions. The court declared the 1875 Civil Rights Act "void."[37]

Only one justice on the Supreme Court dissented from the *Civil Rights Cases* decision. Justice John Marshall Harlan wrote in his dissent that the court's opinion seemed "entirely too narrow and artificial. I cannot resist the conclusion that the substance and spirit of the recent amendments of the Constitution have been sacrificed by a subtle and ingenious verbal criticism." Mia Bay noted in *Traveling Black* that the Black community was devasted by the *Civil Rights Cases* decision and the loss of the Civil Rights Law. One of the five lawsuits included in this decision involved railroad travel. She quotes Frederick Douglass's view that the court had just given a "Railroad Conductor, more power than it gives to the National Government." Douglass wrote a letter to Justice Harlan to express "gratitude and admiration" for his dissenting opinion in the *Civil Rights Cases*.[38]

In addition, a new federal agency, the Interstate Commerce Commission (ICC), which had at first seemed to offer hope of fair treatment for all, didn't live up to those expectations for many years. Created in 1887, the ICC oversaw interstate business dealings, including in public transportation, to assure that "it shall be unlawful for any common carrier ... to subject any particular person ... to any undue or unreasonable prejudice or disadvantage in any respect whatsoever."[39] Despite that mandate, during its first sixty-eight years the ICC ruled in favor of racial segregation in transportation by accepting the "separate but equal" framework used in transportation laws passed by Southern states. The ICC seemed concerned only about seeing that separate facilities were equal rather than seeing that separating people based on skin color might subject Black travelers to "undue or unreasonable prejudice."[40]

The power of the Fourteenth Amendment was diluted even further when the separate but equal policy won the Supreme Court's stamp of approval in its 1896 *Plessy v. Ferguson* decision. This case involved a Black shoemaker and education rights activist in New Orleans, Homer Plessy. He took part in a campaign of civil disobedience organized by a dedicated group of local Black and Creole businessmen and journalists who created a Citizens' Committee. They set out to challenge the constitutionality of Louisiana's 1890 train segregation law, which used the separate but equal policy. Homer Plessy agreed to be arrested in 1892 by sitting in a train car for white passengers. This let Citizens' Committee lawyers challenge his arrest, first in Louisiana courts and then in the US Supreme Court. They argued that the train segregation law violated the Fourteenth Amendment by limiting the rights of a citizen without due process of law.[41]

Instead, a majority of the Supreme Court's justices supported a policy of "equal but separate," claiming that train segregation "neither abridges the privileges or immunities of the colored man" and that if anyone thinks it does, it is "solely because the colored race chooses to put that construction upon it." The justices also took a limited view of the Fourteenth Amendment, stating, "The object of the amendment was undoubtedly to enforce the absolute equality of the two races before the law, but, in the nature of things, it could not have been intended to abolish distinctions based upon color, or to enforce social, as distinguished from political, equality, or a commingling of the two races upon terms unsatisfactory to either."[42]

John Marshall Harlan dissented from this opinion, too. His dissent contained eloquent words: "Our Constitution is color-blind, and neither knows nor tolerates classes among citizens. In respect of civil rights, all citizens are equal before the law. The humblest is the peer of the most powerful." His words would surface years later during Sarah Keys's quest for justice. But in 1896, Harlan's eloquence failed to halt the forward motion of a policy that became known by the catchy phrase "separate but equal." The *Plessy v. Ferguson* decision provided the legal underpinning for decades of segregation laws that affected nearly all aspects of life in Southern states and in some Northern and Western states, too. However, the "separate but equal" facilities provided for Black citizens were almost never equal in quality to those for white people.[43]

A follow-up Supreme Court decision expanded on the difficulty of winning a ruling against train segregation with a case that concerned a railroad company's rules, not a state law: the 1910 case *Chiles v. Chesapeake & Ohio Railway Co.* It concerned James Alexander Chiles, a Black lawyer in Lexington, Kentucky, who had to switch trains on a trip from Washington, DC, to Kentucky. He bought a first-class ticket that he thought would give him first-class seating for the whole trip. He was forced to sit in a non-first-class car for Black passengers when he switched trains in Kentucky because of the train company's rule that limited first-class cars to white passengers traveling within the state. As an interstate passenger, he thought the ticket should apply for the whole ride.[44] The court decided against him, saying that the railroad company had the right to make rules about seating, noting that "regulations which are induced by the general sentiment of the community for whom they are made and upon whom they operate cannot be said to be unreasonable." By "community," the judge most likely meant only Kentucky's white community.[45]

Moving Backward

Streetcars became the next target for white officials committed to racial separation in public spaces. More than thirty years before, as noted earlier, spontaneous protests by Black communities in several Southern cities had ended streetcar segregation. But in the early 1900s, Southern legislatures revived Jim Crow's grip on this aspect of everyday life by passing new laws that reimposed streetcar segregation.

Once again, Black communities protested. But the protests were different than in the 1860s. Instead of sit-ins in which Black riders boldly claimed seats on whites-only cars, the new protests featured boycotts. People expressed their displeasure by walking to work and other destinations instead of riding in a segregated streetcar. These boycotts, which were organized by Black activists, occurred in more than twenty cities in thirteen states, with some lasting for many months. In Richmond, Virginia, and Nashville, Tennessee, the boycotts went on for about two years. The goal was to inflict financial harm on streetcar companies as a way to force a change in policy.[46]

Boycotts were chosen instead of civil disobedience to avoid provoking violence from white streetcar conductors. One of the organizers of Richmond's 1904 boycott, Black newspaper editor Maggie Lena Walker, described those conductors as "hot headed and domineering young white men."[47] They had a lot of power in deciding where people could sit, depending on their whims or the demands of white riders. Co-organizer of the Richmond boycott, John Mitchell Jr., another Black editor of a local newspaper, urged boycotters to "avoid any clash or disorder . . . WALK and STAY OFF."[48] This was wise advice during a period when the numbers of lynchings of Black citizens across the South were increasing. His newspaper, the *Richmond Planet*, kept a running tally of those lynchings.[49]

The new streetcar laws didn't require separate cars for each group, as on trains. In some states, Black riders had to sit in the back of a streetcar; in others, in the front. In Louisiana, there was a movable sign the conductor (or any white passenger) could place on the back of a row of seats behind which Black riders could sit.[50]

In Nashville, the boycott lasted for two years while Black business leaders also created their own streetcar company, Union Transportation Company. At first it used steam-powered streetcars and then switched to more reliable electric cars, but charging the batteries was problematic because the local power company ran the segregated streetcars and didn't like competition. Batteries for the Black-owned streetcar company were sometimes "damaged" during recharging. The city also levied a huge new tax on privately owned streetcars, which led to the end of Union Transportation.[51]

None of the early 1900s boycotts ended streetcar segregation. In Charlotte, North Carolina, there weren't enough riders to cause enough financial pain for the streetcar company to change. In Richmond and Montgomery, where financial pain did cause streetcar companies to briefly end segregation, the states passed new laws that forced streetcar segregation to resume.

In addition, other post-Reconstruction laws in several Southern states had effectively disfranchised Black voters. There were no elected officials looking out for Black rights to support the boycotters' requests. There was little hope of appealing for help to the ICC or the US Supreme Court. Both had shown they were solidly in the separate but equal camp.[52]

When it was clear the streetcar situation would not improve, many boycotters reluctantly went back to riding streetcars, although Virginia boycott leader John Mitchell Jr. apparently never did. Professor Blair LM Kelley, whose book *Right to Ride* describes these early twentieth-century boycotts, notes that they "planted the seeds of resistance," adding that boycotters "may have been forced to tolerate a segregated world, but these protests remind us that toleration was not consent."[53]

New Bus Challenges

After World War I, when the price for a new form of transportation, automobiles, started going down, some members of Black communities could afford to buy a car and avoid the humiliation of traveling on segregated streetcars and railroads. However, travel by auto had its own drawbacks, especially on long journeys, given how difficult it was for Black travelers to find places to stay, eat, and refuel in a country where many businesses refused to serve Black customers. However, automobiles used as jitneys, a kind of informal taxi service, provided transportation for those who couldn't afford to buy a car but could pay for a jitney ride across town. Streetcar companies didn't like losing customers to jitneys and often had local officials put jitney drivers out of business by making them pay steep licensing fees and taxes.

One group of Black jitney drivers in Winston-Salem, North Carolina, made the transition to driving buses, a new type of public transportation that began to be used in the 1920s. In 1926, twenty-one of the Winston-Salem jitney drivers stopped competing with each other for customers and joined together under the leadership of Clark Campbell to create the Safe Bus Company, the state's first Black-owned transportation company. Soon they began offering rides on thirty-five buses. In 1968, the city asked Safe Bus to serve all the city's residents, and then the city bought Safe Bus in 1972. Its staff became part of the Winston-Salem Transit Authority.[54] Safe Bus rides had been popular with East Winston residents, with one woman explaining, "We didn't have to sit in the back of the bus riding Safe Bus because it was owned by Blacks."[55]

Greyhound, the first major US bus company, also started as a jitney service in 1914, driving miners in Minnesota to their jobs. It then transitioned to buses and by the mid-1930s was one of two main bus companies in the United States, along with Trailways, that offered interstate bus service. By that time, eleven Southern states had passed new laws requiring segregated seating on buses. Those laws were modified versions of the laws for streetcars, requiring that Black riders sit in certain sections of a bus.[56]

North Carolina tried for a while to keep Black riders from riding *any* buses. In 1925, when Black businessman Berry O'Kelly complained about not being allowed to board a bus, a white-owned Raleigh newspaper suggested that Black riders should just wait until bus companies provided buses for them. In 1929, the North Carolina Interracial Commission investigated, asking the state's Corporation Commission to make rules enabling Black riders to travel on buses. The Interracial Commission was told that this wasn't possible because a 1927 North Carolina law about bus companies had recently been amended to state that buses were not common carriers.[57]

The amended law's text said that "nothing contained in this act or the law amended hereby shall be construed to declare operators of busses and/or taxicabs common carriers."[58] If buses aren't common carriers, then they can't be required under common law to serve all customers. The Interracial Commission appealed that decision. In 1930, a judge on North Carolina's Superior Court issued an order stating that buses are indeed common carriers and that new rules should be written to accommodate riders of both races. New rules were issued allowing all to ride buses in North Carolina, with a headline in a Virginia newspaper popular in Black communities declaring, "N.C. Buses Must Carry Colored, Court Decides." However, those new rules required separate but equal seating.[59]

Northern and Western states didn't have bus segregation laws at that time. Even so, Black passengers often experienced unfair treatment in some of those states, especially on interstate buses. One judge tried to end that behavior in Indiana in 1927 when he required a bus company to pay Laura Fischer $500 for the mistreatment she received when she was forced to sit in the back of a bus in Richmond, Indiana.[60] The judge told Fischer there "are no Jim Crows in Indiana."[61]

But mistreatment continued in the North, particularly in Chicago. The national office of the NAACP and its Chicago office kept receiving complaints about segregated buses, with many concerning Greyhound buses. As noted earlier, the NAACP didn't have the resources then to mount the kind of massive legal action that might resolve all those incidents. It tried to persuade Greyhound to tell its drivers to stop discriminating against Black passengers. When that didn't work, the NAACP issued a press release encouraging Black passengers to stand up for their rights and file their own personal lawsuits if needed.

Isabella Smith tried to do that during a 1934 trip to Philadelphia from Maryland, but she wound up being forcibly removed from the bus and spending a night in jail until a Maryland judge canceled the charges against her.[62] The judge stated, "Maryland jim crow laws do not apply to interstate customers." This confirms what the Supreme Court decision in Irene Morgan's case noted, that once Morgan's bus had crossed into DC and on into Maryland, she could have sat anywhere.[63]

The NAACP became increasingly alarmed about news reports of bus drivers shooting and killing Black soldiers on buses during World War II. Several of these tragedies occurred in 1942, before Irene Morgan was dragged off a bus and jailed in Virginia for refusing to give up her seat to a white passenger.

Lawyers with the NAACP had been looking for a case they could argue successfully. They had rejected another possibility in 1940, also in Virginia, that initially looked promising. Pauli Murray, not yet a lawyer but already an equal rights activist, was arrested with a friend in Virginia for refusing to move to the back of a bus. She contacted the NAACP, whose lawyers met with her and her friend, Adelene McBean, that night in jail. When Virginia officials learned that the NAACP was involved, they charged the women with disorderly conduct, not with breaking the state's segregation law. That ended the NAACP's hope of using this situation to launch a court case against all segregation laws.

Luckily, when Irene Morgan reached out to the NAACP, she had already been charged with violating the state's segregation law. Thus, NAACP lawyers had found the case they needed.[64]

A Step Forward

Given this saga of unjust treatment of Black travelers and the difficulties in winning justice in court, it's remarkable that NAACP lawyers achieved a positive outcome in *Morgan v. Virginia*. They cited the Commerce Clause as a basis of their argument, which helped their case because it emphasized that the federal government did indeed have a constitutionally recognized oversight role, thus sidestepping the limits past court decisions had placed on that role as a result of discussions about the meaning of the Fourteenth Amendment.

They also helped the case by citing something judges always like to hear about—a legal precedent. The one the NAACP cited, the 1877 *Hall v. DeCuir* decision, might seem an unlikely choice. Although it featured logic similar to what the NAACP lawyers would use, the earlier case actually supported segregation and had not benefited the Black woman, Josephine DeCuir, who was the aggrieved party.

She had been a passenger on a Mississippi River steamboat that traveled between New Orleans and Vicksburg, Mississippi, in 1872. The steamboat company refused to let her use one of its private rooms, which were for white women only. She filed a lawsuit against the steamship company, citing an 1869 Louisiana law passed during the early days of Reconstruction that said transportation companies could not discriminate against people because of race or skin color.

Josephine DeCuir won in Louisiana courts but lost in 1877 at the US Supreme Court, which based its decision on the Constitution's Commerce Clause, using the same reasoning NAACP lawyers would use for Irene Morgan—that only the US Congress could regulate interstate commerce and travel. The Commerce Clause argument applied in Josephine DeCuir's case because the steamboat traveled in both Mississippi and Louisiana waters, making hers an interstate journey. A steamboat company traveling in Mississippi waters could thus not be forced to obey Louisiana's anti-discrimination law. Ironically, this 1877 Supreme Court decision that supported racial discrimination would be used nearly seventy years later to try to end it.[65]

By 1946 the justices on the Supreme Court had a more liberal outlook than those who had endorsed the separate but equal policy in earlier years. After Franklin D. Roosevelt became president in 1933, he began appointing justices who shared his views on equal rights. By early 1941, several conservative justices had retired from the court and were replaced by Roosevelt appointees. That year, in a case about segregation on trains, *Mitchell v. United States*, the court's justices ruled unanimously in favor of requiring a railroad to provide equal services for its first-class Pullman sleeper customers so that Black passengers who bought first-class Pullman tickets would enjoy the same services as white first-class travelers. However, because that ruling applied only to first-class train travel, that decision had no impact on bus travel and did not help the great majority of Black train travelers. Even so, it showed that this cohort of justices was moving in a new direction. The new trend continued three years later when the court issued a ruling in the *Smith v. Allwright* case that ended whites-only primary elections in Texas.[66]

The Supreme Court continued the forward momentum with *Morgan v. Virginia*. But it was not a perfect, airtight case. There were issues with its wording and concerns about whether it would be enforced and adhered to as effectively as it seemed to have been for Sarah Keys during her earlier bus trips home to North Carolina.

3

Test Rides

DESPITE THE JUBILANT RESPONSE TO IRENE MORGAN'S victory in Black newspapers and the hope it inspired in Sarah Keys's father and others, many had concerns about what kind of real-life impact it would have. One major shortcoming was that it applied only to interstate travel and had no impact on other kinds of transportation that affected a much larger portion of the Black community: streetcars and local buses that didn't travel into other states.

It was also unclear whether this history-making court decision would be enforced. A year after the decision was announced, an interracial group of civil rights activists—eight Black men and eight white men—decided to test the effectiveness of *Morgan v. Virginia* by taking a series of bus trips in Southern states during two weeks in April 1947. They bought tickets for regularly scheduled Greyhound and Trailways buses that would be traveling in several states in the upper South: Virginia, North Carolina, Tennessee, and Kentucky.[1]

The test rides were confined to those states because the organizers of this campaign feared the testers might suffer violence if they ventured farther south, where a number of brutal attacks on Black passengers had occurred during the 1940s. One especially tragic incident happened shortly before NAACP lawyers presented their arguments for Irene Morgan's case at the US Supreme Court in March 1946. A few weeks earlier, on February 12, 1946, Sergeant Isaac Woodard, dressed in his army uniform, was returning home after serving honorably during World War II, taking a bus from Augusta, Georgia, to Columbia, South Carolina. Sergeant Woodward was blinded for life during that bus trip. A white police officer in South Carolina beat Woodward severely because, according to the sergeant's testimony in the trial about this incident, he didn't use the word *sir* when speaking to the officer and then tried to defend himself against the officer's attack. The officer was indicted and faced trial but was acquitted by an all-white jury.[2]

During the 1947 test rides that set out to gauge the impact of *Morgan v. Virginia*, a pair of activists—one Black and one white—would board a bus to see whether a Black tester and his white colleague would be allowed to sit in the front seats. Before beginning these tests, participants spent two days in Washington, DC, receiving training in nonviolent protest techniques, learning how to stay peaceful throughout the bus rides even when provoked. They also received guidance on how to explain the *Morgan* decision to bus drivers and fellow passengers who might not have heard about it yet. All of the participants started their test trips on April 9, 1947, departing from Washington, DC, on Greyhound and Trailways buses.

This test-ride campaign was called the Journey of Reconciliation. All the bus riders were dedicated to the strategies of nonviolent civil disobedience and direct-action protest (such as sit-ins or boycotts). The organizers of the Journey of Reconciliation were members of two groups inspired by the nonviolent civil disobedience campaigns used by Mohandas Gandhi in India. One of the groups was the Fellowship of Reconciliation (FOR), a pacifist organization founded during World War I. The other group was CORE (Congress of Racial Equality), started in 1942 by members of FOR.

Before the start of the Journey of Reconciliation test rides, CORE had already held successful nonviolent protests by holding sit-ins at Chicago restaurants. Those early successes inspired Bayard Rustin, a Black activist founder of CORE and a FOR member, to team up with a white FOR member, George Houser, to test the effectiveness of the *Morgan* ruling while also trying to educate people about that Supreme Court decision. They wrote a report at the end of the Journey of Reconciliation bus-ride experiment to summarize the results.[3]

The testers traveled on more than twenty buses. On most of the trips no one was arrested. On six bus rides, a total of twelve men were arrested. Both Black and white testers faced arrest for disobeying a bus driver's directive about where to sit. Local officials later dropped charges in eight cases, usually following a court review. Three men who were arrested in Chapel Hill, North Carolina, were sentenced to three weeks of hard labor. They included Bayard Rustin and two white testers, Igal Roodenko, a conscientious objector from New York, and Joseph Felmet, a conscientious objector from Asheville, North Carolina. They endured terrible conditions working on chain gangs. Rustin wrote a five-part series about this experience, "Twenty-Two Days on a Chain Gang," which appeared in the *New York Post* and *Baltimore Afro-American* newspapers. The article led to an investigation of North Carolina's prison camp policies.

Testers also took four train trips to see if *Morgan v. Virginia* had any impact on train travel. No arrests occurred during the train travel; on one train ride the testers had to sit in the Jim Crow car, but on the other train trips they sat in a regular coach car along with white passengers.[4]

The final report on the Journey of Reconciliation concluded that there was great confusion among both bus drivers and passengers, with many not having heard about the *Morgan v. Virginia* decision. If they had heard of it, they often did not understand what it required. One driver of a Greyhound bus explained to a passenger that he didn't force a Black passenger (one of the testers) to move to the back of the bus because of a recent court case. But on another bus ride, a Trailways driver explained why he wouldn't allow the Black tester to sit in the front because "I have my orders," noting that he was working for the bus company and followed its seating rules.[5]

There was no violence connected with the arrests on the buses and only one violent event, which occurred at the Chapel Hill, North Carolina, bus station. Earlier, when testers had first arrived in this university town the day before, on Saturday, April 12, they were hosted by a local white pastor, the Reverend Charles M. Jones, and greeted warmly by an interracial group. The testers went to an interracial meeting at the university that evening and attended Sunday services the next morning at the pastor's church. They then prepared to travel by bus to Greensboro. However, the bus's departure was delayed. When the bus failed to leave the station while the bus driver processed arrests for several testers, a group of angry white taxi drivers gathered outside. They were opposed to desegregation. One taxi driver hit a white Journey of Reconciliation tester. Before the situation deteriorated farther, Rev. Jones helped the testers escape, bringing them to his home. He then arranged for local college students to drive the testers by car to Greensboro. The pastor and his church received threats, which fortunately lessened after a few days.

The testers had also met with enthusiasm and support in Greensboro and Knoxville, where there were interracial meetings with people who were interested in eliminating segregation. Other positive experiences occurred. On one trip, a white woman in Tennessee spoke up in support of the testers and managed to persuade a bus driver not to arrest them. During the tense situation at the Chapel Hill bus station, another white woman refused to sign a witness card to support the bus company's decision to arrest the testers. Also hopeful was the courage shown by Black passengers who took seats toward the front of a bus when testers were allowed to sit there.[6]

The project's final report summarized the difficulties experienced on some of the rides: "It was generally apparent that the bus companies were attempting to circumvent the intentions of the Supreme Court in the Irene Morgan decision by reliance on state Jim Crow Laws, by company regulations, and by subtle pressure." The report also noted that most of the passengers the testers encountered on these test trips didn't seem greatly concerned about the whole seating issue. Fellow passengers had not shown "from facial expressions that they were for or against the action which the group was taking."[7]

The report acknowledged that more education and testing was needed to help people understand the *Morgan v. Virginia* court decision. Unfortunately, CORE did not have resources at that time to launch additional educational bus-seating campaigns. More than ten years later, however, CORE would play a major role in ending transportation segregation with a differently organized and greatly expanded type of nonviolent direct-action bus campaign, the Freedom Rides. In addition, Bayard Rustin would play a major role in helping to organize a very different kind of event, the 1963 March on Washington for Jobs and Freedom.[8]

Overall, Bayard Rustin and George Houser felt encouraged by what they saw during the 1947 Journey of Reconciliation. As they explained in their report on this experiment, "We believe that the great majority of the people in the upper South are prepared to accept the Irene Morgan decision and to ride on buses" with Black passengers. They cited a comment from a white woman who at first didn't want to sit next to a Black man but did so anyway: "I'm tired. Anything for a seat."[9]

There wasn't much press coverage of the Journey of Reconciliation in major newspapers. But readers of the *Baltimore Afro-American* received an enthusiastic account of it from two reporters who spent a week with the testers. "History was definitely made," the reporters wrote, adding that seeing white and Black riders sitting next to each other "made the solution of segregation seem far simpler than it ever had before."[10]

Worth a Try

Despite the optimism in the Journey of Reconciliation's final report, the riders' experiences revealed drawbacks to *Morgan v. Virginia*. There was a lack of clarity in its text which caused trouble for some of the Journey of Reconciliation testers and would also cause trouble for Sarah Keys during her trip home in 1952. The decision's text had specifically outlawed the use of segregation *legislation* to determine bus seating. But were bus company segregation *rules* also prohibited? Some bus drivers thought they were, as testers discovered during the Journey of Reconciliation. Other bus drivers felt confident about ignoring the Supreme Court's decision in order to enforce their employers' Jim Crow seating rules. Adding to the confusion, a bus company's rules were often not posted in bus stations, so it was hard for both riders and drivers to know what those rules were.[11]

It's also not uncommon for Supreme Court decisions to promise more than they can deliver. Two years after *Morgan v. Virginia*, a totally different decision, *Shelley v. Kraemer*, seemed like a game-changer but proved less effective than initially hoped. It concerned "restrictive covenants," which were used at that time to prevent certain categories of people, often Black or Jewish home-buyers, from moving into a neighborhood. The Supreme Court ruled in 1948 that the government couldn't force people to go along with such restrictions, but the court didn't rule that having such restrictions was illegal. So people in a neighborhood could *voluntarily* agree to block others from moving in, leading to unfair residential exclusions that continued for many years.[12]

Even though there was some uncertainty and lack of clarity in its wording, *Morgan v. Virginia* offered a glimmer of hope. The NAACP's *Crisis* magazine called this court decision "the beginning of the end of Jim Crow transportation." The *Norfolk Journal and Guide*, a major Southern Black newspaper, called it "one of the most highly significant" of all Supreme Court decisions.[13]

Sarah Keys's father was born around the same time that *Plessy v. Ferguson* was decided. For five decades, he had coped with the fraud of "separate-but-equal" rules and laws. *Morgan v. Virginia* may have given him hope that a crack had at last emerged in the hold segregation had on so many aspects of daily life.

During the first few years after *Morgan v. Virginia*, there were additional steps forward. In December 1946, President Harry Truman issued an executive order creating the President's Committee on Civil Rights. He had reportedly been shaken by news of the brutal beating and blinding of Sergeant Woodard earlier that year and by increased reports of racial violence and discrimination. This executive order was one of several new civil rights initiatives his administration would take. The committee he created was authorized "to inquire into and to determine whether and in what respect current . . . means possessed by Federal, State, and local governments may be strengthened and improved to safeguard the civil rights of the people."[14]

Two years later, in July 1948, President Truman issued another executive order calling for an end to racial segregation in the military. That same year, the Fair Employment Board of the US Civil Service Commission was created to investigate incidents of discrimination in the federal workforce. On April 6, 1949, Louis Johnson, the secretary of defense, issued a formal "directive" to all branches of the armed forces calling for "equality of treatment and opportunity for all persons in the Armed Services without regard to race, color, religion, or national origin." This would have a direct impact on Sarah Keys, who would enlist in the Women's Army Corps (WAC) in 1951.[15]

The Fort Dix army hospital in New Jersey, where Sarah was stationed in 1952, had a fully desegregated WAC unit. "Ft. Dix was well integrated," she recalled years later. "Not only on the job, but the living quarters, too. I made white friends. I remember two girls in particular. A girl from Ohio and a girl from Massachusetts."[16]

Her father, in the advice he gave her, had offered a hint that there might be problems with *Morgan v. Virginia*. He told her, "When you board a bus from the North, you can sit any place." But he had also advised her to make sure the bus goes "straight through" with no changes, so she wouldn't be hassled by the driver.[17]

In 1952, when she bought her ticket at the Trenton, New Jersey, bus station, she didn't know about legal loopholes or unclear judicial rulings. She had traveled by bus to and from North Carolina after leaving home in 1948 to move to New Jersey. Although this 1952 trip would be her first time returning home since becoming a WAC, she had made other trips before joining the military. Indeed, on one trip northward, she received a positive message from a white bus driver that seemed to suggest that change was indeed on its way. As she boarded an interstate bus in her hometown's bus station, she recalled that "the driver said to me, 'You sit right here behind me.'"[18]

She had also done other traveling since leaving home. After she had completed ten weeks of basic training at Fort Lee in Virginia, she and other WAC recruits traveled to Texas for further training. "We traveled on a train that was integrated," she recalled. "I don't know if it was just this group of WACs that traveled on this integrated train, but that's how it was."[19]

She had become used to travel going well. "When I got on the bus that morning in Trenton, that didn't come back to me"—the Morgan case. She wasn't thinking about the Supreme Court or civil rights history. "I just did what I was accustomed to do. I had been traveling by bus before and never had any problem."[20]

4

Heading Home

THE BUS THAT PRIVATE FIRST CLASS Sarah Louise Keys boarded in Trenton on August 1, 1952, rolled into Virginia late that night and stopped to pick up additional riders. Sarah saw men in military uniforms boarding the bus. There weren't enough seats for all of them. Some navy sailors had to stand.

"I'm chatting a little with the Marine sitting next to me," she recalled many years later. This friendly young white man was on his way to Camp Lejeune in North Carolina, not far from her hometown. Then she drifted off to sleep.[1]

Just after midnight, the bus made its first stop in North Carolina, at a bus station in Roanoke Rapids, a small city just over the border from Virginia. "I had never heard that name before," she explained years later. Her hometown was still about a hundred miles farther south.[2]

She recounted the events of that bus ride home many times over the years—to the author of this book during dozens of phone conversations from 2004 to 2023 as well as in interviews with news reporters, in speeches at public forums, in an oral history interview recorded for the Military Women's Memorial in 2006, and in a video recorded in 2019 for a group of Black educators in Roanoke Rapids trying to find a way to honor her.

With each retelling, her account has been remarkably similar. Those events seem to have become emblazoned on her memory. So had the fear she experienced. Each retelling caused her emotional distress—so much so that, at age ninety-two in the fall of 2021, she declined to tell a North Carolina Public Radio reporter about the events of that August 1952 bus ride. He was doing a story about new honors she had just received, but agreed to use a video she had recorded two years earlier to find quotes to include in his report.[3]

The account presented on the next few pages uses her own words to describe what happened to her in Roanoke Rapids in August 1952. It is a composite based on the many interviews or talks she has given, mostly made a great many years after the incident she describes. By then she had married and changed her name to Sarah Keys Evans.[4]

Sarah Keys Evans Remembers

When her bus reached the bus station in Roanoke Rapids just after midnight, in the early morning hours of August 2, 1952, a new driver took charge of the bus. He walked down the aisle collecting ticket stubs from the passengers. During this long bus trip, at each new stop the driver would collect a small stub that had the name of that stop on it.

"As the driver was walking down the bus, he said to me that he wanted me to move to the back," Sarah recalled. She was just waking up, but she remembered saying to him, "'I'm comfortable sitting here' and that was all I said to him."

The driver took the ticket stub from the Marine sitting next to her. "He didn't take my ticket," she recalled. "It did not enter my mind then that something was happening."[5]

She noticed that the driver was white, but so were the drivers on earlier bus trips she had taken. "I was tired. It was around midnight. I wasn't going to get up and walk through a crowd to stand. You're just anxious to get to where you were supposed to be."[6]

The new driver went on collecting tickets. When the driver passed by her seat again, Sarah recalled, "I crossed my arm over the Marine to give him [the driver] my ticket, and he said, 'I'm not taking your ticket.'" The driver got off the bus.[7]

A few minutes later he came back onto the bus and told everybody, "I want everyone on this bus to get off, except that woman that refused

4.1 Private First Class Sarah Keys in her Women's Army Corps dress uniform in the early 1950s. Courtesy Sarah Keys Evans.

to move to the rear. She can stay here until this bus moves out, but it's not going any place tonight."

"It was sort of like a shock," Sarah recalled years later. She remembered thinking to herself, "I can't stay on this bus by myself." This had never happened to her on any of her earlier bus trips.

Everyone stood up and started getting their luggage down from the overhead bins. "So I stood up." A white sailor was standing in the aisle. "He said, 'Can I help you with your luggage?' I said, 'Yes, thank you.' He took it down and set it on the floor. I walked out, and he walked out. I never saw that sailor again. Out of all those people, he was the only one that seemed to just want to help where he could—help a person, a lady, a woman who was dressed in a uniform."[8]

As she thought back on those events more than fifty years later, she concluded, "That was really the nicest thing that happened to me that night."[9]

The other passengers lined up to get on another bus. Sarah did, too. When she got near the front of the line, the bus driver said again, "I'm not taking your ticket. You're not riding this bus."

She thought maybe there was something wrong with her ticket. "So I turned and went into the bus station. As I entered the station, the lights dim," she recalled.

Sarah walked over to the ticket window. The white woman selling tickets shut the window's curtain and refused to talk to Sarah.

"I turned around quickly," Sarah remembered. She saw a man standing there. "A man with the broom, sweeping, the porter, a tall Black guy. He said to me, 'Miss, don't you know where you are?' I'll never forget those words."[10]

That's when she got scared. She thought to herself, "Oh, Sarah, you are in trouble."

She knew bad things could happen to Black people who were all alone at night in a small Southern town. That's one reason she had moved away after high school—to get away from that kind of danger.

"I went back out to the line because there were a couple of people still to get onto the bus," she recalled. "I said to the driver again, 'Is there something wrong with my ticket?'"

"No," said the driver. "But you're not riding on this bus tonight."

She turned around and saw three white policemen.

"Is this the one?" a policeman asked the bus driver.

"Yes," said the driver.[11]

She was puzzled about why the police were there. Later, she realized that "the driver apparently had gone into the station and called the police and explained the situation. There was never any commotion. Everything outside was quiet with everyone getting off the bus." One of the policemen "took hold of my shoulder and said, 'You're coming with us.'"[12]

There was an officer on either side of her. "They didn't beat me up or drag me or anything. I certainly was not going to be fighting them. I was so frightened," she remembered.[13]

"You really have to keep your head in situations of that sort," she would explain decades later to a New York NPR interviewer. "I was in my early twenties, never having experienced anything like that before," she noted. "But I knew what the army rules and regulations were, and I just kept putting one foot in front of the other, trying to listen to everything that was being said to me. There really was no one for me to talk to. There was no one there to defend me. I was just overwhelmed." In an interview for an army magazine many years after her arrest, she said she had come to see that "fear is one of the things that said, 'Just don't say too much. Just keep moving along with the policeman here.'"[14]

"So I slow-walked with them to the squad car. They put me in it. We drove down a dark highway. They didn't have streetlights."

"Where are you taking me?" Sarah asked the police officers.

"We're taking you to jail," one said.

"To jail! For what?"[15]

"We can get you for anything. For disorderly conduct," he said.

"But nothing happened," Sarah remembered telling the police officers.

"Well, we don't really even have to get you to jail," said one officer.

"I froze," Sarah recalled, describing the terror she felt when she heard that threat. She was afraid they might kill her. She had heard stories of that happening to other Black people accused of doing things they didn't do. She knew that it had even happened to soldiers wearing military uniforms.[16]

According to University of North Carolina professor Dr. Blair LM Kelley, who while speaking at a 2022 forum for educators about Sarah Keys Evans, explained that "to be arrested and be Black in the Jim Crow South means any number of terrible things can happen to you. It's important to remember the context in which she was raised. She would have been told the importance of not being arrested. Many people never returned from a jail cell or from an arrest. Even though she knew she was right, even though she was brave, even though she was a soldier in her uniform, she still had that knowledge of all the suffering and the difficulty that came before her. In that moment, it must have been the most frightening thing she could think of."[17]

As the police car continued making its way down that dark road, Sarah said she began to pray silently to herself. "I kept asking God to keep my mind open because I was so frightened."

When they reached the police station, "I went before the chief of police and he said, 'I'm locking you up for the night.'"

Sarah asked, "For what?"

The police chief replied, "We can get you for disorderly conduct."

"Oh, let me call my grandparents," she said. She knew that people who are taken to jail have the right to make one phone call. She asked if she could call her grandparents because her parents didn't have a phone. The officer said he would phone for her. Sarah gave him their phone number. He pretended to call, but she learned later that her grandparents never received the phone call.

"I was put in a large jail cell, with a filthy, dirty mattress on the floor and a sink in the corner with a dim light," she recalled. "A policeman took me there, or the jailer. He slammed the door. It was like my heart was going to give out on me. There was no one in there with me. Fear was so overwhelming. I thought my chest would pop open."[18]

The mattress on the floor "was dirtier than any that you see discarded on the street. I said to myself, 'I can't touch that. I can't lie down or sit down.' I wouldn't even wash my hands in the sink. So I paced the floor all night." She was in her dress uniform that she had put on so proudly many hours before in New Jersey, wearing high-heeled shoes with one-and-a-half-inch heels. She did not want to sully that uniform by getting anywhere near that mattress.

"I asked God to help me. What is happening to me? What are you going to say to your family? You are in jail! Why would I come to jail for the steps and moves that I have just made? All night I'm walking and pacing and crying, walking and pacing and crying."

The next morning, Saturday, "the sun began to peek through the bars. The jailer came to the gate. He had a sandwich and he gave me the sandwich. He said, 'You better eat. Don't make like you're too good for it.'" Sarah didn't want to touch anything in that cell. She never ate that sandwich.[19]

The jailer took her to the chief of police, who asked, "What kind of outfit is that you're wearing?"

"I'm in the army. This is the United States Army WAC uniform," Sarah explained.[20]

She was still frightened standing there before the police chief, but it was daylight so she wasn't as afraid as she had been the night before. "I didn't have any fear of being a little more vocal," she remembered. So she told the police chief, "You mean to tell me you don't know the color of the United States Army uniform?"

"That's why you spent the night in jail," he answered. "Because you're too damn smart."[21]

"I felt my face sizzle," recalled Sarah. She knew there were white people who didn't like to see Black people do well. Seeing a young Black woman in an army uniform seemed to make that police chief angry. Instead of earning this young woman the thanks and praise often given to those serving in the military, especially during wartime, this official responded to Sarah's uniform with scorn and hostility.[22]

She began to think that maybe she shouldn't have spoken up like that. She explained later that she had the same kind of feeling you have "when you're growing up and you know that there's something you should have done very different than whatever it was that you had done. Before you're called out on it by a parent or a teacher or whatever, you can sort of feel the worries and the punishment coming. I started to get really, really nervous. I'm still thinking: 'How and why, how did I get there?'"[23]

Then the police chief said, "If you have $25, you can go." That would be like asking for about $200 today. Luckily, she had brought enough money with her to pay the fine.

Even though Sarah was scared, she once again spoke up, telling the police chief, "If you had asked me for $25 before, I wouldn't have had to spend a night in jail."

Speaking up this way again provoked the police chief. "I don't like you," he said. "Keep quiet or you could get your face slapped."[24]

He told her that the next week the local court would be meeting and "you can come back and try to get your $25 back."[25]

Sarah gave them her money. Policemen took her back to the bus station. "They put me on the slowest bus going to Washington, North Carolina," she recalled. They forced her to sit in the back of the bus. She stayed in that seat. She just wanted to get out of that town.[26]

As the bus rolled along, Sarah worried about how she could possibly explain to her family what had happened to her. "What mother would want people to know that her daughter went to jail?"

This was supposed to be a triumphant homecoming, to show her family that she was successfully making her own way in the world, earning a good salary, being independent, doing important work to help her country, all while gaining a new sense of self-confidence. Instead, Sarah had been treated with disrespect and charged with disorderly conduct. She had experienced total fear.

The bus made so many stops along the way that she didn't get home until early Sunday morning. Her family had expected her to arrive the day before. She knew they would be very worried.[27]

A Shocking Surprise

Her treatment at the police station was similar to the disrespect faced by other Black women who had been blocked from entering the ladies cars on nineteenth-century train trips because they weren't regarded as "ladies" in the eyes of a train conductor, as described in chapter 2. The disrespect Sarah Keys experienced had an added element of mockery to it, by not giving her the courtesy customarily shown to a member of the US military in uniform.

The disparagement and danger she experienced in Roanoke Rapids was a direct result of a major loophole in the *Morgan v. Virginia* decision: its lack of clarity about whether the Supreme Court's decision applied to bus company rules as well as to state legislation. That gave Southern bus companies a green light to issue their own segregation rules, something the Journey of Reconciliation testers had discovered as well. Not all bus drivers enforced their bus company's segregation rules. She was unlucky that night in Roanoke Rapids to find one who did.[28]

Sarah Keys would help close that loophole, but it would take more than ten years.

5

"The Quietest of Us All"

SARAH LOUISE KEYS WASN'T THE kind of person anyone would ever think would spend a night in jail. "She was the quietest of us all," said her younger sister Cornelia (Connie) Keys Hargrave, now a retired schoolteacher. "Sarah would never do anything that would create any kind of problem."[1]

Sarah was shy as a child. She was also a hard worker. She had to be, growing up on a farm. The family's farm was on the outskirts of Washington, North Carolina, a riverfront city on the banks of the Pamlico River, not far from the state's southeastern Atlantic Ocean coastline. Often called Little Washington, to avoid confusion with the nation's capital, this town was founded in the 1770s and gained its name in 1775, the first town named for George Washington before he became president.[2]

Sarah's father, David Artis Keys Sr., grew up in that same town on a dairy and pecan farm owned by his father, Elijah Keys, on land that had been owned by Sarah's great-grandfather. David Keys's mother managed a little farm stand in their backyard and also rented out rooms for visiting teachers and clergy because no hotels at that time would accept Black customers.

After serving in the navy during World War I, David returned home and bought his own farm in an area of town called Clark's Neck, not far from where he grew up. That's where Sarah Louise Keys was born on April 18, 1929. When she was still very young, her father moved his growing family to a larger farm in another rural area of town called Keysville, named for some of his ancestors. Sarah grew up on this Keysville farm, along with her three sisters and three brothers. Originally a produce farm, it later focused mainly on tobacco. Two sisters of grandfather Elijah Keys owned farms in that area, too, and lived there with their families.[3]

Sarah had been told that her ancestors came from a variety of backgrounds: African, white European, and Native American. Several of her relatives have taken the DNA test offered by Ancestry.com, and their results confirm this mixed background for their family. Some relatives have done genealogical research to gain a better sense of the family tree. "It is hard to track Black people through census records," explained Joan Dudley, a daughter of Sarah's oldest sister, Marie. That was especially true when looking for people who might have been enslaved, although some of the family tree researchers found that many Keys ancestors had not been enslaved. Making genealogy searches even harder, early census takers were white. They spelled "Keys" in many different ways—Keyes, Keas, Kease, and Keys. Sarah's family used "Keyes" when she was a young girl but switched to "Keys" when she was a teenager. Sarah had also heard that some Keys relatives came from Nova Scotia. Slowly, she and her nieces tried to piece together bits and pieces of family history.[4]

One thing is clear: They had always been a family of hardworking, independent-minded people. Her father was determined to find multiple ways to take care of his family, realizing how risky farming can be, depending as it does on good weather for a plentiful harvest. He did construction work for others to provide additional income during tough times. Finding good-paying construction jobs in segregated Washington, North Carolina, could be hard for Black men. He often traveled out of state for extra employment—to New Jersey or to Washington, DC. During World War II, he worked at the Navy Yard in Norfolk, Virginia.

He and his wife did their best to shield their children from some of the negative aspects of Jim Crow segregation that permeated life throughout the South at that time. Sarah's father made the bold move of helping to create an excellent new academic-oriented school for his children. (Details of this achievement will appear in chapter 7.) That school provided opportunities and broadened horizons for his children and others in the Black community.

During the mid-1930s, when Sarah was very young, her father also helped widen opportunities for the Black community by participating in the Works Progress Administration (WPA), one of the Roosevelt administration's New Deal programs. It was one of the first official efforts to try to lessen the grip of segregation on job opportunities. The WPA provided jobs, often construction jobs, for thousands who were unemployed as a result of the Great Depression. Her father was briefly signed up by this federal agency to work as a foreman for the WPA in his hometown. "He was in charge of hiring, doing payroll, helping to build roads," Sarah recalled. He landed that job because of an influential white woman in town whom Sarah always referred to as "Mrs. Leach."

"I don't know who her family was and how she became such a prominent woman in that town to get things done, but she got him the job at the WPA," explained Sarah. "She recommended him. He was a very smart man. He did a lot of reading. Many of his teachers were still here and put in a good word for him." Her father had told her that Mrs. Leach had come to know him when he was a young boy. "My father grew up with her boys. They all played together on the waterfront. The young boys in town would jump off the pier into the river and swim and crab and play all day in the summer." This prominent woman had already helped him in another way several years earlier, when he had decided to leave town as a teenager and look for more opportunities in the other Washington, the nation's capital (described in chapter 7).

"He was proud of working for the WPA. It was the only thing going then for jobs and training for young Black people. It was important work, helping the country recover from the Great Depression. To make sure that Black people had a share in it. But the WPA didn't last long," Sarah noted.[5]

The WPA had rules that tried to prohibit some of the on-the-job discrimination Black workers faced at that time in states like North Carolina. That aspect of the WPA's mission—to create a fairer work environment for Black workers—may have led to the program's decline in North Carolina, where not only was there strong support for segregation among white officials, but many of them also opposed Roosevelt's whole New Deal program. They justified their opposition to the WPA by saying that its programs were too expensive and interfered with private businesses. In 1937, North Carolina officials closed regional WPA offices across the state; only the office in Raleigh, the state capital, remained open.[6]

So David Keys continued his own search for local construction jobs until the opportunity arose during World War II to work as a cement mason at the Navy Yard in Norfolk, Virginia, a logical choice for a navy veteran. The Navy Yard was more than a hundred miles from his farm, too far to commute on a daily basis, but the pay and opportunity for steady work made this an attractive choice. "He would come home once or twice a month to see how the farm was going," Sarah remembered, "especially at harvest time." He wanted to see if the person he hired to manage the farm "was carrying out what the two of them had decided on."

After the war, he had good luck finding construction jobs in Washington, DC, that paid better than the odd jobs he could find in North Carolina. "They were beginning to let Blacks join the union," explained Sarah. "He was a cement mason. He helped build many buildings in Washington, including the Washington Cathedral." He also began finding construction jobs farther north in New Jersey, where his brother lived. On the day of Sarah's 1948 high school graduation, her father was working on a big job in New Jersey. He couldn't take time off to make it home and see her give the welcoming address at the graduation ceremony. "I knew that's where he was and that what he was doing was important," explained Sarah.

While her father was away doing those extra jobs, Sarah, as the second-oldest of seven children, helped her mother, Curley Vivian Wooten Keys, take care of daily chores on the farm. "My mother was a great manager and housekeeper," Sarah explained. "A very strict mother, and a very good house supervisor." Her mother planned ahead, such as by cooking tomatoes from the harvest and putting them up in cans to have during the winter. "We always had a pantry full of canned tomatoes." Sarah added that her mother also "had a special talent for designing and decorating. She could see an outfit, . . . go home, do up the pattern, and sew it up. She would pick out something that she wanted to see me in, and she'd go make it. She would get out her brown paper and pins and cut it out and measure and she would be on her way." Her mother made sure her children were dressed well. "I always liked neatness. That's how my mother trained us. We didn't do chores on the farm with holes in our clothes. You had to be right to go out, because you had employed help."[7]

"Mom always made our uniforms," Sarah's sister Connie added. "We attended a parochial school and had to wear uniforms. Mom was also very creative in making window treatments and bed coverings, too. She had a great appreciation for beauty—and a great appreciation for education. She stressed the importance of doing well in school so that you would graduate and get your diploma."[8]

Sarah and Connie's grandmother—David Keys's mother, Sarah Tankard Keys—was also a capable manager. She was born in 1868 after the Civil War ended and so was never enslaved herself, although her own mother had been born into slavery before the Civil War on a plantation owned by the Tankard family. Limited in education and nearly blind, Sarah Tankard Keys set prices for her backyard farm stand in terms of how many nickels or quarters would be needed, perhaps so she could feel the edges of the coins, to make sure she was being paid correctly. "She was a good businesswoman," said Sarah (who was named for her grandmother), adding that she "knew how to earn a living. She learned it from her mother who was a good seamstress and from her father who had his own business. They put to use whatever they had learned up to that point that could be used to make an independent living for themselves."[9]

Young Sarah Keys would become a good businesswoman herself one day. She got started as a child, doing chores on the family farm before and after school. "I liked to learn to do anything that would take me outside of the house, even how to milk the cow," she recalled. She also joined her school's marching band, and after finishing her chores in the afternoon, she practiced piano and then also French horn. Sometimes she practiced her horn in the barn with one of her brothers, who played trumpet.

There weren't many kids her age near their farm, but she had fun with her sisters. One of her favorite things to do when they were preteens and teens was to fix their hair. She learned how by watching the hairstylist at a beauty parlor in town that they visited on special occasions. "I'd sit by the window and watch the hairstylist, how she was working," noted Sarah. "I was very good at catching onto new things. The stylist would call my name when it was my turn to have my hair done. I would say, 'That's OK.'" She'd let the stylist take another customer in order to keep watching for a while longer before it was her turn so she could use what she had learned to style her sisters' hair at home later. "I was always interested in what this hairdresser was doing, how popular she was. You could talk to her about your parents, how you were getting along," she recalled. And sometimes the hairdresser would offer helpful advice, too. "We all had appointments to go into the beauty salon and get our hair done. That was a real treat. In between times I would do their hair. I would do my own creations. At thirteen years old I asked my mother if I could take care of my own hair. She said yes. From then on, I was creative in that area."[10]

A Good Listener

Young Sarah also loved sitting on the porch with her father when he was home on Sunday afternoons, listening to him tell stories. "Everybody else would be doing their thing in the yard, jumping rope or whatever games we played. I would be there asking Daddy questions while he was reading his newspaper or a book. He had *National Geographic Magazine* and a set of encyclopedias. When we were growing up, if you asked Dad a question, he would say, 'That's what the encyclopedia is for,'" she recalled.

She loved hearing his stories, but she noted another reason she retreated to the porch to sit with her father. "Not even I knew why I wouldn't be jumping rope for as long as they would. I'd get tired fast and just sit on the porch with Daddy." After a while, her mother grew concerned and took her to a see a doctor, who found that Sarah was anemic. "My mother and I would take a bus and go to the clinic on Saturdays to get medication for my anemia."[11]

Some of the stories her father told her delivered important messages about the value of standing up for what's right and also having the courage to be independent and find your own opportunities, ideas that would prove important later in her own life.

One of his stories described the surprising history of "the little caves on our farm," Sarah recalled. "We used to see the caves when we were working on the farm." He told her how more than sixty years before she was born, when there was slavery in North Carolina, those caves helped people escape from slavery, giving them a place to hide as they tried to gain freedom. By hiding in those caves, "they were freed and lived there on that farm, on the land in this community," explained Sarah. Back then, that farmland was owned by free Black farmers. "Not all blacks in this country from its inception were slaves," noted Sarah.[12]

"Keysville was always a community of free Black people," explained Leesa P. Jones, a distant cousin of Sarah's who founded the Waterfront Underground Railroad Museum in Washington, North Carolina, in 2016. She has been researching the history of the Black community there and found that "they owned that farmland in Keysville. Freedom seekers would have gone to that farmland for protection and help. Caves and trenches may have been used to hide them. Many may have stayed there instead of going on to other places. The farms offered them jobs." Hiding freedom seekers was illegal. Bounty hunters would try to find escapees and punish them, as well as those who aided them. But free Black farmers in Keysville were willing to take those risks.[13]

"In 1836," Leesa Jones noted, "Southy Keys, a free Black man and wealthy ship caulker in this riverfront town, bought scores of acres of land in that portion of Washington we now call Keysville." She found courthouse records that in 1849 and 1850 Shadrach Keys also bought land. He may have been Sarah's great-grandfather. A book on the history of Washington, North Carolina—*Washington and the Pamlico*—reports that a man named Southey Kease (or Keys) owned "considerable property" in the Keysville area before the Civil War. It's not known if he was an ancestor of Sarah Keys, in part because of the varied ways nineteenth-century record keepers spelled family names. *Washington and the Pamlico* features recollections from many local residents. It is an anthology about the history of that city, created in 1976 in honor of the US bicentennial.[14]

According to research that Warren E. Milteer Jr. presents in his book *North Carolina's Free People of Color, 1715–1885*, court records in Beaufort County—the county that includes Washington and Keysville—show that in 1854 a man named Southy Keys was granted permission to have a young free Black man apprenticed to him to learn caulking. The Milteer book also reports that in 1855 this same court granted two other Keys landowners the right to have apprentices: Isaiah Keys, a free Black landowner, was approved to teach farming skills to an apprentice; and Shadrack Keys gained an apprentice to whom he would teach the cooper's trade of making wooden casks. John Hope Franklin, in *The Free Negro in North Carolina, 1790–1860*, noted that in 1847 a man named Southey Kease agreed to teach an eight-year-old boy how to be a caulker, an important skill in shipbuilding areas like Sarah's hometown and other cities along the Eastern Seaboard of North Carolina.

Young free people of color whose parents were unable to provide for them or teach them a skill could be "bound out as apprentices," either with Black craftsmen or with white families. Some free Black parents sought apprenticeships for their children, but others opposed them, needing their children's help working at home. These apprenticeships often included literacy training, which was important because the public school system North Carolina set up in 1839 specifically prohibited Black students from attending, whether enslaved or free. Before 1838, teaching an apprentice to read had been required until the creation of North Carolina's public schools the following year, when that requirement was rescinded at a time when slaveowners began fearing that literacy might lead to slave revolts.

Some apprentice masters, however, did continue the earlier practice of teaching reading.

The Franklin book also reports that although free Black young people were officially excluded from the state's new public schools, some still managed to receive instruction, including even in a "school," perhaps organized by the free Black community. In addition, that book provides 1850 US Census data for North Carolina, listing "100,591 whites and 217 free Negroes in school," with two free Black children attending school in Beaufort County. Those reports of free Black school attendance were made by families, apparently, not by boards of education. That same census showed that 43 percent of North Carolina's free Black citizens were literate.[15]

As a child, Sarah had also heard stories about another community of free Black farmers not far from Keysville—in Wootentown. That's where Sarah's mother, Curley Vivian Wooten, grew up. According to *Washington and the Pamlico*, Wootentown is a "community on land originally owned by Harkness Wooten" in the early nineteenth century. This free Black landowner and his descendants continued living there, including after the Civil War. A road from Washington to Wootentown was named Brick Kiln Road because Wootentown had clay deposits that were good for making bricks. Skilled free Black artisans created high-quality bricks in the town's kiln.[16]

There were other communities of free Black people in North Carolina before the Civil War. In 1860, North Carolina had about 331,000 enslaved residents—a third of the state's total population—as well as 30,000 "free people of color," about 3 percent of the population. The term "free people of color" was used by officials at that time, but it was also a name that those who fit that category used to describe themselves pre–Civil War, according to Milteer's book *North Carolina's Free People of Color*. The category "free people of color" included all who were not considered white: both those of exclusively African or Native American ancestry, or a mixture of both, as well as those with some white forebears, a description that matches Sarah Keys's background. Professor Milteer's book notes that communities of free people of color in North Carolina were located mainly in the western Piedmont area, as well as in the eastern areas including Keysville and Wootentown.[17]

Even in areas with established communities of free people of color, such as in Keysville, most of the Black people in neighboring vicinities were enslaved. Slavery in North Carolina had started in the mid-1600s. The barrier islands off the coast near Sarah's hometown made it difficult for ships to bring people captured in Africa directly to that part of North

Carolina. Often, captives who had been brought to other parts of the United States were sold to North Carolina landowners and transported to the state. There they were forced to work on farms or plantations for no wages, under profoundly difficult conditions, with little chance for most of them or their descendants to break free. Often enslavers used brutal forms of punishment to control those they enslaved, as individuals who had been enslaved in North Carolina recalled in oral histories recorded during the 1930s for the Federal Writers Project, archived at the Library of Congress.[18]

The enslaved in the Washington, North Carolina, area grew and harvested tobacco, rice, cotton, and other crops. Some had to handle the dangerous work of tending kilns where pine wood was burned to create tar and pitch. Others prepared harvested products to be shipped from the port of this riverfront town and sold elsewhere. Some worked on boats or as shipbuilders. This was one of the busiest ports in North Carolina before the Civil War.

Despite their hard work and importance to the state's economy, the enslaved had no rights. Families were torn apart when individuals were sold separately. They were not allowed to vote, to meet in groups without white supervision, or to be out on the street at night without written permission from the enslaver. Learning to read was forbidden and could lead to serious punishment for teacher and student. An enslaved man named Scipio, who lived in North Carolina, was killed for teaching reading to a young enslaved boy, who was then beaten severely, as noted in James D. Anderson's book on Black education. He also notes that despite the dangers, about 5 percent of those who were enslaved did manage to learn to read.[19]

Sarah, recalling stories she had heard years earlier, felt that some enslaved people had indeed learned to read surreptitiously. "Behind the curtains in the house, in the slaveowners' house," she said. "White folks' kids taught Black folks to read and write. It wasn't done out of doors. Those who knew how taught the ones who didn't. They were teaching each other. They learned to read and write and make music and sing."[20]

According to John Hope Franklin, Quakers in North Carolina were firmly opposed to slavery and as early as 1771 had begun teaching some of the enslaved to read and write, later even opening a school for enslaved children. Those efforts ended in 1830 when the North Carolina legislature made it illegal to teach an enslaved person to read and write, strengthening the earlier official prohibition in place from 1818. White enslavers feared that if those they enslaved could read, they might find ways to escape.

Legislators actually mentioned this fear in the law restricting education for the enslaved that was passed during the 1830–1831 session of the North Carolina General Assembly. The introduction to that law said that "the teaching of slaves to read and write has a tendency to excite dissatisfaction in their minds and to produce insurrection and rebellion to the manifest injury of the citizens of this state." Some of the enslaved managed to flee regardless, escaping on boats that sailed from the Washington harbor or hiding in the Great Dismal Swamp located more than a hundred miles north of Keysville. Others, as noted earlier, found safety in caves on Keysville farmland.[21]

It's not known exactly how the pre–Civil War Keysville farmers whom Sarah's father mentioned in his stories had gained their status as free people. According to *Washington and the Pamlico*, descendants of early Keysville residents reported to the book's authors that their ancestors were born free. Professors Milteer, Franklin, and others suggest various ways individuals could gain the designation "free people of color." Some had never been enslaved, having entered North Carolina as free people. However, in 1826 a North Carolina law put an end to that option by prohibiting any additional free people of color from entering the state. Others in North Carolina were considered free if their mothers had been free. Having a white mother gave a person free status, no matter who was the father. A few may have become free during the American Revolution by serving with American forces in the Continental Army, an option offered to enslaved people as a way to enlarge the size of the force battling the British. North Carolina records for the Revolutionary War show that only fifty-eight of its soldiers were enslaved. At least a few of them were given freedom after the war. It's possible that others gained freedom by earning enough money doing extra jobs to pay off their enslavers. But that became costly after 1855, when the legislature required that a bond worth a thousand dollars (about $38,000 today) be posted in order to emancipate anyone.

White officials made manumission—freeing the enslaved—difficult to achieve. In North Carolina, it could occur only if sanctioned by a court or government official. Also, the enslaved person had to have performed some type of "meritorious service," with few specifics as to what that might entail, leaving the decision to the whim of local officials. Quakers who were opposed to slavery formed a manumission society and tried to find ways to free the enslaved. One approach was to purchase enslaved individuals in order to free them. In 1827, the state Supreme Court's chief judge criticized that strategy, but Franklin's book says efforts still continued to try to free the enslaved.

For those who did manage to gain freedom, it was important for them to keep a certificate or other document stating that freedom had been granted because of the risk of being accused of being a runaway and sold back into bondage. Those who had always been free also needed to have documentation because their free status could be challenged, too. A few free people of color became slaveholders themselves, often in order to purchase relatives and set them free, but that became illegal in 1861, when free people of color were prohibited from being slaveholders.[22]

Free people of color had some rights in North Carolina, but those rights kept being eroded. Slaveholders in North Carolina and other Southern states were alarmed by slavery uprisings in Haiti in the 1790s, an 1811 rebellion in Louisiana, and an 1831 insurrection led by Nat Turner in Virginia. They feared additional uprisings might occur, perhaps fomented by free people of color living in their state. Even more concerning to white landowners, according to John Hope Franklin, was a pamphlet written in 1829 by David Walker, a free Black man from Wilmington, North Carolina, who had moved to Boston. His "Appeal in Four Articles" described the "wretchedness" of slavery and said the enslaved would be justified in trying to oppose slavery with force. When copies of his articles reached North Carolina in 1830, the legislature passed a law forbidding the circulation of any written materials that would encourage insurrection among both enslaved and free people of color.

In 1835, insurrection-wary officials revoked free people of color's right to vote, a right granted in the state's 1776 constitution, which was completed on December 23, 1776, when equal rights were on many Americans' minds after that summer's signing of the Declaration of Independence. But later fears of uprisings overrode earlier egalitarian ideals.

In addition, people of color were no longer allowed to sell goods outside of their own county and were forbidden to return to North Carolina if they left the state for more than ninety days. Laws also denied free people of color the right to preach in public, buy or sell liquor, attend a public school, or have a gun without obtaining a permit. However, until the Civil War they retained the right to own property and to file complaints in court.[23]

Despite these restrictions, the number of free people of color in Sarah's hometown increased from eight in 1800 to more than two hundred by 1860, comprising about 13 percent of the town's total population, according to local historian Ray Midgett. This was a slightly larger percentage than in the state as a whole. In addition, *Washington and the Pamlico* notes that there were twenty-one free Black farmers in the Washington area before the start of the Civil War. A similar increase in free people of color occurred in the state as a whole. From 1830 to 1860, the number of free people of color in North Carolina increased more than 50 percent, from 19,543 in 1830 to 22,732 in 1840 and then to 30,463 in 1860. That was a larger increase than for those who were enslaved in the state, which rose from 245,601 in 1830 to 331,059 in 1860, as reported by John Hope Franklin.

Communities of free people of color were important to the economy of their areas. In 1860, North Carolina was still a rural, agrarian state. According to Franklin, nearly three-quarters of North Carolina families were not slaveholding families. Of those that were, more than half enslaved fewer than ten individuals. Many non-slaveholding farmers hired free people of color as low-wage farm workers and as skilled craftsmen, such as masons, brick makers, painters, caulkers, and carpenters. Free people of color also filled needed roles in the shipping and fishing industries of coastal areas, including in the busy port city of Washington. Free women of color played important roles in the local economies as seamstresses, weavers, dressmakers, and bakers. As Franklin noted, the free Black farmer, "living in the inarticulate and relatively sparsely settled countryside, steadily rose in economic independence and, consequently, in the respect—somewhat disquieted, perhaps—of his fellows."[24]

Taking a Bigger Risk

In addition to the danger Keysville's free Black landowners faced by sheltering freedom seekers in caves on their land, they took a bigger risk by signing up to fight with Union forces during the Civil War, helping bring an end to slavery altogether. Some white residents in the eastern coastal area of the state where Keysville is located did not support seceding from the United States. But other white North Carolinians did, and the secessionists prevailed. North Carolina became the second-to-last state to secede, doing so in May 1861, one month after Confederate forces attacked Fort Sumter in South Carolina and initiated the war. But as David C. Williard notes in his article "North Carolina in the Civil War," "several thousand North Carolinians, especially those living in the state's coastal and mountain regions, remained loyal to the United States and resisted the Confederacy's control over the state."[25]

Union forces won early victories in North Carolina during the Civil War, beginning with seizing control of Hatteras Island in August 1861. Six months later, General Ambrose Burnside's troops arrived by sea to take control of Roanoke Island and then sailed south to win a March 14, 1862, victory in New Bern, a railroad hub of strategic importance. New Bern already had a community of free people of color and remained under Union control for the rest of the war.

Later that month, Union troops took control of two nearby cities: Plymouth and Sarah's hometown of Washington. A year later, in March 1863, Confederate forces tried but failed to retake Washington. The Union commander there, Major General John G. Foster, said local Black men "applied to me for arms, and to strengthen my lines I armed about 120, all that I had arms for." At least two of the Black volunteers, who served as boatmen, died helping ferry Union reinforcements in order to keep Union forces in charge in Washington. This was several months before official Black Union Army battalions were organized.[26]

Enslaved people in nearby areas made their way to New Bern, "through woods and swamps from every side," using any means possible, noted one Union officer. One enslaved woman and her children used a dugout canoe to travel down the Neuse River to New Bern, according to David Cecelski. Others escaped in a dinghy while their "owner took potshots at them from shore."[27]

A Black Union Army scout, William Henry Singleton, organized an informal militia of about a thousand newly freed men in New Bern. They became frustrated when they weren't allowed to join the Union Army. They were also treated with disrespect by some Union Army officers. That began to change after President Lincoln issued the Emancipation Proclamation on January 1, 1863. It declared an end to slavery throughout the Confederacy and allowed Black men to serve in the military. On January 3, 1863, with Union troops still in control in Washington, North Carolina, a Union officer read the Emancipation Proclamation aloud from the steps of the city's Presbyterian church.[28]

By then, fugitives from slavery had set up shantytown dwellings on the outskirts of New Bern. Many of the men would become members of the Union Army, along with free men of color, thanks to an agreement that Abraham Galloway worked out with military officials. In 1857, Galloway had escaped from slavery in Wilmington, North Carolina, stowing away on a ship bound for Philadelphia. In the North, he became an advocate for abolition and then returned south to serve the Union Army as a spy and a recruiter.

In the first months of 1863, however, recruiting was not going well in New Bern until Abraham Galloway had local army officials promise that

Black recruits would receive the same pay as white soldiers. Officials also promised to help the families of Black recruits while the soldiers were away fighting, including providing education for their children. In addition, he made the army agree that it would try to make Confederate forces treat captured Black soldiers as prisoners of war instead of enslaving or executing them. That would be hard to enforce, but the fact that army officials showed a willingness to try led to successful recruiting. Also helping with recruitment was General Order No. 252 that President Lincoln issued in July 1863, which said that if any captured Union soldiers were enslaved, a captured Confederate soldier would face hard labor. However, Confederate mistreatment of Black troops still occurred, causing the Union Army to stop prisoner exchanges with the Confederates.

From late May 1863 onward, as a result of Abraham Galloway's negotiating, more than 5,000 Black soldiers were recruited in New Bern and at recruiting stations in nearby Plymouth and Washington. They served initially in the 1st North Carolina Colored Volunteers, later renamed the 35th Infantry US Colored Troops (USCT). Others served in the 36th and 37th Infantry USCT divisions. They were among the more than 190,000 Black soldiers and sailors who fought on the Union side. Black women encouraged men to sign up. In New Bern, a Colored Ladies Relief Association raised money to help soldiers' families. Black women in Washington, North Carolina, made a regimental flag for one regiment, according to a book on Black Civil War troops by James K. Bryant.[29]

Sadly, Black recruits often faced the mistreatment many feared. A tragic example occurred in Plymouth, a recruiting site for the 37th USCT. From April 17 to 20, 1864, Confederate forces launched an attack on Plymouth with 10,000 infantry troops, backed up by a devastating new weapon of war, an ironclad battleship that sank a Union ship, damaged another, and bombarded the city. The much smaller Union force of 2,800 surrendered on April 20th. Confederate soldiers then looted the town.

Even worse, they massacred Black soldiers, both those taken prisoner and others who had fled the battlefield, often trying to hide in nearby swamps, along with terrified local Black women and children. It is hard to know how many died in this massacre. A 1995 study by two Civil War historians, Weymouth Jordan, Jr., and Gerald W. Thomas, estimates that at least one hundred were killed in this way, but the total may be higher.

Because of the defeat in Plymouth, the Union general in nearby Washington received orders on April 26, 1864, to evacuate. He sent his troops, including his Black soldiers, to New Bern, along with Black refugees and their families. As they fled, some Union soldiers did what Confederate soldiers did in Plymouth—they looted the town. Then on April 30, 1864, as the last Union troops fled, a fire broke out that destroyed many buildings in Washington, including the Catholic church, and other churches as well. Many residents had already left earlier in the war. "The town was desolate and ruined," according to *Washington and the Pamlico.*

The Union Army later condemned the looting but not the burning of the city, according to a recent account by historian Ray Midgett. He noted that in 1910 some churches "received compensation for their losses" from the federal government.

Sarah Keys's father would find a way to help create a new Catholic church in Washington more than sixty years later.[30]

According to a book by James K. Bryant on the history of the 36th Infantry USCT, the company's roster included four men named Keyes or Keys. The military records presented in that book showed that these four soldiers had all been "born free" and had signed up in June or July 1863. They continued to serve until June or July 1866, except for Benjamin Keyes, who mustered out in June 1865. He and James Keyes are listed as having been farmers in Washington, North Carolina. William Keyes, identified as a farmer, is listed as coming from Beaufort County (the county that includes Washington) and may also have been in the 35th Infantry, according to another book on the battalions.

Shadrach Keyes's registration information for the 36th Infantry says he was a carpenter from nearby Martin County and was wounded during a battle in Virginia in September 1864. Sonya Keys, Sarah's niece, discovered during her genealogy research that Sarah's great-grandfather was named Shadrach Keyes, although it hasn't been determined if he was the same Shadrach Keyes who was in the 36th Infantry.[31]

Whether or not these Keys/Keyes soldiers were related to Sarah, clearly people of color in her hometown had a long history of standing up for what's right—and a history of service in the military, sending an important message about citizenship and equal rights. As Frederick Douglass remarked in a speech he gave in 1863, once a Black man "can get upon his person the brass letters U.S., . . . an eagle on his button, and a musket on his shoulder, and bullets in his pocket, there is no power on earth which can deny that he has earned the right of citizenship in the United States."[32]

Other Stories with a Message

Sarah's father didn't tell her stories about those Keys soldiers in the Civil War. The records of their army service came to her attention during the research for this book. "It was surprising. Maybe they were related in some way," Sarah said.[33]

Her father did, however, explain the new dangers that Keys's ancestors faced after the end of the Civil War, when the Ku Klux Klan began to attack and threaten Black communities, starting in 1868 in North Carolina. The Klan, along with other groups of armed white men, terrorized Black communities to try to bring back whites-only rule. "My father and my grandfather used to tell us stories of the Klan. The stories, they were usually things that had happened in the past. They were never in our community. You didn't think of being fearful of that," said Sarah.[34]

Her father's stories had illustrated his and his ancestors' strategy for dealing with situations that needed fixing—taking a firm, positive, nonconfrontational approach—a strategy he would suggest to her years later when trouble came her way.

The most significant change that he brought to his local community, however, was the excellent school he helped start, attended by Sarah, her siblings, and other young Black people. The next chapter describes what education for Black students was like in North Carolina during the years before he decided to help create that school in 1927, two years before Sarah was born.

6

Education Backstory

NORTH CAROLINA

THIS CHAPTER TAKES A LOOK AT EVENTS in North Carolina from Reconstruction onward that helped prompt Sarah's father, David A. Keys Sr., to take a stand on the creation of a new school for Black students in his hometown in 1927. Education for Black people was a major topic during those post–Civil War years, first as something to be encouraged and expanded upon and, later, as something some officials tried to limit in scope and content.

For a brief period at the start of Reconstruction, educational opportunities blossomed for people of color in North Carolina. The Freedmen's Bureau, established by the federal government in 1865 to oversee the postwar transition in the South, helped set up schools to provide education for the formerly enslaved who had been denied a chance to learn to read. These schools were often staffed with Northern teachers and funded by Northern benevolent and religious organizations. Freedmen's School teachers and staff also included those who had been free people of color before the Civil War and were already educated. According to LeRae Umfleet's *A Day of Blood*, one of those prewar freemen, John P. Sampson, whose family was wealthy before the war, became a clerk to the head of schools for the Freedmen's Bureau in Wilmington, North Carolina. Later, he worked as a local official and then as a lawyer in Washington, DC.

Prewar free people of color also created organizations to help the newly free while also working to influence official policy in the state and, later, running for elected office.

However, after the Civil War, even before the Freedmen's Schools started, Black communities in North Carolina and elsewhere in the South had set up their own schools, organized by Black churches and staffed by Black teachers. Called Sabbath Schools, their classes often met on evenings and weekends. They educated thousands of eager learners, ranging from young children to great-grandparents. By 1868, the African Methodist Episcopal (AME) Church had forty thousand students in its Sabbath Schools across the South. Educational efforts had also started before the war ended as Union forces gained control in the Outer Banks and in New Bern. Those who had freed themselves began to receive instruction from soldiers and others who volunteered to teach.

Some in the white community were not pleased with efforts to educate Black people, fearing this might upend the existing social situation. Schools for Black students and their teachers were sometimes attacked, but the thirst for learning persisted.[1] John W. Alford, the superintendent of Freedmen's Schools, was impressed with the students' determination "to educate themselves. . . . They have within themselves . . . a vitality and hope, coupled with patience and willingness to struggle, which foreshadows with certainty their higher education as a people in coming time."[2]

Black leaders in North Carolina, including Abraham Galloway (mentioned earlier as a recruiter for Union forces), had been busy even before the war ended trying to make sure the postwar South would treat all fairly. He and other activists traveled to Washington, DC, in April 1864 to meet with President Lincoln and members of Congress to persuade them that after the war, Black people should have full rights as citizens, including the right to vote. The Black delegates who met with President Lincoln in the White House included Jarvis M. Williams, a baker from Sarah Keys's hometown of Washington, North Carolina, who before the war had been a free person of color. However, a year later, after Lincoln was assassinated, his replacement, former slaveholder Andrew Johnson, opposed Black voting rights and allowed Confederacy supporters to regain control in North Carolina and other Southern states. Those officials tried to recreate the prewar social situation, offering few rights to people of color and forcing newly freed families to work and live under conditions not much different from those during slavery.

Galloway and other Black leaders, both the newly freed as well as others who had been free before the war, met in the state capital, Raleigh, in 1865 to create the North Carolina Equal Rights League. They drew up a list of moderate policies for white officials to consider in order to create a fairer situation, such as providing a way for the newly freed to earn a living, as well as education for their children and help reuniting families split up during slavery.

White officials ignored those suggestions and issued their own new constitution and a Black Code that did not allow Black men to vote, banned interracial marriage, and made it easy to arrest people of color if they could not prove they had a job, which could lead to them being forced to work in unjust circumstances.[3]

When the US Congress saw this happening across the South, it stepped in to put an end to President Johnson's approach by passing, as noted earlier, the Military Reconstruction Act of 1867, which marked the start of the ten-year period known as Reconstruction. That law called for federal troops to be stationed in Southern states and required those states to write new constitutions, with Black men taking part in the elections that would select delegates to the states' constitutional conventions. In North Carolina, Galloway and fourteen other Black men were elected to help create the new constitution. Most of that constitutional convention's 120 delegates were members of the Republican Party, Lincoln's party, including eighteen Northern Republicans who had moved to North Carolina after the war.

The constitution they wrote in 1868 was revolutionary. It gave Black men the right to vote and also made voting easier for everyone—Black and white—by no longer requiring voters to own property. It also said voters should elect local officials rather than allow politicians to appoint them.

In addition, the 1868 Constitution called for something North Carolina had never required before: free, tax-supported public schools for all, including for Black youngsters. North Carolina had started public education for white students in 1839. Now the mandate widened. Black and white students wouldn't be going to school together, however. There would be separate schools for Black and white students. Still, for the first time children of color had the right to an education. Local communities would be in charge of providing funds for that education. For Black students this meant that, in some areas, their public schools received less funding than schools for white students. Also, the publicly funded schools for Black students were generally grade-school level because the State of

North Carolina didn't create its first official public high school for Black students until 1918.[4] Even so, W. E. B. Du Bois noted, "Public Education for all at public expense was, in the South, a Negro idea."[5]

In an election in 1868, Republican candidates did well, winning the governorship with the election of William W. Holden, a white newspaper editor who had criticized the Confederacy during the Civil War and tried to start a peace movement in 1864. All but one of the state's representatives who were elected to serve in the US Congress that year were Republicans, as were two-thirds of the members of the state legislature, including Abraham Galloway and nineteen other Black candidates. Among them was John A. Hyman, who had once been enslaved and would win election to Congress in 1874 as North Carolina's first Black US congressman. All the Black members of the newly elected 1868 legislature came from the eastern part of the state, where Black citizens made up the majority of the population, although in the state as a whole, white citizens outnumbered people of color by a two-to-one ratio.[6]

The 1868 constitution and electoral victories raised the spirits of the Black community, especially because of the emphasis on education. The new schools set up for Black students used the same kind of academic curriculum being taught then in New England schools, emphasizing reading, writing, math, and history. Although the Black schools tended to receive less funding than those for white students, religious organizations tried to fill the gap by setting up private schools for Black young people and by founding universities for Black students. They also set up teacher training academies, which often provided high school–level instruction along with teacher training skills. These academies were the only option for Black students to receive high school–level instruction in some communities until North Carolina created its first official high school for Black students in 1918.[7]

Obtaining a good education was often a patchwork effort, as it was for Sarah Dudley Pettey, born in New Bern, North Carolina, in 1869. The life story of this pioneering feminist is told in Glenda Elizabeth Gilmore's book *Gender and Jim Crow*. Sarah Dudley Pettey would become a teacher, newspaper columnist, women's rights advocate, and a champion, with her husband, of the kind of education that David A. Keys Sr. would also endorse many years later.

Sarah Dudley Pettey's educational journey began at home, where she was taught to read by her mother, who had been enslaved. Then this young girl completed six grades at one of New Bern's new elementary-level public schools for Black students, mandated by the 1868 Constitution. "Graded" schools were a new development in education at that time, gaining interest elsewhere in the country, too. They were an improvement over the earlier "common school"—one-room schoolhouse approach—where students of different ages were taught together.

At age twelve, Sarah Dudley Pettey spent a year at the new coed New Bern State Colored Normal School, where she had high school–level classes along with teacher training. At age thirteen, she spent a year at Scotia Seminary, a Presbyterian school for girls started in 1867 in Concord, North Carolina. It had both white and Black teachers. Then she returned home to work as an assistant principal at one of New Bern's graded public schools.[8]

The curriculum in the schools she attended was based on the classical instruction offered at the time in New England schools and colleges. In fact, Luke Dorland, the white educator who founded the Scotia Seminary, based the school on Mount Holyoke College in Massachusetts. Mary McLeod Bethune, a future Black educator and NAACP leader who also studied at Scotia Seminary, said its classical curriculum taught her that "the color of a person's skin has nothing to do with his brains." Other colleges for North Carolina's Black students started by religious organizations between the 1860s and the 1890s used a classical curriculum as well. Those schools, which continue to educate students today, include Shaw University in Raleigh, Biddle Memorial Institute (now Johnson C. Smith University) in Charlotte, Saint Augustine's in Raleigh, Bennett Seminary (now College) in Greensboro, and Livingstone College in Salisbury. Shaw University added two professional schools not long after opening: a medical school and a pharmacy school.[9]

Vibrant Black communities began to blossom, with Black lawyers, doctors, business owners, writers, craftsmen, preachers, and teachers creating new opportunities for many by offering Black citizens more access to legal, medical, crafts, educational, and religious services. By the 1890s, New Bern's large prewar free Black community had joined with the newly freed to turn New Bern into a thriving city, with three Black lawyers and the first Black private bank in the state, founded by eight local Black leaders. New Bern also boasted Black butchers, carpenters, and general merchants. All eight of the city's barbers were Black. In addition, it was home to influential Black educators, including Sarah Dudley Pettey and her husband, Bishop Charles Pettey, who in about 1900 had done well enough to buy a hotel, which became a popular health resort, in Wilkes County in western North Carolina, located not far from where Charles Pettey was born into slavery.

However, for many in North Carolina's Black communities, life remained hard, particularly for those among the newly freed whose only way to survive was by becoming sharecroppers, continuing to plant and harvest crops for white landowners as they had done during slavery. The legal arrangements sharecroppers had to accept were overwhelmingly favorable to the landowners, who gained the lion's share of earnings from sharecroppers' harvests. This system also kept sharecroppers in continuous debt to the landowners for equipment and supplies, making it hard for sharecroppers to build savings and find ways to become independent.[10]

Downward Spiral

Sarah Keys's landowning ancestors in Keysville may have avoided the hardships of sharecropping, but they must have been concerned when the hope-filled postwar era began to crumble in the 1870s. By 1871, wealthy white members of the Democratic Party regained control of the state legislature and set out to bring back whites-only rule.

Their return to power was accomplished in part by a reign of terror and intimidation launched by members of the Ku Klux Klan, which in North Carolina was based in the central Piedmont area. The Civil War had devastated the state's economy. Wealthy white people who had been in control before the war felt that their financial concerns weren't being addressed by the new Republican-led legislature, with its elected members, Black and white, who advocated for Black rights.[11] As W. E. B. Du Bois wrote in his book about the Reconstruction era, those disgruntled wealthy whites set out "to draw the color line and convince the native-born white voter that his interests lay with the planter-class and were opposed to those of the Northern interloper and the Negro."[12]

They began a campaign of fear and intimidation aimed at ending Republican control. It led, in 1870, to the murder of a white Republican leader in a county courthouse in the northern part of the state. That same year a prominent Black leader was lynched. Hooded Klan members launched nighttime attacks on Black homes and burned dozens of schools for Black students. This made many white people leery of voting for Republicans and persuaded some people of color to fear voting at all in the upcoming election.[13] Essie Harris, a Black man in Chatham County who was seriously injured when Klan nightriders shot into his cabin one night for ninety minutes, reached this decision: "I do not expect to vote anymore. It is not worthwhile for a man to vote and run the risk of his life."[14]

The election of 1870 saw Democratic Party candidates gain control of the legislature, which then impeached and removed Governor Holden for having tried to rein in the Klan. In 1875, the state legislature, controlled by Democratic Party delegates, created a new constitution for the state, undoing the 1868 Constitution's reform that had required local officials to be elected. Instead, local officials were now appointed by those interested in undoing Reconstruction's advances. In addition, interracial marriage was made illegal. Schools for Black students continued to be less well funded than those for white young people. By the time US troops withdrew from the South in 1877, ending the decade of Reconstruction, white supremacists were firmly in control in North Carolina.[15]

Help from the federal government receded. As noted in chapter 2, in 1883 the US Supreme Court said the Civil Rights Act of 1875 was unconstitutional because of the limited way in which the justices interpreted the Fourteenth Amendment—that only individual states, not the federal government, could make rules and laws about the rights and privileges of a state's citizens or businesses. As a result, Congress could not intervene to counter restrictive new race-based segregation laws passed by majority-white legislatures in North Carolina and other Southern states.[16]

There was a brief reprieve in the mid-1890s when supporters of Black rights made a comeback in North Carolina politics. Republicans—both white and Black, including Black sharecroppers—joined forces with the new Populist Party to create what became known as the Fusion coalition. The Populist Party had started when low-income white farmers decided to create their own political party because they felt wealthy white Democrat officials were helping banks and businesses, not farmers. This Fusion coalition of Republicans and Populists elected enough candidates in 1894 to win back control of the legislature and in 1896 to elect a Republican governor. That legislature revived some reforms from 1868, including the one about voters electing local officials. As a result, Black men began serving as local postmasters, firemen, and aldermen.[17]

Those reforms incensed wealthy white Democrats, who plotted how to regain control of the legislature in the 1898 election, devising a plan that would use racial fear, terror, and voter suppression.[18] As Democratic lawyer Furnifold M. Simmons noted in describing their victory plan, "This is a white man's country and white men must control and govern it."[19]

Democrats whipped up racial fear among white Populists to persuade them to vote for Democrats in order to save the white race and protect white women. White newspapers printed cartoons depicting Black officials as monsters. The state's main newspaper, Raleigh's *News and Observer*, led the charge. Democratic speakers claimed Black politicians were taking over, which was unlikely, as the legislature at that time had five times more white legislators than Black ones.[20]

"It will be the meanest, vilest, dirtiest campaign," boasted Daniel Schenck, a Democratic Party leader.[21] He was right. During the 1898 election, white mobs intimidated Black and Republican voters, destroyed ballots cast for Republicans, and stuffed ballot boxes with fake votes for Democrats, leading to Democrats winning control of the legislature.

Efforts to regain control went farther, however, in Wilmington, the state's largest city, located about a hundred miles south of Sarah Keys's hometown. More than half of Wilmington's citizens were Black, and they had created a thriving community, getting along well with the city's white residents. Wilmington had a Black-owned newspaper, the *Daily Record*, whose editor, Alex Manly, was not shy about writing in favor of Black rights. In August 1898, in response to an article in the city's white newspaper that called for the lynching of Black men who had relationships with white women, he wrote an editorial criticizing white men who abused Black women. Manly's editorial outraged white Democratic Party leaders across the state. They targeted Wilmington for special punishment during the 1898 election.

An armed white group, the Red Shirts, terrorized Black people in Wilmington. On election day, November 8, 1898, white supremacists interfered with the counting of votes in Wilmington to guarantee that Democrats won seats in the state legislature. Two days later, Democrats tried to ensure they would never be defeated there again. Although Alex Manly escaped, a mob of more than a thousand armed white people burned down his newspaper's building. Such groups roamed the city, killing Black leaders and other people of color. Some Black people tried to fight back but were no match for the mass of white attackers and the local militia, which brought a machine gun mounted on a wagon into Black neighborhoods. Black women and children fled into nearby woods and swamps.

News reports said twenty-five Black citizens were killed that day in Wilmington. Experts feel the toll was over a hundred, with bodies likely thrown into the Cape Fear River.[22] A leader of the massacre, Colonel Alfred M. Waddell, said this might happen in a speech he gave a few weeks earlier, when he vowed to end Black rule, "if we have to choke the current of the Cape Fear with carcasses."[23]

Waddell was installed as the city's mayor that day, even though the mayor's office was not up for election that year. He simply forced the city's white Republican mayor to resign, along with the city's board of aldermen, Black and white, in what is thought to be the first successful governmental coup in US history. Black firefighters were dismissed and replaced with white men.[24] The next Sunday, a local white pastor proclaimed that "whites were doing God's service."[25]

The Wilmington massacre delivered a clear message that it would be risky to oppose the Democratic Party's agenda in North Carolina going forward. Sarah Keys's father was only two years old when the Wilmington massacre occurred. It wasn't talked about in public for a long time. But the repercussions of that 1898 coup set the stage for what would follow.

Disfranchisement

In the years between the Fusion coalition victories of 1894 and the Wilmington Massacre of 1898, the US Supreme Court issued its *Plessy v. Ferguson* decision in 1896 (discussed in chapter 2). It gave the federal government's stamp of approval to the concept of separate but equal, which provided the legal underpinning for decades of Jim Crow segregation.

Once white supremacist legislators regained control in North Carolina in 1898, they continued what they had started earlier during their first return to power in the 1870s, when they had passed laws that required segregated schools and prisons and outlawed interracial marriage, as noted in Richard A. Paschal's book on Jim Crow legislation in North Carolina. In the 1890s and the early twentieth century, they passed laws in line with those of other Southern states, such as the 1899 law that instituted segregation on railroads and steamboats. Another law required racially separate teacher training institutes. A 1901 law said North Carolina's state library had to provide separate areas for Black people.[26] A 1903 school segregation law included this phrase that made it clear there would be no chance for any compromise on the issue: "No child with negro blood in his veins, however remote the strain, shall attend a school for the white race."[27]

Laws passed in 1907 segregated streetcars and road crews. By then North Carolina had become involved in convict leasing, which other Southern states had been doing for many years. This allowed the state to earn money from businesses that paid for the right to have North Carolina's prisoners work in chain gang–type crews to build railroad tracks and roads. Many of the prisoners forced to do this work were Black men who had been arrested for minor offenses. The convict leasing crews often worked in dangerous conditions, resulting in prisoner deaths.

White-owned businesses felt emboldened to establish their own discriminatory rules, such as not allowing Black customers to eat in a restaurant's dining room, requiring them to order takeout, often from a back door. Movie theaters made people of color sit in the balcony, reserving seats downstairs for white customers. Stores wouldn't let Black customers try on clothes before making a purchase. Some cities and towns set up separate park areas for Black and white residents, separate water fountains and restrooms, and even separate Bibles for people to place their hands on when promising to tell the truth in court. Access to financial resources was limited for the Black community, including obtaining loans from banks and government agencies, making it hard for these families to become homeowners. The farm services agency was segregated, with Black farmers receiving less assistance than white farmers. As David A. Keys. Sr. discovered, finding good-paying jobs to supplement his farm income often required traveling to DC and New Jersey.[28]

Even before many of the new restrictions were imposed, the state's new leaders found a way to limit opposition to the Jim Crow restrictions they planned to legislate. In 1900, an amendment was added to the North Carolina constitution that made it hard for Black men to vote. Fewer Black voters meant that there wouldn't be many lawmakers elected who would look out for the interests of people of color.

The 1900 amendment didn't actually state that ending Black voting was its purpose. This would violate the Fifteenth Amendment to the US Constitution. Officials avoided mentioning race by making prospective voters pay a steep poll tax and take a reading test that required an applicant to write from memory randomly assigned sections of the US Constitution. A voting registrar had total control over which excerpts would be chosen and whether an applicant passed. White men, however, didn't have to take the literacy test because of a grandfather clause first used two years earlier in Louisiana as a way to suppress the Black vote. This clause said that men could skip the reading test if they were a descendant of someone eligible to vote in 1867. Since no Black men could vote in North Carolina or other Southern states in 1867, only white men were allowed to skip the test.[29]

Just before the 1900 election, in which voters would choose whether to approve the new amendment, the Democratic Party published an information sheet to explain to white voters why they should vote for it: "The chief object of the Amendment is to eliminate the ignorant and irresponsible Negro vote . . . [and] to protect forever the entire body of the uneducated white vote of the state in their right to vote."

In 1900, North Carolina voters overwhelmingly approved the disfranchising amendment. Red Shirts again terrorized Black voters and stuffed ballot boxes with fake votes, both for the amendment and for the state's new Democratic governor, Charles B. Aycock.[30] The *Messenger*, Wilmington's white-owned newspaper, proclaimed that the 1900 election results were "a glorious triumph for white supremacy."[31]

Governor Aycock said in a speech given before the election: "When we say the negro is unfit to rule we carry it one step further and convey the idea that he is unfit to vote. To do this we must disenfranchise the negro."[32] The new amendment lived up to the governor's expectations. In the 1896 election for governor, 87 percent of Black men voted. In the elections that took place after the new disfranchisement amendment went into effect, the percentages of Black men who managed to register to vote had dropped radically—to about 4 percent in both 1902 and 1904. According to Richard A. Paschal, "The estimated percentage of black votes in the 1904 governor's race was effectively zero."[33]

Governor Aycock gave a speech in 1903 noting that disfranchisement had "solved the negro problem." He announced: "Let the negro learn once for all that there is unending separation of the races, that the two peoples may develop side by side to the fullest but that they cannot intermingle." He added that the white race was "the dominant race. . . . When the negro recognizes this fact we shall have peace and good will between the races."[34]

Alabama, Virginia, Georgia, and Oklahoma also used the grandfather clause to limit Black voting. In 1915, the US Supreme Court banned this policy for violating the Fifteenth Amendment. In response, some states simply added new restrictions. North Carolina still used its difficult-to-pass literacy test.[35]

The racial-fear crusade launched by wealthy white Democrats ended the start of an alliance among working-class people—white and Black—that had begun to form during the Fusion era. Lower-income white residents lost out as a result, according to historians Barbara and Karen Fields in their book *Racecraft*. Anti-Black propaganda ended that earlier alliance, which had been based on those two groups' shared economic interests.[36] Historian C. Vann Woodward noted that the white supremacist victories in the South were not only about solidifying white control but were also about "which whites should be supreme."[37]

A Shift in Education

In Governor Aycock's 1903 speech boasting of his many successes, he added, "We must educate not only ourselves but see to it that the negro has an opportunity for education."[38] However, that did not mean that education for Black children would soon become equal in quality to that provided for white students. The legislature began to fund public elementary schools for Black children in 1910, but the funds provided for school buildings for Black students was one-tenth of what was allotted for white children's schools. Black teachers received half of what white teachers earned. The spending per pupil was nearly twice as high in white schools, with $17.25 spent per pupil on white students' education and only $9.28 for Black students. By 1949 these disparities contributed to a marked difference in high school graduation rates in the state, with the number of white students who graduated from high school twice as high as the number of Black students.[39]

However, there was a new challenge for Black education that arose one year before the 1896 *Plessy v. Ferguson* decision solidified the idea of "separate but equal." The new 1895 educational proposal didn't follow that mandate. Instead, it called for a new kind of education for Black students that would not be at all equal to the education most white students received.

Instead of using the classical education curriculum taught in Northern states that most Black schools in North Carolina followed at the time, the 1895 proposal would instead train Southern Black students to develop practical skills that would be of use to a South whose economy was still based largely on agriculture, such as skills useful in harvesting and processing crops and also in working as household servants for those who oversaw the marketing of those harvests.

This new policy was introduced to great fanfare in a speech delivered by Black educator Booker T. Washington on September 18, 1895, before a predominantly white audience at the Cotton States and International Exposition in Atlanta, Georgia.[40] He suggested that the South could prosper if Black citizens would "cast down your bucket where you are" and develop skills in "agriculture, mechanics, in commerce, in domestic service, and in the professions" that can help the Southern economy thrive. He wanted fellow Blacks to learn that "there is as much dignity in tilling a field as in writing a poem."[41] He used poetic language but offered few details that day about the curriculum he thought would be best for Black students in the South. His approach came to be known as "industrial education" or, as it is often called today, vocational education.

Booker T. Washington was born into slavery in 1856. After Emancipation, he learned to read as a boy in the informal Black-taught schools described at the beginning of this chapter. He was introduced to the idea of having Southern Black students focus on industrial education as a teenager, when he enrolled in 1872 at Hampton Normal and Agricultural Institute in Virginia. It had been founded in 1868 by Samuel Chapman Armstrong, who grew up in Hawaii as the son of a missionary, attended Williams College in Massachusetts, and after graduation enlisted in the Union Army, serving as a brigadier general for a regiment of Black soldiers. After the war, this white veteran worked for the Freedmen's Bureau. The American Missionary Association then helped him start the Hampton Institute to train Black teachers to work with newly freed people of color.

The policies at the Hampton Institute reflected General Armstrong's views about Black people.[42] He thought they weren't ready for Northern-style classical education because, in his opinion, they lacked "foresight, judgment and hard sense."[43] But he felt they could "develop those guiding instincts and institutions that the Anglo-Saxon has reached through ages of hard experience."[44] He also opposed Black Southerners taking part in politics or in efforts to achieve equality, feeling they should focus instead on what they were already good at and had experience with: farm labor tasks they had engaged in during slavery, which could help bring prosperity to them and to the South. At Hampton Institute, he trained Black teachers to teach those kinds of practical skills by having the teacher trainees engage in vigorous farm labor themselves.[45] The emphasis was on industrial rather than academic learning. One student at Hampton Institute in 1878, who was dissatisfied with the academic classes, noted that this part of the curriculum was not rigorous, involving "going over what I had learned in a primary school."[46]

Washington later became a teacher at Hampton. In 1881, he moved on to head a new teacher training school in Alabama, the Tuskegee Institute, which used the same approach as Hampton—helping teachers hone their farming skills, prioritizing industrial learning over academic classes.[47] In 1902, the director of Tuskegee's Academic Department described the academic program by noting that the academic instruction offered for the lowest class at the institute's day school was "the equivalent to a fourth grade class in the North," while the senior class was similar to "the first or second year . . . in a northern high school." To him, the importance of Tuskegee's Academic Department was its "technical utility" in providing skills that would help students master industrial skills.[48]

In 1900, Booker T. Washington made a similar argument when he delivered an address to the National Education Association. He said, "It is a positive sin to take a black boy from an agricultural district and send him to a school or a city where he is educated in everything in heaven and earth and has no connection with agricultural life, with the result that he remains in the city in an attempt to live by his wits. . . . You will find that in proportion as we give industrial training in connection with academic training, there go with it a knowledge and a feeling that there is a dignity, a civilizing power, in intelligent labor," providing the student with "a certain amount of self-reliance or backbone he would not get without such effort on his own part."[49]

During the 1880s, some Southern Black schools became interested in this new approach and supported the idea of adding vocational classes. But most Black schools continued to offer classical education, with vocational training as an extra.

Others in the Black community strongly opposed the vocational education policy. Many who raised concerns had spent their lives promoting classical education for Southern Black students, including Bishop Charles Pettey, the husband of educator Sarah Dudley Pettey. He was at the exposition in Atlanta when Booker T. Washington gave his "cast down your bucket where you are" speech. Bishop Pettey gave a speech there that day, too, but it didn't gain much public notice.[50] Later, in 1897 at a gathering in Mobile, Bishop Pettey delivered another speech. In it he said that to fully advance, Black people needed a full education that included "classical training" in order to reach "the topmost round of intellectual manhood." He wanted Black students to "soar high, far beyond the cloudy pathway of all present astronomers and there blaze like the sun." He too had started anew after slavery and studied at Biddle Memorial Institute in Charlotte. There he learned to read Latin and Greek as part of its classical curriculum, became a bishop in the AME Zion Church, and established a normal school to train teachers to bring classical education to others.[51]

Many Northern Black leaders, including W. E. B. Du Bois, opposed prioritizing vocational education.[52] William Monroe Trotter, editor of a Black newspaper in Boston, said the Tuskegee policy would mean the "relegating of a race to serfdom."[53]

At that time, most white Southern landowners generally opposed any kind of education for Black people, as James Anderson reports. Southern planters focused on their own financial well-being and feared that education would make Black workers dissatisfied with doing the kind of field labor those planters needed them to do. In 1905, North Carolina's labor commissioner asked the state's white farmers if they approved of compulsory education for Black students. Ninety percent did not.[54] They felt that "educated Negroes, in nearly all cases, become valueless as farm laborers." Another participant in that survey, the head of education in Sampson County, noted that schools for Black children "may be fatal to the cotton crop" because harvesting cotton depends "upon the labor of children for pickers."[55]

But the Tuskegee proposal was popular with another group of white people—Northern millionaires, such as oil baron John D. Rockefeller; George Eastman, the founder of Eastman Kodak; William Henry Baldwin Jr., a railroad executive; and George Foster Peabody, a successful investment banker who did well betting on the new Edison Electric Company.[56] George Peabody thought vocational education could "help the Negro fit his environment" and noted the benefit to Southern whites, pointing out that the South needs Black workers' "labor and would be practically bankrupt without it."[57] He and other wealthy Northerners wanted the South to be prosperous, which would help maintain the stability of the overall US economy while also, of course, benefiting their own investments.

In addition, limiting Black education to skills important in farming would directly benefit white landowners, which might help win their support.[58] Railroad executive William Baldwin noted another benefit: Industrial education allowed Black workers to "willingly fill the more menial positions, and do the heavy work, at less wages, than the American white man or any other foreign race which has yet come to our shores," leaving the more complex tasks to white laborers.[59] Fitting Black workers into such a niche might also help discourage talk about equal rights.

Wealthy Northerners began giving large donations to Tuskegee Institute. They also made it clear they would refuse to make donations to Southern colleges for Black students that declined to embrace the industrial training model. Some colleges that had previously offered strictly classical education began to let those donors know they were on board with the new focus.[60]

In a 1902 report edited by Du Bois on the role of industrial classes in Southern colleges, Shaw University said that although it had no plans to become a trade school, it would offer industrial programs along with its academic educational courses and noted that it could offer more industrial options if it received financial help. Scotia Seminary, the school Sarah Dudley Pettey attended, began highlighting its "domestic arts" program.

Saint Augustine's Normal School in Raleigh started calling attention to its printing, carpentry, and bricklaying programs. Even Bishop Pettey's alma mater, Biddle Institute, noted that every student would now spend an hour a day in industrial courses. Livingstone College requested financial help from the Rockefeller-funded General Education Board so it could expand its industrial training courses. However, those schools didn't abandon classical academics while they added industrial extras. Livingstone graduates continued to become doctors, lawyers, and teachers.[61]

To encourage the use of the new industrial education approach they found attractive, Northern philanthropists created foundations that provided funds to help Southern schools make the transition. Nathan C. Newbold was eager for the philanthropists' help. This white educator had been working as the superintendent of graded elementary schools—both those for white students and those for Black young people—in several small cities, including Washington, North Carolina, when he was appointed in 1913 as North Carolina's first state agent of Black rural schools with a mandate to bring industrial training to those schools.[62] He firmly believed in this mission, as he explained to a white teacher who wondered why he would spend his time helping Black people. He replied, "If I do my duty as I conceive it, I shall . . . add to the dignity, the self respect and the humanity of the State as a whole."[63]

The first official report he wrote in 1914 showed that Black rural schools needed help: "The average negro rural school house is really a disgrace to an independent civilized people. To one who does not know our history, these school houses, though mute, would tell in unmistaken terms a story of injustice, inhumanity and neglect on the part of our white people."[64] He added an optimistic spin to his report by pointing out that twenty-five years earlier, white schools had been in bad shape, too, but had since improved. He felt progress was possible, especially since philanthropic foundations were ready to help.

The General Education Board paid his salary. The Anna T. Jeanes Fund paid for Black teachers trained in industrial education techniques to begin "improving education" in rural North Carolina. This foundation had been endowed with a million dollars from a Philadelphia Quaker woman's family inheritance. It covered half of the Jeanes teachers' salaries. County boards of education helped fund the rest of the teachers' pay.[65] All the Jeanes teachers were women because the director of the Jeanes Fund said he would only pay for female teachers, as "we have never had a man on the list that measured up to the work which women accomplish."[66]

The Jeanes teachers began visiting rural schools and communities. They often served as social workers in addition to being regular teachers. They did some teaching and gave children demonstrations in cooking, sewing, taking care of animals, and farming skills. They visited students' homes and gave guidance to parents on public health issues. They encouraged students' entrepreneurial spirit by helping them sell some of the fruits and vegetables they grew. In the spring, the Jeanes teachers organized popular festivals. One of these teachers, Annie Welthy Holland, a Black woman, was so capable that Newbold hired her as his assistant to coordinate Jeanes activities statewide. The program started with nineteen Jeanes teachers. By 1917, rural North Carolina communities had thirty-five Jeanes teachers, more than in any other Southern state.[67]

Soon the Jeanes teachers began helping with another project, organized by the Rosenwald Fund, created by Julius Rosenwald, a Chicago businessman and president of Sears, Roebuck, and Company. He became a strong supporter of Booker T. Washington after reading his 1901 autobiography, *Up From Slavery*, and joined the Tuskegee Institute's board. He wanted to help build small, sturdy schools for Black students in rural Southern communities that either didn't yet have schools or had schools that were rundown and inadequate, often one-room schoolhouses. He worked with the Tuskegee Institute's architectural design department to create architectural plans for small schools that could be built easily. Leading Tuskegee's architectural design department was Wilmington, North Carolina, native Robert Robinson Taylor, the first Black graduate of the Massachusetts Institute of Technology and the country's first accredited Black architect. Hired in 1892 as an instructor in architectural drawing and architecture at Tuskegee, he introduced its students to up-to-date architectural design techniques, including the use of blueprints. He also designed many of the buildings on the Tuskegee campus.

The first six of these Rosenwald schools were built in 1914 in rural areas of Alabama whose Black communities enthusiastically raised additional funds to make construction of the schools possible and were glad to have them. Booker T. Washington invited Julius Rosenwald to visit those schools. The school-building had gone so well that Rosenwald contributed $30,000 to help build a hundred more schools. The Rosenwald program was then offered to North Carolina and other states. North Carolina's first Rosenwald school, the Warren Grove School, was built in 1915 in Chowan County.

The Rosenwald Fund would contribute about $300 to build each school. The local community had to raise funds to cover the rest of the cost, serving as an important partner in the process. Often Black communities had to contribute much more than twice as much as the Rosenwald Fund, a process known as double taxation. They already had to pay regular school taxes and then had to contribute additional money to build and maintain a Rosenwald school. Most were glad to do this in order to have new school buildings.

Jeanes teachers and Newbold were enthusiastic supporters of the Rosenwald project. So were the rural Black communities where the schools were built. The Jeanes teachers raised funds for the schools and often helped build them. By 1932, when the Rosenwald Foundation ended its school-building project, North Carolina had built 787 Rosenwald schools in rural parts of the state, along with eighteen homes for teachers, and had also held eight industrial education workshops—the most of any Southern state. One of these schools was located in a rural area not far from the Keysville section of Washington, North Carolina.[68]

The Rosenwald Fund played an important role in improving education in rural communities. As James Anderson notes, "In 1932 more than one-fourth of all black schoolchildren in the South were taught in Rosenwald schools."[69] Eric Medlin offers another impressive statistic in his article on North Carolina's Rosenwald schools. The schools' focus on basic reading and math skills, along with vocational instruction, helped decrease the Black illiteracy rate in North Carolina "from 30.1% in 1900 to 5.5% in 1950."

Civil rights activist John Lewis, who later became a US Congressman, is one of many prominent Black leaders who received their elementary school education in a rural Rosenwald school. In the introduction he wrote for a book by Andrew Feiler on the history of those schools, he praised "the partnership of Julius Rosenwald and Booker T. Washington, who together harnessed these deeply help passions in African American communities to bring a better education to generations of students like me."[70]

However, the Rosenwald Fund ended its school-building program in 1932, partly because of the negative reaction it received in Little Rock, Arkansas, and New Orleans, Louisiana, when it tried to have those cities use Rosenwald money to build Black high schools that focused on industrial education. In Little Rock, local Black lawyer W. A. Booker objected. He wrote to the Rosenwald Fund about its plans to open a school in Little Rock named "Negro Industrial High School."[71] In his letter, he said, "Our people here have been waiting patiently over a span of years for a real high school, one that would not be a subterfuge; one that would give a thorough educational training and literary background, and a curriculum upon which a college education could be well predicated."[72]

The new school, with some Rosenwald help, opened in 1929 in Little Rock but with a different name: Paul Laurence Dunbar High School, named for the famous Black poet. The school offered three tracks: an academic track, an industrial curriculum track, and a combination track. Little Rock parents encouraged their children to enroll in the academic track. Few students enrolled in the industrial track, although many took a vocational course while mainly focusing on academic courses. In New Orleans, school officials refused the Rosenwald Fund's offer in 1931 to build a strictly vocational Black high school.

From 1928 to 1932, the Rosenwald Fund switched to making a different arrangement with some cities, including Winston-Salem, contributing funds to create an industrial "department" in a Black high school rather than centering the whole school on industrial education. By then, some Black high schools offered classical academic instruction in several Southern states, including Alabama, Arkansas, Kentucky, Maryland, Missouri, Tennessee, Texas, and Virginia, as well as in North Carolina.[73]

In 1921, North Carolina created a formal Division of Negro Education in its State Department of Public Instruction. Black schools and teachers in the state continued to receive less state funding than white schools.[74] White elected officials continued advocating for vocational-focused education for Black students, with Governor Cameron Morrison saying in 1921 that Black students were receiving "as much education as you are ready for. You cannot use the highly organized system that is provided for whites."[75]

Nathan C. Newbold, the white director of the new Division of Negro Education, advocated for improvements but reached a discouraging conclusion in 1938 when he observed "that it is natural and logical for intelligent Negroes to exhibit a feeling of unrest, whether wisely or unwisely, over conditions which to them seem to mean there is no hope for equality of educational opportunity for them in a great State like North Carolina."[76]

A Different Path

Rosenwald school-building projects in rural areas did not get started in North Carolina until the year after Sarah Keys's father, David A. Keys Sr., at age eighteen, had finished his education in Washington, North Carolina.

On May 20, 1914, he received a diploma from an educational program in his hometown: "Washington Industrial High School, Colored High School." This was not a state-funded high school and most likely did not offer the range of academic courses offered in today's high schools. The program seemed to follow the Booker T. Washington policy of providing instruction in industrial, or vocational, skills.

An official state-sponsored high school didn't open in this Washington until 1924, when David Keys was twenty-eight years old. That new 1924 high school initially didn't go up to twelfth grade and at first "was based on the Booker T. Washington model with a strong vocational component for the boys," said Alice Sadler, curator of that city's P. S. Jones African-American Education Museum.

Soon young David Keys would have an opportunity to experience a very different kind of education at one of the best classical education high schools for Black students in the country. That helped him envision the kind of education he wanted his own children to have, which he explained to his daughter Sarah in the stories he shared with her while they sat together on their porch as she was growing up.[77]

7

"Can Anything Be Done for My People?"

WITH THE JIM CROW ERA FIRMLY IN PLACE, Black families had to find ways to cope with its many restrictions. Parents did their best to help their children develop into self-confident young people despite the limitations. The Black community tried to provide opportunities that would help make up for those that Jim Crow denied. "Restaurants were segregated, but there were a couple of restaurants that were operated by Black folks," said Sarah Keys Evans, thinking about what her hometown was like while she was a child. "The others, we didn't go to, absolutely not."[1] The school Sarah attended there, which her father helped create in 1927, also provided options that were otherwise unavailable.

The idea to start that school grew out of a decision her father made as a teenager in the early 1900s to leave home and move north in search of more opportunities, foreshadowing what Sarah would do years later. David Keys's choice to leave home was influenced by the many restrictions imposed by segregation in his hometown as well as by the limited nature of the schooling available there.

As noted earlier, local funding for public schools led to Black schools generally receiving less money than schools for white students, including in Sarah's hometown. In 1897, a year after Sarah's father was born, there was a proposal to increase taxes in his hometown to provide more funding for both the white and the Black schools. When that plan was defeated, local white educator John Small solicited funds on his own from the city's residents. As president of the Washington, North Carolina, School Board and a former Beaufort County superintendent of public instruction, he was able to obtain enough donations to fully fund both the white and the Black schools for two years. A few years later, a similar education-focused tax increase proposal did pass. In the early 1900s, bond issues were approved to create a new school building, completed in 1906, with areas for Black students separate from those for white students.

Earlier, John Small had appointed local Black educator Louis R. (L. R.) Randolph as the principal of one of the city's schools for Black students. He was popular in the Black community and praised by a local white newspaper, which in 1891 called him "one of the leading colored educators of the State." Born in Washington, North Carolina, he attended school and a teacher's college in nearby New Bern, followed by studies at Lincoln University in Pennsylvania. He went on to serve as principal of his hometown's school for Black students until his death in 1908, when Presbyterian minister Dr. A. G. Davis became principal.

In 1913, a local newspaper article suggests that there was a focus on vocational skills in the instruction offered in the town's school for Black students. The news article describes an exhibit by that year's Black graduates, showing off their accomplishments in sewing, cooking, and construction. The article notes all items showed careful workmanship and that the work of these Black students "is making itself felt in the home life of the community among the best, white citizens . . . all articles made were useful."

The text of that 1913 article is on display in the P. S. Jones African-American Education Museum, which opened in Washington in 2023, organized by retired educator Alice Sadler. Near the museum's display of that article, curators added a comment noting that the school described in that article prepared Black students "for work in service of Washington's white residents." The curatorial comment adds that in later years the curriculum for Black students in the city's public schools broadened, especially during the 1930s after an official state-sponsored Black public high school opened there.

However, those broadened curriculum changes had not occurred by 1914, when eighteen-year-old David A. Keys received his diploma from "Washington Industrial High School, Colored High School." This was a different school than the one L. R. Randolph and Dr. A. G. Davis led. According to local historian Leesa Jones, the school David attended was started by a Baptist pastor, Reverend C. E. Askew, whose name is listed on David's diploma as the school's superintendent. Leesa Jones notes that Reverend Askew had helped bring Booker T. Washington to visit the city in 1910. The name of the school on David's diploma implied that it followed Booker T. Washington's educational philosophy of industrial, vocational training, instead of providing a classical academic curriculum.[2]

Young David Keys would soon experience the classical education option when at about age eighteen he headed to Washington, DC, located about three hundred miles away. Years later, Sarah recalled that her father had told her he was partly inspired to move to DC by an older friend who several years earlier had also moved there because of the city's greater opportunities for Black people. The wealthy white woman in his hometown who would later help him find a job with the WPA also helped with his plan to move to DC, according to stories Sarah's father told her. It has been hard to identify precisely who this helpful woman was, although there have been multiple efforts to do so.

Sarah remembered that this woman was named "Mrs. Leach."[3] Her father told her this woman "had family that was living there" in DC—including a woman married to a navy official who agreed to let young David Keys live in her house rent free if he made two promises. He loved to tell about the agreement he made with this woman, noting that she said, "David, you can stay here. But there are two things you must do. You have to make breakfast in the morning, and you have to finish school." He liked to cook, so he agreed.[4]

Sarah recalled her father saying that his sister secretly helped him pack his bag and "he slipped out of town. I don't think his father would have agreed that he should leave town at that age. My father left to embark on the rest of his adventurous life. He had a traveling mind."[5]

He also told Sarah that while living in DC he was able to attend an excellent high school for Black students, which today is called Dunbar High School, named for the well-known Black poet. It gained that name in 1916, when David would have been living in DC. This school (previously called the "M Street School") opened in 1870 and was the first official high school for Black students in the United States. It used a rigorous academic curriculum and was regarded so highly that some Black families moved to DC so their children could attend.[6]

Black parents who could afford to would sometimes send young people to a better school in another city or town "after eighth grade to finish their schooling. Some went off to private school," said Sarah.[7] Her own mother spent a year living in Virginia in order to attend a Catholic boarding school when she was frustrated by the lack of a high school in her hometown of Wootentown. Sarah's sister Connie explained that their mother's hometown school, like many for Black students in that area, "didn't go further than eighth grade. Since her Aunt Mary, who was a teacher, taught at an all-girls' boarding school for Black students, mom was given an opportunity to attend and further her schooling."[8]

Dunbar High School gave David a new idea of what education could be. It's not clear how long he was a student there and at what grade level. Carrie Thornhill of the Dunbar Alumni Association reported that Dunbar High School has no pupil records from the early 1900s. There are also no Dunbar yearbooks in the DC public library for that time period. His stay in DC was cut short, however, when the United States became involved in World War I. He left Dunbar to join the navy.[9]

David served as a cook while stationed at a naval training base in Rhode Island. He was one of more than 6,750 Black people who served in the navy during World War I, while 380,000 served in the army. The military was segregated then, with white and Black recruits serving in different units. Most Black units were not allowed to engage in combat missions. One exception was the Harlem Hellfighters, who took part in combat after being assigned to serve with the French military, which welcomed their help.[10]

Segregation was especially strict in the navy during World War I, despite its being integrated a few years earlier in 1898, during the Spanish-American War. During that earlier war, even though Black sailors were limited to roles as cooks, stewards, and other noncombat duties, they still "messed and berthed with shipmates from a variety of races and ethnicities, including white sailors, Japanese, Chinese, and Filipinos," according to a report from the Naval History and Heritage Command.[11]

Integration in the navy ended when Woodrow Wilson became president in 1913. Born in Virginia, he exhibited the attitudes about race relations that many white Southerners still had at that time. He segregated the entire federal government and its workers, including the navy. Recent research by Berkeley professors Abhay Aneja and Guo Xu highlights the long-term negative economic impact that policy had on Black workers.[12]

President Wilson chose an especially strong supporter of segregation as his Secretary of the Navy, Josephus Daniels from North Carolina. Born in Washington, North Carolina, Daniels grew up in the nearby city of Wilson after his father's death during the Civil War. As the owner and editor of the largest newspaper in North Carolina, the Raleigh *News and Observer*, he helped fuel the white supremacist campaign that led to the 1898 massacre in Wilmington and the passage two years later of the constitutional amendment that disfranchised Black voters.[13]

Secretary Daniels justified the segregation of navy personnel by claiming, incorrectly, that "it has been customary to enlist colored men in the various ratings of the messman branch . . . and in the lower ratings of the fireroom; permitting colored men to sleep and eat by themselves."[14]

David Keys experienced some difficulties in the navy, which Sarah attributed to his "doing too much. He was always helping other people. That was just his personality. He was there to teach the other sailors how to read. He would write letters for the guys. Because a Black person is not supposed to do too much, just do what you're assigned to do, and then go sit down in the hold."[15]

He may have found strength to cope through his Catholic faith, which he had been introduced to after leaving home. By the time he returned home from his navy service, he was a committed Catholic. It might have been hard for him to tell his parents, who were Baptist and Methodist. "Both his parents supported their son," explained Sarah. "They were proud of him." They even let him hold Catholic services in the living room of their home, where he sometimes taught catechism to children.[16]

During the early years of the twentieth century, David Keys had experienced the sharp contrast between opposite poles of the white community's attitudes toward Black people: the restrictions imposed by North Carolinian Josephus Daniels and those with similar beliefs as well as the helpful support provided by others, including his hometown benefactress and the DC woman who let him live in her home, allowing him the opportunity to explore new possibilities. These experiences gave him good training in how to navigate between those two extremes. He passed this skill along to his daughter Sarah.

"Can Anything Be Done for My People?"

For a while, David Keys was one of his hometown's only Black Catholics. Soon there were others, but there was no Catholic church in town, for either Black or white worshippers. The city's only Catholic church had burned down in 1864 during the Civil War and was never replaced. To attend Mass, one option was for David to get up early on Sundays to drive to New Bern and have Mass at St. Joseph's, a Catholic church for the

Black community there, founded in 1887. Mass for Black Catholics was also sometimes held in Washington, North Carolina, in a room rented in a local building that served as an out-mission of the New Bern Catholic congregation, with a visiting priest from St. Joseph's officiating in the Washington outpost.[17]

In the early 1920s, during one of the Catholic services in the rented room in Washington, David Keys spoke up, according to an account in *Washington and the Pamlico*, a book on Washington, North Carolina, history. At that service, he is said to have asked, "Can anything be done for my people?"[18]

The brief mention in *Washington and the Pamlico* of David Keys's question doesn't say whether Black and white Catholics were having Mass together when he asked his question of the visiting white priest, Reverend Charles Gabel. But an article about white priests who engaged in that kind of out-mission work during the 1920s in North Carolina noted that they "followed the accepted rules of racial segregation of the time." That same article explained that other priests on an evangelical tour in nearby Plymouth and Bayboro in 1926 were threatened by the KKK, which was known for holding both anti-Catholic and anti-Black views. Most likely the service where David asked his question was only for Black Catholics.

David's question captured the interest of Reverend Gabel, leading to discussions among white clergy in New Bern. One of the main priests at St. Joseph's, New Bern's church for Black Catholics, was Father Charles Hannigan. He asked David what he thought about starting a Catholic school for Black children in Washington. This priest may have made this suggestion in part to try to increase the number of Catholic families in town, but a parochial school could have benefits for all the city's children of color, whether Catholic or not.

The city's first official state-sponsored public high school for Black students would soon open in 1924, named the Colored High School. At first, it didn't go all the way to twelfth grade and initially emphasized vocational instruction for male students but would broaden its curriculum later, according to Alice Sadler, curator of the P. S. Jones African-American Education Museum.[19] A new Catholic school, however, could follow a different model, the one used in Catholic schools elsewhere, going from first grade to twelfth grade and teaching a classical academic curriculum. In addition, with funding from the church and Catholic-focused philanthropists, a parochial school might offer features a regular public school couldn't afford.

7.1 The father of Sarah Keys Evans, David Artis Keys Sr., as a young man. Courtesy Cornelia Keys Hargrave.

The idea of creating this new school interested Sarah's father. It would provide more educational options for Black students and keep others from having to leave home, as he had, searching for better possibilities. Catholic schools had a history of filling educational gaps for Black students in the South, as Sarah's mother discovered during the year she spent at a Catholic boarding school.

Sarah's father agreed to find a site for the new Catholic school. He had advice from a wealthy white woman who was friendly with his parents (not the same woman who helped with his move to DC and his gaining a position with the WPA). This other helpful woman wasn't a Catholic, but she supported his efforts and helped him locate a site for the school. In 1925, the bishop of the diocese in Raleigh arranged to have a Mother of Mercy "mission" set up in Washington, North Carolina. This was an

7.2 Children at the Mother of Mercy School in Washington, North Carolina, in the 1940s or early 1950s. Courtesy Archives of the Congregation of the Sisters, Servants of the Immaculate Heart of Mary, and the Passionist Historical Archives, Scranton, Pennsylvania.

outreach missionary effort that would provide pastoral care and support, help grow the local Catholic community, and oversee the plans for building the new school for Black children. Father Hannigan was given charge of this mission. He traveled twice a week to Washington from New Bern to oversee this project.

By September 1927, the Catholic school's building had been constructed on the site David Keys had helped locate. The Mother of Mercy School was ready to welcome its first fifteen students. Enrollment grew quickly, reaching one hundred students three months later. Although this was Washington's first Catholic school for Black students, St. Joseph's

Catholic Church in New Bern had already opened its own school for Black students in New Bern the year before.[20]

In 1927, the same year the Mother of Mercy School opened, David Keys married Curley Vivian Wooten. According to their daughter Connie, her parents met thanks to an introduction from a cousin of his, Zebedee Bonner. The Bonner family also became members of the new Mother of Mercy community and sent their children to the Mother of Mercy School.[21]

The year after the school opened, *The Sign* magazine, a national Catholic publication, started a fundraising campaign for the Mother of Mercy School that allowed the school to double its classroom space and enlarge the school's grounds. In 1937, the school graduated its first class of high school students, with five students achieving that milestone.

Mother of Mercy's teachers were white nuns who came from a religious community based in Pennsylvania—the Sisters, Servants of the Immaculate Heart of Mary (IHM), Scranton, Pennsylvania. Four sisters from that community came to North Carolina in 1927 to begin teaching at the school, according to Sister Beth Pearson, archivist for the IHM Center.

The Mother of Mercy School also had a chapel where religious services were held for the community's Catholics—with both Black and white Catholics attending together while a white priest officiated. In 1928, a white priest from the order known as the Congregation of the Passion, Father Mark Moeslein, was sent to serve as pastor for this new mission's congregants. Passionist priests continued to serve as pastors there for decades.

Father Moeslein was a strong advocate for ending segregation in the Catholic church. In 1927, the year Mother of Mercy opened, he wrote an article in *The Sign* describing the third annual convention in New York City that year of the Federated Colored Catholics. In his article, he "lamented the lack 'of Catholic laymen and women of the white race' at the meeting." He then listed the changes he believed the Catholic church needed to make: an end to segregation in Catholic churches, schools, and seminaries. He also criticized the policy of posting Black priests only to Black congregations. It would be more than twenty-five years before the Catholic church in North Carolina embraced suggestions like his and officially desegregated.[22]

Two years after Mother of Mercy School opened, Curley Vivian Keys gave birth to her and David's second child—Sarah Louise Keys, born on April 18, 1929, joining older sister Marie, born the year before. A month later, on May 26, 1929, Sarah was baptized at the chapel in the Mother of Mercy School, with Father Mark Moeslein officiating. He also officiated when Sarah was confirmed at that same chapel on December 7, 1941, a significant date for another reason, the day of the attack on Pearl Harbor that brought the United States into the Second World War. "We were all worried whether my father would have to go in the service again," Sarah recalled. "He didn't. Anyone with over four children did not have to go." But he contributed to the war effort by doing construction work at the Norfolk Navy Yard during the war. He would be away from home working there but would take leave periodically to check on the farm, especially during planting and harvest times.[23]

Catholicism had a long history in Washington, North Carolina. The state's first Catholic church had opened there in 1828 and was consecrated in 1829. After this church, along with much of the town, burned down during the Civil War in 1864, Catholics had to attend services in other towns, in their homes, or in rented rooms until the Mother of Mercy School and chapel opened. A whites-only Catholic church, St. Agnes, opened there in 1929. Later, a whites-only parochial school followed as well. But the Mother of Mercy School chapel remained open for all, white or Black.[24]

Mother of Mercy School provided such a good education that the Keys children put up with walking an hour each way to get there. The school was located in the more downtown area, three miles from their farm. "My father had a Dodge truck, but he used it for business," Sarah explained.[25] Sometimes she and her siblings would stop off on their way home at their grandparents' house, which was near the school, especially if the weather was bad. When Sarah was growing up, school buses weren't provided for students attending private and parochial schools, nor for Black children attending the local public schools. Until the late 1940s, school buses in Washington, North Carolina, transported only the area's white students.[26]

In Keysville, "we were the only Catholics out there," recalled Sarah. Their neighbors, some of whom were her relatives, were either Baptists or Methodists. "When we came back from school, a couple of us would walk home together. We knew how to dodge the group that would be waiting to tease us about going to a Catholic school and being taught by nuns."[27] The attitudes of those teasers changed, however, when a Black Catholic priest came to visit the Mother of Mercy School. "My family invited him to dinner," Sarah said. "On that occasion, my father took him around to visit the neighbors in Keysville. Two of them were sisters of his father who lived out there. The young people fell in love with the Black priest. That changed their attitude a little better about Catholics."[28]

Making the walk to school worth the effort, the Mother of Mercy School offered courses that weren't initially taught in the public school for Black students, such as instruction in Latin, French, and music. "Some of the nuns were absolutely wonderful," recalled Sarah. "Others did not want to be there. They had to go where they were assigned. Most of them were very smart. They came from Pennsylvania and New York. They always brought very good material to teach the children—dance and the arts."[29] She especially loved Mother of Mercy's excellent music instruction, which was not offered at the public high school at that time. "We were the only one that had a flourishing music department. We shared concerts with them for their special occasions, basketball, football, whatever." The Mother of Mercy band, with Sarah on French horn, also performed at the town's January First Emancipation Proclamation Day Parades.

"The public school had a reputation of turning out very good students. So did the Catholic school," said Sarah. "The principal of the public school had a very friendly relationship with the principal of the Catholic school. They worked together." She added that "I saw how comfortable my grandparents were with us being Catholic and their son being Catholic. When we spent weekends with them, the first order of the day was getting us to church on Sunday. My grandmother was always a big supporter of the Catholic church and would recommend to anyone she could to send their kids to the Catholic school. People did love to have their children get early education at the Catholic school. For me and most all in my family, we went all the way through high school there."[30]

There is no official data comparing the Mother of Mercy School with the other schools in town. However, in 1937 Mother of Mercy was listed as one of the state's accredited high schools. Its students reportedly performed well in statewide scholastic competitions, winning first and second place in a Latin competition, for example, and third place in a competition on American literature. "This standard of excellence was maintained all the years the school remained open," according to *Washington and the Pamlico*.[31] In 2021, Sister Beth Pearson, the archivist for the Pennsylvania religious order that provided teachers for the school, reported that she had found a letter in their files from one of the Passionist priests who served the Mother of Mercy parish. The priest wrote that he and the students were of the mind that the Mother of Mercy high school "was much better in quality than the public schools." A 1953 news article recently on display in the lobby of the former Mother of Mercy School building included a photo of Sarah Keys Evans's younger sister, Cornelia, who graduated that year and was one of six finalists in a statewide youth oratory contest.[32]

Local officials also noticed a difference in the education that the Mother of Mercy School provided. In 1929, two years after the school opened, the University of North Carolina conducted a survey for North Carolina's newly formed Division of Work Among Negroes, created in 1925. This agency was led initially by Lawrence A. Oxley, a Black social science teacher at St. Augustine's College in Raleigh who later served in the Roosevelt administration's Department of Labor. This was the first state bureau in the country set up specifically to look into social issues regarding Black people. The 1929 survey solicited the opinions of officials in each of North Carolina's counties, asking about their attitudes toward Black people on such issues as how much and what kind of education they should receive. The new Mother of Mercy School was mentioned by one of the white respondents, the superintendent of welfare in Beaufort County, the county in which the school was located. In his response, he "criticized the Catholic school in Washington, North Carolina, because the nuns treated blacks as equals," as was noted in a report on this survey. That Beaufort County official said that the egalitarian behavior of the Mother of Mercy nuns "is causing the negroes to be more uppity."[33]

Other white officials who participated in that 1929 survey agreed that education for Black students should be limited to preparing them to be farm workers and laborers. One court clerk from Burke County, in the western part of the state, repeated in his survey answer a phrase that apparently was often used at that time: "Educate a negro and you ruin a good servant." Another survey respondent said educating Black students past seventh grade was "a waste of time and money," and another noted that Black students "should be taught to be better cooks, farmers and laborers."

These white officials evidently endorsed the vocational educational philosophy developed by Booker T. Washington and his Tuskegee Institute, which was key to the efforts of the Rosenwald Fund to build small vocational-focused schools in rural areas. The Rosenwald Fund provided the University of North Carolina with the funds for that 1929 survey on local officials' attitudes about Black education.[34]

By 1932 when the Rosenwald school-building program ended, there were more than 780 Rosenwald schools in rural North Carolina, more than in any other state. One was near Sarah's Keysville home, the River Road School. Its small wooden building had two classrooms in which two teachers taught students from grades one through seven. This school had no electricity, running water, or indoor toilets, with heating for the two classrooms provided by an iron stove. Limited as they were in size and scope, the

7.3 The science laboratory in the Mother of Mercy School in Washington, North Carolina, in the 1950s. Courtesy Archives of the Congregation of the Sisters, Servants of the Immaculate Heart of Mary, and the Passionist Historical Archives, Scranton, Pennsylvania.

Rosenwald schools provided something that had not been available earlier in rural areas of North Carolina and of other Southern states: education for young Black children. The River Road School closed in 1952, by which time there was a public elementary school for Black children in town.[35]

The Mother of Mercy School provided a different kind of education than Rosenwald schools. With its larger and better-equipped brick building, which included a library and science lab, Mother of Mercy teachers focused on giving students a classical academic education. "Our teachers would try to get you on the highest level. You had to match the best and compete," Sarah remembered. "I was very proud of that education. I got

7.4 The library in the Mother of Mercy School in Washington, North Carolina, in the 1950s. Courtesy Archives of the Congregation of the Sisters, Servants of the Immaculate Heart of Mary, and the Passionist Historical Archives, Scranton, Pennsylvania.

teased a lot in the army that I didn't have a Southern brogue and spoke proper English. My parents spoke well at home. I was taught by white folks." She recalled that during ninth grade, one teacher "gave up a half hour of her lunchtime to tutor me." It wasn't that young Sarah was slow at reading but that she tended to fall asleep while reading, a problem that would cause difficulties for her years later when she gave nursing school a try before deciding to join the Women's Army Corps.[36]

The Mother of Mercy school did, however, offer a nonacademic course: home economics, which was also being offered then in Northern schools focused primarily on classical academic education. On her high school graduation day in 1948, Sarah noted proudly that "I received an award for Best in Home Economics." However, the main focus of the Mother of Mercy curriculum was academic excellence.[37]

Mother of Mercy School also provided options for the Black community that were otherwise not available to families like Sarah's. The town's public library was segregated until the mid-1960s. "I never went to that public library," said Sarah. "We had our own library in the school." She recalled that the high school seniors and the alumni worked hard raising money for the library. "We sold chicken dinners on Sundays to buy books for the library."[38]

In addition, the school invited the wider community to attend its concerts and plays. Their band and choir concerts were "the best," said Sarah. "The town turned out for that. The auditorium was filled with mostly Black folks, but there were white people, too. Some were friends of the school's benefactors." In addition, Mother of Mercy showed movies "at Christmas and Easter," said Sarah, "right in the school, for a nickel. So we wouldn't have to go to the movies." The local movie theater required that Black people sit upstairs, while white customers sat downstairs, except for special shows for the Black community. "I didn't like sitting upstairs," explained Sarah. "That meant that we were different from the people that were privileged to sit downstairs." When Mother of Mercy showed movies, nobody had to worry about those Jim Crow seating rules.[39]

The school's benefactors were wealthy individuals in New York and Pennsylvania who believed in the school's mission and donated money to support it. They also helped provide extras that many other schools might not have. "When the benefactors would come to visit, we'd put on performances and plays. The choir and the music department would shine," recalled Sarah. At the end of these performances, "the Mother Superior would say, 'Would the Keys stand.' That was their way of letting those visitors know who the Keys family was"—the family whose father had helped create the school.

The introductions at those events also led to a change in the spelling of the family's name, which until the 1940s had sometimes been spelled "Keyes." When Sarah and her siblings were asked to stand at celebrations for the school's benefactors, the speaker would emphasize the "es" at the end of their name. "We got tired of that," Sarah said. "So we asked my dad, 'Can we spell our name Keys instead of Keyes? We get tired of the teachers introducing us as the *Key-es*.' So just in school, we started spelling it 'Keys.' That's how that came about."[40]

Gradually, other schools for Black students in North Carolina—including the Colored High School that opened in 1924 in Washington—began offering the kind of education that Mother of Mercy was providing: a solid academic education to help prepare graduates for a wide range of careers.

In one private school in North Carolina, its Black director, Charlotte Hawkins Brown, found a way to teach an academic curriculum despite pressure to have a vocational program. Born in North Carolina in 1883, she moved as a young child with her mother to Cambridge, Massachusetts, part of an early Black migration from the South by those fleeing the post-Reconstruction era's increase in Jim Crow segregation. She attended schools in Massachusetts and then studied at a normal school there to prepare to become a teacher. A member of the American Missionary Association (AMA) persuaded her that she was needed as a teacher in the South. So Charlotte Hawkins Brown returned to North Carolina in 1901 to teach in an AMA school in the town of Sedalia, near Greensboro. The school soon closed. So she started her own school, the Palmer Memorial Institute, named in honor of a Harvard professor's wife, Alice Freeman Palmer, who had helped pay her normal school tuition in Massachusetts.

At that time, Northern philanthropists and North Carolina education officials were enamored with the Booker T. Washington "industrial" schooling philosophy. To obtain needed funding, Charlotte Hawkins Brown claimed that her Palmer Memorial Institute was an industrial school. But right from the start she also taught a rigorous academic curriculum. By the 1940s, her school had become a top academic-focused private boarding school for Black students.[41] One of her teachers explained the school's policy: "You could teach anything you wanted when you got in your school. You came inside your class room and you taught them Latin and French and all the things you knew."[42]

Black public school educators began speaking up for change. As noted in *Fragile Democracy* by James Leloudis and Robert Korstad, teachers began joining the North Carolina Teachers Association union, which, aided by the NAACP, called for Black teachers' salaries to be equal to those of white teachers. In 1944, their campaign succeeded in North Carolina, thanks in part to a 1940 ruling in the US Court of Appeals for the Fourth Circuit in Virginia, which said racial differences in teachers' pay violated the Fourteenth Amendment.[43]

In 1951, a lawsuit filed in Durham, North Carolina, called for equal funding for Black and white schools. It proved successful, with a judge ruling that Black students had to be provided with "substantially equal facilities to those furnished white children."[44] That same year, a lawsuit filed by Black parents in Pamlico County, just south of Sarah's hometown, said their children should be allowed to attend white schools if facilities provided for Black schools didn't improve. The state legislature realized that this lawsuit threatened to end segregated schooling. So in 1953, it approved funds to build better schools for Black students in order to preserve segregated schooling.

Soon victories like the one Sarah Keys would win a few years later, along with a landmark Supreme Court schools decision, made it harder for those officials to continue to preserve the unfair educational status quo.[45]

Coping and Excelling

Sarah had learned from her father that sometimes it's important to take a stand that might be dangerous or considered unusual but that could help make things better in the long term. She and her siblings also learned from him how to navigate in a Jim Crow world, as they watched him try to shield them from some of the harshness of its restrictions.

One area where he took a stand involved the local movie theater, with its rule about people of color sitting upstairs. When Sarah was young, she and her siblings would go to the movies and have to sit upstairs. After a while, her father seemed to change his attitude about when, and under which circumstances, to bring his children to that theater. Her sister Cornelia (Connie) Keys Hargrave, who was five years younger than Sarah, recalled that while she was growing up: "Our dad did not want us to be subjected to that kind of indignity. This was something that he felt he had some control over. The movies were not a place where we were taken unless there was something very special and the cast was basically an all-Black cast. Then there would be a special showing and we could sit any place for a 'colored' people's showing of the movie. I always appreciated his concern in protecting us."[46]

Connie was also impressed that her father and mother always voted, despite obstacles imposed by their state constitution. They and increasing numbers of Black citizens managed to navigate the restrictions and register to vote. "Dad was a voter, and I remember him encouraging neighbors to vote," recalled Connie. "He would even drive them to register to vote. That made a lasting impression. I have never missed an election."[47]

During the 1940s, Black communities in nearby areas organized voter registration campaigns, such as the effort started by Dr. George K. Butterfield Sr., a dentist in Wilson, a town about fifty miles west of Sarah's. He and others would help people memorize the US Constitution so they would be ready for the literacy test when they registered to vote. In 1953, Dr. Butterfield won election to Wilson's Board of Commissioners, the first

Black official to be elected in that town for more than fifty years. His son later became a US congressman who would speak at a ceremony honoring Sarah Keys Evans in Roanoke Rapids over sixty years later.[48]

Sarah and her siblings also saw how their father dealt with segregation at church. Sarah's family and other Black Catholics in town couldn't go to services at St. Agnes, the whites-only Catholic church that had been built there two years after the Mother of Mercy School opened. But St. Agnes members and other white Catholics could attend mass at the little chapel inside the Mother of Mercy School "if they wanted to go to a Mass at a different time than at their own church. Anyone was welcome to come to our church," said Sarah.

However, when white people attended Mass in the school's chapel, they took communion before Sarah's family and the other Black parishioners. "Whites getting communion in your own church ahead of you, that's how the prejudice was. As a child, growing up, I saw this," recalled Sarah. "The nuns and the priest were nice enough. But as children, sometimes we would talk it over among ourselves, coming from church on Sundays, about whites getting communion before we did."[49]

This was an example of the balancing act required of families like Sarah's. There were benefits of having a school and church staffed by white nuns and priests who broadened educational horizons. But the situation also required careful navigation.

One Christmas Eve, the discrimination from white Catholics became too much for Sarah's father to accept or ignore. He chose a firm yet orderly and nonconfrontational way to react, the same choice he and Sarah would make later in response to her 1952 arrest.

That Christmas Eve, the local all-white Catholic church had invited the choir at Sarah's school to sing at its midnight Mass on Christmas Eve because, as Sarah explained, "We had an excellent choir." Her father's cousin, who had a daughter in the choir, drove Sarah and the other choir members to St. Agnes so they could perform. The cousin then "sat in the back of the church in the last row," noted Sarah, to be ready to drive the choir home after the service.

"All of a sudden, the director of the choir kept looking at us, at the Keys. Why was she looking at us? When the Mass was over, she asked what was my cousin doing sitting back there. She got very angry because my cousin was sitting in the back of the church. We could have walked, but it was midnight. Why walk when you can ride?," asked Sarah. "We related what went on to my dad."

Despite the unpleasantness of the Christmas Eve incident, "the next morning, we went to church at our own church, which we always did on Christmas Day, and sang Mass," said Sarah. However, immediately after the Christmas Day service, Sarah's father spoke with the principal of Mother of Mercy School in the office. He said he was writing a letter to the bishop. He told exactly what the letter to the bishop would say—that his children would not be singing midnight Mass anymore at the church where only white people were welcome. He said that from then on, "we should have midnight Mass at our own church where all the people of the town, Black and white, Catholics and non-Catholics, could attend that service if they wanted to." Her father made sure his family would not be insulted like that again. Midnight Mass at Mother of Mercy "was always full after that," according to Sarah.[50]

Her father also demonstrated the wisdom of reacting calmly and discreetly when Sarah was reprimanded by one of her schoolteachers while she was in eighth or ninth grade. Students were supposed to line up in front of the school each morning before the bell rang and then say the Pledge of Allegiance before going into school. That morning, as she neared the end of her three-mile walk to school, "I was about a half block from the playground of the school, and I was running because there were certain spots that we knew if we didn't run from there we wouldn't get there in time," recalled Sarah. "The bell had rung. I was still trotting to get into this line. A nun was standing on the fire escape, watching everybody. She called my grandmother's house, which was about a block away, and told her to mention to my father if he came by before school closed, to come by that day because she wanted to talk to him about me. So he did. The nun told him that when the bell rang, I stopped running and went to walking. I'm standing up there listening to her tell him this story. She said, 'David, I want you to punish her.' (Because I was a little bit late!) He looked at her and said, 'Sister, I will take care of it.' We picked up my other siblings from my grandmother's and we came home. I didn't say anything for a while. Later I said, 'Daddy, that nun, she was wrong. I would not walk if I knew I was a little late. If you punish me, I will run away from home.' He said nothing about it then, and he did not punish me."

Sarah said she and her father talked about that incident "many years later and laughed about it. Sometimes, I think I had a reputation of being a little defiant," Sarah noted. "I did not know that until my middle sister mentioned that" when they were both adults, reminiscing about their childhoods. Even so, Sarah said she would never have talked back to the nun directly. "We were not allowed to do that. There would be punishment. That's why I just listened" as the nun spoke. But when Sarah was back home, in a safe environment, she was willing to be a bit defiant and speak out against an unfair accusation. This reflected what she had learned by watching her father counter unfair situations. It was a rehearsal for how she would respond to her unjust arrest at the Roanoke Rapids bus station. She waited until she got home to defend herself, first to her father, and later to others, and then to the wider world when she had a supportive attorney by her side.[51]

Other unfair things happened in her hometown while she was growing up that troubled her, incidents she kept to herself. "One time they had a program on the radio. You write a story on a card with a hundred words or less and you could win a box of silk stockings during World War II," said Sarah. "I won, and my brother and I went to collect my award. They were supposed to let you say your name and school on the radio. But it took them a long time to come out and decide to give me my award. I wasn't allowed to say anything on the radio. Those little, small things, quiet things. We never talked about that. It made an impact. I knew some of the things there were terribly wrong. You just didn't go about talking about it a lot."[52]

Leaving Home

Sarah loved her family. She loved the farm and her school, too. But she had learned from her father's stories—and from his having to search for extra jobs elsewhere—that there was no future for her in that town. "I always knew I would not remain there," she said. "There were no jobs. There was segregation and prejudice."[53]

However, she had also seen that "some whites and Blacks were friendly in that town."[54] She had found that was especially true of the women. "They always knew what was going on around the whole town. They were always there for each other. I think if we heard a little bit more of that kind of story, there wouldn't be so much time spent on division." She had experienced this watchfulness during the long walks she took to and from the Mother of Mercy School. If women (both Black and white) who lived in houses along the way hadn't seen all the Keys children walk by in the morning, they would be concerned that something was wrong. Women "in the evening . . . would be standing outside by their little picket fence saying what happened. That's how people looked after each other."[55]

She noted that "there were whites who voiced their opinions and wished that segregation was not as it was at that time. They could not voice it loudly. I don't think anyone in that town would have asked me to go to the back of a bus. Of course, there weren't very many buses there to go to the back of." Speaking out against segregation in a Southern state was dangerous back then, even for white people.

Her father illustrated the tightrope that needed to be walked when he told her about a farmers' meeting and luncheon in a nearby town that he had been invited to attend. He and another Black farmer got a ride to the event from a white friend of the other farmer. When they started to walk into the event, Sarah recalled that her father said that at first he "turned to go one way, away from the man that had given him a ride." But that white man said, "Dave, where are you going? You're with me. You're coming and sitting with me. Don't worry about a thing." So that's what her father did and "nobody asked him to move," Sarah noted. "Small things like that would happen. But a white man had to be very brave . . . to just say, you're my friend, and we're talking, and you're gonna be sitting with me." She remembered also one of the Mother of Mercy nuns telling about a bus trip she took coming back to school after a vacation in Pennsylvania. "A Black man was her companion in the seat next to her. Their conversation was about how they both hoped that one day they could always ride together, everywhere." Sarah would play a role in making that nun's wish come true.[56]

"My parents raised us well and raised us with discipline," explained Sarah. "We knew what our parents expected of us. Out in public, we knew our place. Whites knew their place and Blacks knew theirs."[57] But Sarah yearned for something different, living somewhere that offered more possibilities, more freedom.

Sarah's older sister Marie left home after high school to work in New Jersey. So did Sarah. "Everyone just sort of left home after high school. All of us. My sister who was in New Jersey sent me a bus ticket. I left home two days after I graduated from high school," Sarah said. Her mother was glad for her. "She knew my life would take a different direction than hers," said Sarah. "I always knew that I was not going to hang around for someone to marry me and take care of me."[58]

As she said years later, "Working and being independent was my whole life when I left home. I went to seek a new life."[59]

Many others made the same decision as Sarah and her brothers and sisters. According to statistics in Jeffrey J. Crow's book on North Carolina

7.5 Sarah Keys's high school graduation photograph, 1948. Courtesy Sarah Keys Evans.

history, about 57,000 of North Carolina's Black residents moved to Northern states between 1910 and 1930. Even more—about 222,000—left between 1930 and 1950. North Carolina lost nearly 15 percent of its Black population during the 1940s. Between 1960 and 1980, about 44 percent of Black adults who were born in North Carolina were living in other states, according to data collected by Carolina Demography of the University of North Carolina. Similar departures occurred throughout the South, an exodus known as the Great Migration.[60]

After leaving home in 1948, Sarah at first tried nursing school in New Jersey. Then she moved to New York City, where she found jobs in department stores and in an office. She loved working in the department stores, being involved with the latest fashions.

In 1951 she saw an ad for the Women's Army Corps (WAC) that talked about "traveling and seeing the world and being trained for a job and going to school," said Sarah. The company she was working for, doing an office job, was downsizing. "I was let go. My mind kept going back to this commercial, and I thought I'd see what it was all about. So I went and signed up."[61] She passed the medical test, even though it found that she was still anemic, something she had been dealing with since childhood. A few weeks later, she was on a train to Fort Lee, Virginia, to begin basic training. "I hadn't any idea what I was really in for."[62]

Segregation in the military had ended officially in 1948, three years earlier. Blacks and whites began serving together rather than in separate battalions. Sarah liked that. She had become used to being in an integrated environment at the integrated nursing school she attended briefly in New Jersey as well as at the jobs she had in New York City while living at the Handmaids of Mary convent in Harlem that offered rooms for "working girls," where she stayed before signing up for the WACs. All of her experiences in the WACs—training, living quarters, and work assignments—took place in integrated settings.

She made white friends during basic training in Virginia and also at Fort Houston in Texas, where she was sent next for more training and to wait for a formal assignment. Some of the white girls had never "lived around Black people before . . . but we all did get along." At Fort Houston she learned new ideas from her white roommates on a topic that always interested her, hairdressing. She was surprised to see white WACs do something she hadn't realized was a way to curl hair—they would "pin curl" their hair. The hairdresser she learned from in her hometown "just used hot irons for the hair to curl it, or we used some kind of rollers to roll it up, to curl it," she said. Her first official posting at Fort Dix was also well integrated, and she made white friends there, too. "We learned little things from each other," she said.

Army life could be hard, especially during the ten weeks of basic training. "Had I not been raised on a farm and traveled three miles out and three miles back each day to school, enduring basic training would not have gone as well as it did. I kept thinking, because I had that behind me, that I can do this. Basic training is very difficult. You have to be strong and have lots of endurance." She had to admit, "The farm was not as grueling as basic training. We kept pushing, and we made it."[63]

Her brothers who served in the military "were very proud of me being in the army," she recalled. "My father was very proud, too. He was happy that I was going into something. I can assure you that he thought I was the last person to get involved in something like the army because I was so quiet." Her father was working then on construction jobs in Washington, DC. He would drive "down to visit me when I was in basic training in Fort Lee, Virginia. He kept up with his children."

But Sarah always had the feeling that her mother wasn't happy about this career choice, probably concerned about the danger of military service and about her young daughter being around so many men. Years later, her mother came to see that Sarah had indeed made a good choice.[64]

Sarah's first assignment after basic training was as a receptionist in the army hospital at Fort Dix, New Jersey. In early 1952, an "Inquiring Photographer" reporter for the Fort Dix newspaper asked her, "Is the Women's Army Corps a good career?" Sarah answered that it was "wonderful," adding that a WAC "gains self-assurance." She noted many years later, when she registered with the archives of the Women in Military Service for America Memorial, that because of her service in the WACs, "I was no longer that very shy person."[65] She would need this self-confidence for the challenge she would face in August 1952 as she traveled home to North Carolina.

8

A Plan of Attack

AFTER THE UPSETTING EXPERIENCE OF BEING arrested and jailed in Roanoke Rapids, it wasn't until early Sunday morning, August 3, 1952, that Sarah Keys finally reached her hometown. Nobody from her family was there to meet her at the bus station. They didn't know why she hadn't arrived the morning before, as expected. There had been no way for her to phone her family when police officers placed her on the bus after her night in jail. This was long before the era of cellphones. After the bus arrived in Washington, North Carolina, "I got a taxi from town, there at the bus station, out to this little community where I lived. That's how I got home," she said.

She didn't explain to her parents right away what had happened, even though they must have been very worried. Instead, she got dressed to go to a church service at the chapel in Mother of Mercy School, as her family did every Sunday. Her father asked why she was so late getting home. Sarah tried to brush off the question by saying, "It's a long story. The bus was a bit late."

The family went to church in a taxi, "which was always reserved the night before," Sarah explained. On the way, they stopped by her grandparents' home, which was near the Mother of Mercy School where they attended church in the school's chapel. An aunt was also living with her

8.1 Sarah's parents, Curley Vivian Wooten Keys and David Artis Keys Sr., standing in front of their home in the Keysville section of Washington, North Carolina, probably in the 1950s. Courtesy Sarah Keys Evans.

grandparents then. "I asked my aunt if they had gotten a telephone call that night. And she said, 'No.' I didn't say anything more." But during the service, as she sat in the chapel, she realized, "I'm really going to have to tell him this story." She wondered what they would think of a daughter who has been charged with being disorderly.[1]

After taking the taxi back to Keysville, "I imagine my father couldn't hold it any longer. He said, 'Why were you so late getting in last night?' And I start to spill the story."[2]

Sarah and her mother sat on the edge of a bed as she began to explain. Her father sat in a chair and listened carefully. When she reached the part of the story about being arrested, "he jumped up," said Sarah. "He was furious. I had never seen him so angry."[3]

She explained to him that the police had charged her with being disorderly, but she told her parents, "I wasn't disorderly."

"No, daughter, I know you weren't disorderly," her father replied. "That is a term that they use when they cannot find anything else to arrest you for when you are traveling."[4] He described to her some of the difficulties he had faced. "His experience with traveling made him realize that the story I told was true," Sarah recalled. "My father told me there were some drivers who took it upon themselves to seat passengers as they saw fit."[5]

Her father had tried to protect his children from segregation, looking for ways to get around it. To provide a good life for his family, he went to other cities to find good-paying jobs that segregation didn't offer him at home. He helped start a new school to give his children educational opportunities that segregation tried to deny them. He shielded them from insulting treatment at movie theaters and at the whites-only church. He taught his children how to behave in public so they wouldn't ruffle the feathers of segregationists.

Now, segregation had found its way into his family. This latest insult was too much. He wanted to help Sarah challenge the disorderly conduct charge. He also had a wider goal—to try to put an end to segregation altogether. Sarah was with him all the way.

As an avid reader of newspapers, Sarah's father was no doubt aware that the Black community in North Carolina was becoming active in politics, with encouragement from articles by Black journalist Louis Austin, owner and editor of *The Carolina Times*, a Durham newspaper. From the early 1930s onward, Austin encouraged Black business and religious leaders to get involved in registering Black people to vote. By 1940, efforts by Dr. George K. Butterfield and many others throughout the state had resulted in the registration of 75,000 Black voters in North Carolina, according to an article by history professor Jerry Gershenhorn. These voters included men and women, too, now that women had won the right to vote with the passage of the Nineteenth Amendment in 1920. Black candidates also began running for local offices. In 1947, Rev. Kenneth R. Williams won a place on the Winston-Salem Board of Aldermen, the first Black person in North Carolina during that century to win more votes than a white candidate. In 1951, one year before Sarah's arrest, thirteen Black men ran in local elections in eleven North Carolina cities; three won seats on municipal councils.[6]

Those developments may have given Sarah's father a feeling that change was possible. He was ready to challenge the system. So was Sarah.

She explained to her father that the police chief said she could come back that week to speak with officials at a court hearing and try to have the charges dropped and get a refund for the $25 fine. She remembered her father asking her, "Would you like to do that?"

She replied, "Yes, Daddy, if that's what you think I should do."

"Well, that's what we'll do," he said.

"He was short in stature but a giant in character. He would walk the last mile for his child," she recalled years later. "He told me that if any time I felt that I wanted to quit, I could, because we all have choices. As long as he was with me, I would never give up. It was a matter of moral principle. It wasn't the $25. We spent much more than that. It was the principle."[7]

As Sarah noted, "A process was beginning that I had no idea how it would turn out."[8] What kept her going was her firm belief that "I knew I had been unjustly accused of disorderly conduct. I believe in people being treated right and treated fairly no matter what the situation."[9]

Sarah worried, however, about the impact her arrest would have on her younger siblings, who were living at home then. "It couldn't have been a very easy thing for my mother to explain to them how their sister got herself arrested," Sarah noted.[10]

Her sister Connie, seventeen at that time, explained later, "I was aware of what was going on. I was very sad that something like that could happen to someone who was so very dear to me. Of all the people in the world, how could this have happened to her? I felt sadness and also fear, extreme fear. The next year, I went away to college in North Carolina. I was afraid when taking buses. But I think it made me a stronger person. We're different personalities. We're kind of opposites. But knowing how strong she was helped make me stronger as a person. I felt if she could stand up to something she thought was really wrong, Sarah was a good example. There have been times in my life when I really had to dig down and be courageous and stand up for what I thought was right."[11]

Taking Action

Sarah's father went into town and spoke with the Mother of Mercy priest. "The priest told him that due to segregation laws, there really wasn't anything he could do for me," recalled Sarah. "I was a bit disheartened and

8.2 Sarah Keys in the living room of her family's home in the Keysville section of Washington, North Carolina, in 1952. Courtesy Sarah Keys Evans.

was not surprised with how that had gone. The priest was white. As far as he was concerned he was right, within the law. He could have spoken out, but it would not have been safe for him. That was the end of that. I never had a conversation with that priest about any of this myself."

Then her father met with a friend who was a minister at the Baptist church, a Black man married to a cousin of Sarah's mother. "My father was not active in the NAACP. They didn't have it here," explained Sarah. "He became acquainted with people who were members when he went to get help for me. The friend was a member and told him about a lawyer out of Fayetteville and Raleigh who would be able to help us. They talked by telephone. He got a letter from the lawyer saying he would meet us, for what fee, and so forth."

Her father went back into town to find someone to drive them to Roanoke Rapids. Sarah and her father left home very early on the morning of the court hearing to go appear before the magistrate there. Sarah was wearing her army uniform. "The lawyer met us there," recalled Sarah. "He was a very young Black lawyer. I just told him briefly what had happened. He had already heard the whole story on the phone from my dad. Everything went against us." Roanoke Rapids officials kept saying that Sarah had been arrested for being disorderly. They refused to drop the charges or refund the money.[12]

After her ten-day leave ended, Sarah returned to Fort Dix. The lawyer that her father had hired wrote a letter to Sarah's commanding officer requesting an emergency leave so she could return to North Carolina and try again to have the charges dropped. She got the leave and made a second visit to Roanoke Rapids with her father. "That time we took a bus from Washington and spent the night with some acquaintances there and went to court in Roanoke Rapids." The lawyer they had hired didn't show up at the hearing to help her. "The NAACP did not particularly want to get involved," she concluded. Or perhaps the lawyer had another case to argue that day.[13] According to a book by Mia Bay on the history of transportation segregation, the NAACP at that time had limited resources to file cases in court and had to carefully pick and choose the "strongest cases."[14]

For whatever reason, Sarah did not have legal representation on that second visit. "I faced that magistrate that day, no lawyers and no observers. I faced it all by myself that day. That was really an overwhelming feeling," she recalled. What particularly surprised her, however, were the remarks made at the hearing by the man who had been sweeping the floor at the bus station the night she was arrested. At the magistrate's hearing, "He testified that I was disorderly, cursing, and swearing," Sarah recalled. She couldn't understand why he would say something so untrue like that. All during her search for justice, she would hear others say things about her that weren't true. Once again, she did not succeed in having the charges dropped.[15]

But by the time of this second hearing in Roanoke Rapids, Sarah's father already had a new plan. He had asked one of his friends in Washington, DC, for advice. This friend knew people in the DC office of the NAACP. Those contacts helped Sarah's father connect with a young, Black woman lawyer, Dovey Johnson Roundtree, a fellow North Carolinian. Born in Charlotte, she had just graduated from Howard University's law school in DC. One of her professors, Frank D. Reeves, was a lawyer for the NAACP. During law school, she had observed NAACP lawyers doing research in the Howard law library for a big case they were developing against school segregation that they hoped would head to the Supreme Court. She had learned about some of the legal arguments those lawyers were developing for use in the school case.

Sarah's father hoped that this new young lawyer might want to work on a case that could help put an end to segregation on buses. He spoke with her, asking if she would help with his daughter's case. She was delighted to learn more and to offer assistance. Dovey Johnson Roundtree had just set up her own law office with another recent law school graduate, Julius Robertson. This would be one of her and her partner's first cases. She said that Sarah should contact them to set a date to meet if the second visit to Roanoke Rapids didn't go well.[16]

After the failed second visit to Roanoke Rapids, Sarah called Dovey Roundtree, and then she and her father traveled to DC to meet with these two lawyers. "We took the bus, but we didn't have any trouble. I had been to Washington before," said Sarah. When she was first stationed at Fort Dix, her father was working construction jobs in DC. "I would take leave from Fort Dix and visit him, just for a Sunday, and then return back to Fort Dix," explained Sarah.[17] But she had never been in a lawyer's office before. As she entered the office, some of her shyness began to return.

Dovey Johnson Roundtree was in her late thirties, fifteen years older than Sarah. "This was the first woman lawyer I had ever met," Sarah recalled. "Mrs. Roundtree was very talkative. She could talk a mile a minute. I began to feel more comfortable when she said she had been in the service"—as a member of the same branch of the military as Sarah.[18]

Dovey Roundtree had joined the Women's Army Corps during World War II in 1942, the year the army created this women's unit. Members of the WAC units were the first women, other than nurses, to serve as official members of the army. She had graduated from Spelman College in Atlanta a few years earlier and was one of the first Black women to enroll in the WAC's first Officer Training School class. She was also one of the first women, Black or white, to become an officer in the US Army. The WACs continued as a separate part of the army until 1978, when women were at last allowed to serve as regular members of the army.

However, the army wasn't the only thing she and Sarah had in common. Roundtree had also been treated unfairly during a bus trip about ten years earlier when she too was wearing her uniform as a captain in the US Army. She was on a special assignment for the army during the winter of

1943 to recruit more women to join the WACs. One evening, she arrived at the bus station in Miami, Florida, in time to board a bus about to depart that would take her to another Florida city. There she was to meet a fellow officer to start the recruiting mission. Many soldiers and sailors were waiting on the platform to take that bus.

By the time she climbed on board, the section in the back for Black travelers had filled up, but the section in the front for white passengers was still pretty empty. She took a seat in the white section, thinking she could explain that she was on a military mission. But the bus driver said to her, "What do you think you're doing? Don't you see there's somebody waiting for that seat?" She turned around and there was a white soldier, ready to take her seat. She explained that she was on army business and had to take this particular bus in order to meet another army officer. That didn't impress the driver. He ordered her to get off and stand at the end of the long line of white travelers waiting on the platform to board the bus.

She got off and walked to the end of the line. None of the white soldiers in the line saluted her, as soldiers are supposed to do when they see an officer. Those soldiers got on the bus, leaving her standing on the platform as the bus roared out of the station. She had to wait for several hours before another bus arrived that could take her where she needed to go. So she knew the fear and anger Sarah had felt in Roanoke Rapids. This lawyer was determined to stop that kind of unfair treatment from happening to anyone else.[19]

At their first meeting, Sarah told the two lawyers her story. "We agreed that they would do something about it," recalled Sarah. "Mrs. Roundtree was very optimistic. She was upbeat. She was a very bright woman. She had that preacher mentality." In fact, Roundtree became an ordained minister in addition to being a lawyer.[20]

Sarah also observed that "there are some people that you meet, they slightly always remain strangers to you. That was somewhat true of Mrs. Roundtree. With Mrs. Roundtree, it was always more formal. This was a business relationship."[21] In addition, there were differences in their partnership stemming from their army experience: Dovey Roundtree had been a captain; Sarah Keys was a private.

This energetic young lawyer gave Sarah Keys the feeling that everything would work out. The lawyers told her they would handle the details, although they explained that fighting this arrest could take a long time.[22]

The lawyers were impressed with Sarah's determination. Here's how Roundtree described their first meeting in her memoir *Mighty Justice*,

8.3 Dovey Johnson Roundtree (*right*), who served as a captain in the WAC during World War II, at a luncheon at the first WAC Training Center in Fort Des Moines, Iowa. Educator, NAACP vice president, and prominent advisor to President Franklin Roosevelt, Mary McLeod Bethune (*left*), was on the advisory board that created the WAC in 1942. Bethune visited this training center to put a prompt end to the unjust segregation Black WAC members had been experiencing there. Courtesy Library of Congress Prints and Photographs Division.

written many years later: "Sarah was undaunted. She'd come this far, she told us. She wasn't going to back down now. . . . Private First Class Sarah Louise Keys saw herself as a woman wronged, and she spoke with the surety I believe God gives to persons who are telling the truth."[23]

What About the *Morgan* Case?

Why hadn't the 1946 *Morgan v. Virginia* Supreme Court decision protected Sarah? Gradually Sarah and her father came to learn more about the *Morgan* case and about other legal issues. There was indeed a big loophole in that 1946 Supreme Court decision that gave Southern bus companies wiggle room to do whatever they pleased.

The exact words used—or not used—in a court decision can make a big difference. The Supreme Court's 1946 *Morgan* decision said that Virginia's segregation *legislation* couldn't be imposed on riders heading to or arriving from other states. But the decision didn't explicitly say that segregation *rules* a bus company had were also illegal. Some people might not notice any significance in not using the word *rules*. But bus companies noticed. As soon as the *Morgan* decision was announced, Southern bus companies began issuing their own segregation seating rules.

Her father had feared that bus companies might do something tricky like that. That's why he had urged Sarah to buy a ticket for a bus that went straight home, with no changes along the way. Not all drivers for Southern bus companies enforced their company's seating rules, which is why Sarah had no problems on earlier trips. She was unlucky to meet a driver in Roanoke Rapids who did enforce his company's segregation rule. She and her lawyers aimed to close that *Morgan* loophole.[24]

Waiting

Sarah returned to work at Fort Dix while her lawyers got busy figuring out how best to help her. There were articles about Sarah's arrest in some newspapers and also in *Jet*, a magazine popular with the Black community. Sarah thought her two best friends in the army might see those articles and so she told them what had happened. One friend was Black; the other was white. "They were quite surprised. They both said, 'That's terrible!' The Irish girl from Massachusetts thought it was deplorable. They were supportive," recalled Sarah.

Her commanding officer also knew what had happened, but Sarah didn't tell anyone else at Fort Dix. She didn't know what people would think if they heard that she had been arrested. Not everyone would have been as supportive as her two friends were.

The memory of her arrest continued to upset and worry Sarah. The arrest had happened so suddenly and had caught her by surprise. "I knew there was something I had to change in my attention and behavior in order to protect myself," she explained many years later, remembering how that arrest made her feel, both at the time and for the rest of her life. "I started questioning everything in my mind before acting on it or giving an answer. I learned to look at people, to study the faces of the people I met. I learned a lot about strength and about protecting myself, about not just thinking, but thinking it over very thoroughly before you make a comment. I was a very quiet person, but I went under. I used to go on dates, to the movies or bowling. But I never let them know what had happened."

What kept her going was knowing that what she was trying to accomplish—to stand up for "people being treated right and treated fairly," as she phrased it—was important. "I remember getting a letter from a soldier who had been transferred to Europe," she recalled. "He found out about it from *Jet* magazine and wrote me a letter commending me for my strength and courage. It made me feel good to know that it had reached worldwide through some source of communication. It made me feel very good." But still she kept her worries to herself as she waited to hear from her lawyers.[25]

9

Finding a Strategy

THE STRUGGLE AGAINST SEGREGATION IN public transportation has deep roots. From the 1700s onward, many Black people took great risks to protest against this form of discrimination. Over the years, several strategies were used, with varying degrees of success: filing a legal complaint in a court of law or before other governmental bodies, engaging in civil disobedience, launching boycotts or protest demonstrations, lobbying for new legislation. All those strategies would ultimately play a role in allowing Sarah Keys's personal stand for justice to have a lasting impact on civil rights history.

Twenty-three-year-old Sarah had no role in selecting which legal strategy her lawyers would choose. "I knew nothing about law," she said. "I followed their directions." She came to realize years later that as her case got underway in the fall of 1952, her lawyer, Dovey Johnson Roundtree, "probably didn't know how big it would become. When she was introduced, it had been stated that she was a young lawyer right out of law school. But I did not know that they were very new in law practice."

As the case progressed, Sarah saw that "it was not easy for Mrs. Roundtree and her partner. I'm glad I was me and not them. Imagine a young woman lawyer trying to undertake my case and those in front of her who had been her teachers, her instructors and professors. Visualize a woman in that position. I was never close enough to talk with her about this. There are certain people we are not going to let in on how vulnerable we felt at certain specific times. Why should she reveal that to me? To her peers maybe. But to a client? They probably most likely wished that there had been someone else on that bus other than me. Someone who knew something about the game, how it works."

Before long, Sarah did become interested in legal issues and began to enjoy reading books about law—not legal texts, but popular novels. "They give me a lot of insight on how things are supposed to go."[1]

She also picked up some practical know-how from an unusual source many years later, at a medical appointment when she was talking with someone in the waiting room who turned out to be a retired police officer from North Carolina. When she told him about her case and the $25 fee she paid, he mentioned to her that the police officers in Roanoke Rapids had probably spent that $25 before they put her on the bus to continue her trip home. He told her, "Nobody ever gets the $25 back."[2]

When Sarah returned to Fort Dix after meeting with the lawyers, they sent her a brief that had to be notarized for a court filing. "I read it over," Sarah recalled years later, "and there was one little detail that I wish I had said something about it at the time, but not having dealt with lawyers, I just read it and had it notarized and signed and sent back. Goodness knows, I didn't know how briefs went. That one little detail—had I been experienced—I would have mentioned it before getting it notarized. It was stated that I had changed in Washington, DC. I never changed bus. I had a straight-through bus to Washington, North Carolina. It was in Roanoke Rapids that there was the new bus everyone was asked to move onto."

That "little detail" would stay with her case all along. Sarah continued to feel frustrated about this inaccuracy concerning a bus change in DC, which had never happened, as far as she remembered. It would remain a permanent part of her official case materials. This detail probably didn't affect the outcome of her case, but it shows how uncomfortable and reluctant she was at that time to intervene in the legal arrangements.[3]

The rest of this chapter and the next provide an overview of the legal choices her two lawyers made, based on information in Dovey Roundtree's memoir, *Mighty Justice*, and from other sources, too.

At first, her lawyers considered filing a court complaint. Such a strategy had proved effective in one of the first victories against transportation segregation, when educator and church organist Elizabeth Jennings filed an 1854 suit in a Brooklyn court after being roughly thrown off a New York City horse-drawn streetcar for white riders, as described in chapter 2. However, Jennings's remarkable early victory did not immediately end all streetcar segregation in New York City. The path to accomplishing that foreshadows what would also be required a century later with Sarah's case: the need for other kinds of strategies after a legal victory to finish the job.[4]

Sarah's lawyers realized that the court case strategy might not succeed, but there had been some recent partial court victories that gave them hope. One, of course, was the 1946 *Morgan v. Virginia* case, which had started in a state court and was then appealed to the US Supreme Court. In addition, the NAACP's *Brown v. Board of Education* school segregation case had just started to be scheduled for consideration by the Supreme Court. This is the case for which Dovey Roundtree had heard some advance legal planning during law school. She realized that the legal world would soon be abuzz with talk about how to end segregation. That could definitely help a Sarah Keys lawsuit.

First, her lawyers had to choose a court in which to file a complaint. They realized they would never win in North Carolina, given what Sarah and her father experienced when they went to Roanoke Rapids to try to have the charges dropped. Roundtree definitely decided against a North Carolina court filing after reading the transcript from those Roanoke Rapids hearings, with local officials falsely claiming that Sarah had cursed and been so disruptive that incarceration was required.

However, Sarah's bus trip had passed through DC. Even though the bus company that mistreated her wasn't headquartered in DC, perhaps her bus passing through DC would be enough to qualify the bus company as "doing business" there so that a lawsuit in a DC court would be possible. On November 19, 1952, her lawyers filed a complaint in the US District Court for the District of Columbia against the bus companies involved in her journey. Sarah's lawyers demanded a jury trial, hoping to sway a jury by describing the disgraceful way the bus company and local police had treated a young army private in uniform. Roundtree contacted a newspaper reporter she knew who wrote a story about the Sarah Keys case that appeared the next day in the influential Black newspaper the *Pittsburgh Courier*.

Unfortunately, three months later, on February 23, 1953, the US District Court for the District of Columbia refused to take the case, saying it did not have "jurisdiction."[5]

On to the ICC

The next possibility was to file a complaint with a government agency featured in some earlier court cases on transportation segregation: the Interstate Commerce Commission (ICC), the nation's first independent federal regulatory commission. The ICC was created by Congress in 1887 to bring some order to the wildly variable rates that different railroad companies charged to haul goods and animals for businesses and farmers. As noted in chapter 2, Congress had the right to pass the Interstate Commerce Act and create such a commission because of the Commerce Clause in Article 1 of the US Constitution, which gives Congress power "to regulate commerce with foreign nations and among the several states." Originally, the ICC had jurisdiction only over railroads. In 1935, Congress passed the Motor Carrier Act, which expanded the ICC's mission to include interstate bus and trucking companies.

The 1887 law establishing the ICC lists the many ways it can oversee interstate commerce. A Black US congressman from North Carolina, James E. O'Hara, helped add an important feature to the original Interstate Commerce Act, as explained in Mia Bay's *Traveling Black*. He wanted the ICC to have the authority to regulate conditions for passengers on trains and not just deal with regulations for transporting goods or animals. He introduced an amendment to the Interstate Commerce Act stating that all interstate passengers who paid the same fee for a railroad trip from one state to another state should receive the same services and accommodations "without discrimination." He received support from the House of Representative's only other Black congressman, South Carolina's Robert Smalls, but not much encouragement from other Representatives. White congressmen from the South worried that Representative O'Hara's amendment might end railroad segregation. The wording of his amendment was rejected, but the suggestion that the law should include passenger travel still found its way into the act, although in a more limited way than he had suggested. The Interstate Commerce Act stated that "provisions of this act shall apply to any common carrier or carriers engaged in the transportation of passengers or property." The law also stated that railroads could not charge any person more than others were charged for the same service.

In response to concerns from white Southern representatives, the act also states that its provisions would not apply to "the transportation of passengers or property . . . wholly within one State." The ICC's rules would apply only to interstate transportation. Individual states would thus still be able to enact their own rules for travel within their state.

When the ICC's role was expanded to include buses, with the Motor Carrier Act of 1935, the act's rules then applied to interstate bus travel, too. This nineteenth-century Black North Carolina congressman helped allow Sarah's complaint to be heard at the ICC.[6]

Another part of the Interstate Commerce Act was of great interest to civil rights lawyers—its Section 3, which includes the fairness principle, stating that "it shall be unlawful for any common carrier . . . to subject any particular person . . . to any undue or unreasonable prejudice or disadvantage in any respect whatsoever." Sarah Keys had definitely experienced "undue or unreasonable prejudice or disadvantage" in Roanoke Rapids.[7]

However, the ICC was a risky choice. Right from the start, the ICC had ruled that segregation was acceptable, showing support for the idea that travelers could be separated by skin color as long as the separate accommodations for Black and white passengers were equal in quality. Two of the ICC's earliest rulings in the 1880s set forth that policy. One case decided in the commission's first year in 1887 involved educator William H. Councill, then president of what is now known as Alabama A&M University. He filed a complaint at the ICC because he had bought a first-class ticket for a train ride from Tennessee to Georgia but was badly beaten by a railroad employee and white passengers when he refused to leave the ladies car and go to the filthy Jim Crow car. The ICC ruled in his case that although segregation was permissible, because "public sentiment . . . sanctions and requires this separation of races," it also said that the train company could direct "a colored man to a car for his own race" but that the passenger still had the right "to have accommodations substantially equal to those of other passengers paying the same fare," which had not been true for William Councill.

The ICC reached a similar conclusion the following year in a complaint filed by Rev. William H. Heard, who was forced to move from the first-class car to the inferior Jim Crow car when the train reached Atlanta on a trip from Cincinnati to Charleston. In both cases, the ICC ordered the railroad to cease and desist denying comparable facilities for customers paying the same fares.

Unfortunately, the ICC had little enforcement power. Unequal train accommodations continued. By the time the Supreme Court issued its 1896 *Plessy v. Ferguson* "separate but equal" decision nine years after the ICC was established, the ICC had already been routinely upholding the separate but equal policy in cases brought by Black travelers who complained about segregation.

What gave lawyers Roundtree and Robertson hope as they began researching past ICC cases was an argument used in a recent transportation case that suggested success at the ICC might be possible. That case involved a Black US congressman from Illinois, Arthur Mitchell. Born in Alabama, Mitchell became a successful lawyer and businessman in Chicago. In 1934, he was the first Black Democrat elected to Congress. Three years later, he bought a first-class ticket for a train trip from Chicago to Hot Springs, Arkansas. When the train reached Arkansas, he was forced to move out of the first-class car and into a second-class car for Black passengers in order to comply with the Arkansas train-car segregation law. He filed a lawsuit in an Illinois court. That court ruled against him. He then filed a complaint with the ICC, which also ruled against him. He didn't give up. He appealed the ICC decision, and his case wound up at the US Supreme Court, which ruled in his favor in 1941.

The NAACP did not represent him at the Supreme Court. Instead, Congressman Mitchell argued the case himself, along with another lawyer, explaining that when the railroad company had not provided the congressman with the first-class seat he paid for, it had violated both the Interstate Commerce Act and the Fourteenth Amendment's guarantee of "equal protection of the laws."

Congressman Mitchell's Supreme Court victory affected only first-class train passengers and thus had no impact on the great majority of Black passengers. Even so, Sarah Keys's lawyers thought the Mitchell strategy—linking the Fourteenth Amendment to the Interstate Commerce Act—could be an effective strategy to try.

Another railroad case also interested Sarah's lawyers. It too had initially been rejected by the ICC and then made its way to the Supreme Court. This case began in 1942 when Elmer Henderson, a Black official of the federal Fair Employment Practices Committee, was denied first-class dining car access on a train trip from DC to Alabama. After experiencing defeat at the ICC, his case was appealed to the Supreme Court. Henderson's lawyer cited the Fourteenth Amendment in his arguments to the Supreme Court. The court ruled in 1950 that the railroad, in the way it had treated Elmer Henderson, had violated the nondiscrimination clause of the Interstate Commerce Act. But the court did not comment on whether segregation itself was illegal.

Sarah's legal team studied carefully how the ICC had responded to the kinds of arguments used in both the Mitchell and Henderson cases as they planned how they would present Sarah's case to the commission.[8]

There was, of course, another strategy used in both those cases that could not be ignored: persistence. Congressman Mitchell and Elmer Henderson never gave up. Neither did Sarah.

Nor did her lawyers. They had been especially inspired when they had a chance to attend a session at the Supreme Court on December 9, 1952, thanks to two "day passes" given to them by one of their Howard professors who was part of the NAACP's legal team. That day Thurgood Marshall delivered arguments in one of the five school cases that were part of what became known as *Brown v. Board of Education*. He argued forcefully and eloquently in this court session that segregation itself was wrong and demeaning to Black schoolchildren, denying them rights that are guaranteed to them under the Fourteenth Amendment—the right to equal protection of the law.

With the demise of the court case option, Sarah's lawyers decided to try to win a victory at the ICC by using arguments like those they had heard Thurgood Marshall use. They were also determined, as Dovey Roundtree notes in her memoir, "to force the ICC to look with a new eye at the act it was charged with implementing" in order to make the ICC explore the true meaning of the Interstate Commerce Act's prohibition against subjecting anyone to "undue or unreasonable prejudice or disadvantage."

Another positive development occurred in June 1953 as Sarah Keys's legal team was planning the complaint they would send to the ICC. The Supreme Court that month called for a pause in arguments in the school segregation case so that lawyers could explore the meaning of the Fourteenth Amendment, with a focus on figuring out what Congress intended when it wrote that amendment in the mid-1860s. This could help Sarah's ICC case if the lawyers' exploration led the Supreme Court to decide that the Fourteenth Amendment did indeed allow the federal government to be involved in setting policies regarding fair treatment for citizens, unlike the conclusion earlier versions of the court had reached, such as in the *Plessy* case, that only states could make rulings on the behavior of individual citizens.[9]

When Sarah learned from her lawyers that they had switched strategies, she went to Washington to meet with them and hear what was planned. On September 1, 1953, a little over a year after Sarah's arrest, her lawyers, with Sarah's approval, filed a complaint at the ICC: *Sarah Keys v. Carolina Coach Company*. Sarah Keys became the first Black citizen to file a complaint at the ICC regarding bus travel.[10]

The Waiting Begins

One month after her case was filed at the ICC, Sarah's two-year tour of duty in the Women's Army Corps came to an end. She had enjoyed being a WAC and the self-confidence it gave her, especially at her new posting at Fort Knox in Kentucky. About a year earlier, she had asked to transfer from Fort Dix because of an incident in which she thought she had been falsely accused of being late for KP (kitchen patrol). That incident led to her receiving company punishment from her commanding officer (CO). Private First Class Keys worried that perhaps the Fort Dix CO, who was white, treated her unfairly because she knew Sarah was involved in a civil rights case and the CO had not approved. Sarah didn't want to bring a complaint against the CO or discuss her suspicions with anyone. Instead, she decided to move to a new army base where no one would know about her case. "That was my main reason for asking for a transfer," she explained. "I knew that I had to protect myself and keep this thing to myself."

Moving to Fort Knox gave her a fresh start. "No one there knew. I got an assignment that I enjoyed. I worked at the Post Locator, a division that corrects misplaced mail." Just before her two-year tour of duty was to end, the commanding officer at Fort Knox, a fellow Black member of the WACs, called Sarah into her office to say that she had just read in *Jet* magazine about Sarah protesting her Roanoke Rapids arrest. The CO told Sarah, "This is wonderful. Why didn't you come to me and talk to me about this?" Sarah explained about what had happened at Fort Dix and her fears that she had been singled out because of her court case. Sarah was offered a promotion if she would sign up for another two years. Even so, she decided not to reenlist. She wanted to try something new.[11]

The GI Bill benefits she received after mustering out helped her enter a new career. Dovey Roundtree had used the money she received after leaving the army to go to law school. Sarah Keys used her money to learn how to do something she had loved ever since she was a young girl when she would style her sisters' hair at home. She went to a beauty school to become a hairstylist. The school was in Harlem, near where she was living in New York City. For the next year, she worked as a clerk in an office during the day while taking classes at night at the beauty school. "I loved the beauty business," said Sarah.[12]

Several months after Sarah started beauty school, Roundtree phoned to say that the ICC was ready to look into Sarah's complaint. Sarah would have to travel to Washington, DC, to testify before a meeting of the members of the ICC, describing to them what had happened in Roanoke Rapids. She would need to be ready to answer questions from the bus company's lawyers.

Sarah felt nervous about talking to these important government officials. She had never done anything like that before. She phoned her father, who said he would be there in Washington with her, sitting in the section for visitors in the room where the ICC held its meetings. He would bring along William, her ten-year-old brother. That way, she would have some supporters there, rooting for her to do well. Her father was working in Washington then as a cement mason on construction jobs. "But he went back home that weekend and brought my youngest brother with him 'so he could watch the process,'" Sarah explained.[13]

She met with her lawyers just before testifying. They didn't do a mock run-through of the testifying, but as she noted later, "We had gone over the whole thing in her office. They had their stuff together. They knew how they wanted it to start and how they wanted it to end. All I had to do was answer the questions."[14]

The ICC meeting took place on May 12, 1954. It was almost like a trial, with bus company lawyers asking Sarah questions. "I was very nervous," she recalled. The lawyers kept telling her to speak louder. "My voice will go into a very low spin if I'm excited or nervous. I remember very vividly questions that the attorney for the bus company kept asking me. He asked me a few questions and then he'd go back to the same line: 'Weren't you planted to go on that bus? Who planted you? Well now, Miss Keys, didn't someone plant you on that bus?' I had never heard the word 'planting' in the context of what happened to me until the hour I was up there. It seemed like an eternity that I was up there, being badgered about this. They brought that bus driver up to testify at the ICC. Can you imagine they did a thing like that? And they just kept asking me: 'Who planted you on that bus?'"[15]

The lawyer for the bus company was suggesting that a civil rights group had put Sarah Keys on the bus on purpose in order to cause trouble. She knew that wasn't true. As she said many years later, "I didn't set out to do what I did. It just happened."[16]

The bus company's lawyer managed to make her agree that the seat she was asked to take in the rear of the bus was equal in quality to the one in which she had been sitting. He also tried to get her to say that she had shouted and cursed at the bus driver. She remained quiet and polite throughout the testimony. Dressed in her army uniform, she made it clear that she wasn't the kind of person to shout and curse. She told the truth about what had happened on that hot summer night in Roanoke Rapids. Roundtree wrote in her memoir, describing the ICC hearing, "Sarah, calm and exquisitely polite and ever so military in her WAC dress uniform, quietly made a mockery of the bus company's characterization of her. She made me proud that day—proud to be a WAC, representing another WAC who took the uniform and her service as seriously as I myself had."[17]

Finally, the questioning stopped. Sarah met with her father and brother. She felt sad that William had seen the way the bus company lawyer treated her. "William thought that I was really being badgered. He thought, 'Why don't they leave my sister alone? Why do they keep asking the same dumb question over and over again?'" She thanked them for coming. Then she took a train back to New York to wait for a phone call from her lawyers on the ICC's decision.[18]

US Supreme Court Helps

Five days after Sarah testified, the US Supreme Court reached a decision in the NAACP's school segregation case, *Brown v. Board of Education*. On May 17, 1954, all nine Supreme Court justices voted unanimously that segregation in public schools had to end. Dovey Roundtree thought the arguments that helped the NAACP lawyers win the schools' case could also help Sarah win her case. Sarah's lawyers rushed to send the ICC a document pointing out how this new Supreme Court education decision related to Sarah's case—that the court's support for the "equal protection of the laws" clause of the Fourteenth Amendment related directly to the Interstate Commerce Act's nondiscrimination clause.

The NAACP's arguments in the *Brown* case rested not only on the Fourteenth Amendment but also on a new idea its lawyers introduced: that segregation itself was harmful. Thurgood Marshall, the lead NAACP lawyer in this case (who had also been one of the lawyers in the *Morgan* case), described a research study which showed that simply living in a country where people are separated by skin color led Black children to have negative feelings about being Black. That led the children to think that being white is better, which the researchers concluded could harm the children's ability to do well in school.

This study, conducted by two prominent Black psychologists, Dr. Kenneth Clark and Dr. Mamie P. Clark, involved more than 250 Black children between the ages of three and seven. The children had been shown four dolls that were alike except for skin color: two dolls had brown skin with black hair and two had white skin with yellow hair. The children were asked which dolls were nice, which look bad, which they'd want to play with, and which were like them. A majority preferred the white doll. Most said the brown doll "looks bad."

This research helped persuade the Supreme Court justices that school segregation must end. As the court's *Brown v. Board of Education* decision stated, "To separate them [children] from others of similar age and qualifications solely because of their race generates a feeling of inferiority as to their status in the community that may affect their hearts and minds in a way unlikely ever to be undone." The Supreme Court also expressed an opinion on the Fourteenth Amendment. While the justices acknowledged that it's impossible to "turn the clock back to 1868," when the amendment was written, the court said it was possible to consider its current impact on education to determine "if segregation in public schools deprives these plaintiffs of the equal protection of the laws." The court concluded: "We believe that it does."

That led the justices to make a strong statement with a direct impact on the Sarah Keys case at the ICC. It called into question the *Plessy v. Ferguson* decision that the ICC had defended for so long. The Supreme Court's decision in *Brown v. Board of Education* said: "Whatever may have been the extent of psychological knowledge at the time of *Plessy v. Ferguson*, this finding is amply supported by modern authority. Any language in *Plessy v. Ferguson* contrary to this finding is rejected. We conclude that, in the field of public education, the doctrine of 'separate but equal' has no place."[19] With that statement, the court struck a major blow at *Plessy v. Ferguson*'s legal support for segregation that had been used for more than fifty years to justify Jim Crow laws.

In a follow-up brief Sarah's lawyers sent to the ICC in response to the *Brown* decision, they made what they hoped would be a winning argument: that because of *Brown v. Board of Education*'s ruling it could "no longer be doubted" that "any regulation requiring segregation of passengers in interstate commerce on the basis of race is not only unreasonable but unlawful."[20]

Shocking Setback

Four months later, on September 30, 1954, Sarah's lawyers received a letter from the ICC with its decision. Dovey Roundtree was shocked when she opened the envelope.

Sarah Keys had lost!

The ICC's letter rejected all the ideas her lawyers offered. The letter said the Supreme Court's *Brown v. Board of Education* ruling applied only to public schools, not to rules made by a private business, such as a bus company. The ICC letter added that the *Brown* decision "in no way affects or prohibits separation or segregation of the Negro and white races insofar as transportation is concerned."

The ICC letter also cited its own precedents to justify its conclusion, noting that the ICC had always based its decisions on its understanding that the Interstate Commerce Act did not forbid buses from separating people by skin color: "From the beginning, the Commission has interpreted the Interstate Commerce Act as not prohibiting carriers . . . from requiring separation of white and Negro passengers."[21] The ICC letter writer offered the ICC'S own ruling in the Elmer Henderson case as an example of its decision-making consistency without mentioning that the Supreme Court had later overturned the ICC'S Henderson decision.

In addition, the ICC letter said that the Supreme Court's *Morgan* decision was not relevant because it concerned state *laws*, not a private company's *rules*. The ICC letter also supported the *Plessy v. Ferguson* idea of "separate but equal" by taking a narrow view of the meaning of "equal." Although the seat at the back of the bus was said to be equal to the one Sarah had occupied, the writer of this letter seemed oblivious to another aspect of Sarah Keys's trip that was not at all equal. She had not been treated with the same respect and courtesy as the white passengers. Nor had she received the customary respect and courtesy that is generally given to white members of the military in uniform.[22]

Sarah was disappointed when Roundtree phoned to explain what had happened. But this young lawyer had already begun to figure out how to respond and was busy making a plan for what to do next to keep fighting for justice. "I commend her for her spirit and her tenacity," explained Sarah. "Neither one of us gave up."[23]

10

Never Give Up

THE ICC HAD ELEVEN MEMBERS, called commissioners, who were supposed to make decisions on ICC cases, but only one person wrote the letter delivering the negative decision for *Sarah Keys v. Carolina Coach Company*. He wasn't an official commissioner but worked for the ICC as an "examiner," someone who gathered facts for the commissioners in order to write up reports that they could use in making their decisions. This examiner, Isadore I. Freidson, was at the hearing where Sarah testified. Instead of simply preparing a report for the commissioners to consult, he was allowed to decide the case on his own.

Dovey Roundtree thought that was unfair. To find a way to have all eleven ICC commissioners vote on this case, she made use of another strategy that has helped many a legal case: networking.

She asked a friend from her college days at Spelman for help contacting Sarah's congressman, US Representative Adam Clayton Powell Jr. When the congressman heard what had happened at the ICC, he was "outraged," noted Roundtree, especially because that lone ICC examiner hadn't understood the significance of the Supreme Court's *Brown v. Board of Education* decision, apparently not realizing that the court had just overturned the *Plessy v. Ferguson* legal concept of "separate but equal." The congressman contacted the head of the ICC and urged him to remove that examiner, which didn't happen, but the congressman's intervention alerted the ICC to the concerns of Sarah's lawyers. A *JET* magazine article reported the role played by Representative Powell in the October 14, 1954, edition.

Roundtree and her legal partner, Julius Robertson, then got busy writing an "exception" to the examiner's ruling, which had to be filed within twenty days, to make the case for all eleven commissioners taking a second look at *Sarah Keys v. Carolina Coach Company*.[1]

In their appeal to the ICC, Sarah's lawyers used many of the same arguments they had used earlier. This time, they cited more forcefully the Mitchell and Henderson court cases and their links to the Fourteenth Amendment. In addition, her lawyers uncovered and cited a 1949 case from a federal district court based in Ohio, *Whiteside v. Southern Bus Lines*. It highlighted a wider meaning for the text of *Morgan v. Virginia*.

Many had noted that because the 1946 *Morgan* ruling failed to specifically outlaw bus company segregation "rules," bus companies could circumvent the Supreme Court's decision simply by making and enforcing their own segregation seating rules. However, the Ohio-based federal judges in the 1949 *Whiteside* decision noted that *Morgan v. Virginia* had used the word "rule," although in a more general context when it concluded that "seating arrangements for the different races in interstate motor travel require a single uniform rule."

To the *Whiteside* judges, this commonsense use of the word *rule* meant a "way of doing things," which let them decide that it wasn't only state *laws* that could interfere with having a "single uniform rule." So could *rules* made by "private persons" or bus companies.

This 1949 case involved a complaint filed by Elizabeth Whiteside, who had been ordered to move to the back of a bus when it crossed into Kentucky during a trip that had started in Missouri. The court decided that the bus company's use of its segregation rule in Kentucky during Elizabeth Whiteside's interstate trip "constitutes a burden upon interstate commerce." Elizabeth Whiteside's court victory applied only to the four states that were in the federal district of the court that decided her case: Michigan, Ohio, Kentucky, and Tennessee. Even so, Sarah Keys's lawyers thought this court's reasoning could help her ICC case. They included it in their appeal for an ICC rehearing, which they sent to the ICC on October 19, 1954.

They also included a quote from a 1943 Supreme Court decision, *Hirabayashi v. United States*. Although the court had ruled in that case that internment of Japanese Americans during the World War II was allowed because of danger during time of war, the court noted that otherwise such discrimination would violate the "equal protection" clause of the Fourteenth Amendment because "distinctions between citizens solely because of their ancestry are, by their very, nature odious to a free people whose institutions are founded upon the doctrine of equality."[2]

In their appeal to the ICC, Sarah's lawyers again reminded the ICC that because the Supreme Court had just overturned the idea of "separate but equal" in the field of education with *Brown v. Board of Education*, the ICC should overturn it in interstate travel, too.[3] They were explicit in explaining why the school ruling was relevant, noting that the Supreme Court had stated in its *Brown* decision that the forced separation of people due to race "generates a feeling of inferiority." Sarah's lawyers added that this "stigmatizes those persons segregated . . . subjects the person segregated to an unreasonable and constitutionally forbidden discrimination." They added that the Supreme Court had "specifically relegated the doctrine of 'separate but equal' to limbo." Thus, according to the Supreme Court's conclusion about segregation, segregation itself violates the nondiscrimination section of the Interstate Commerce Act.[4]

The attorney general of the United States, Herbert Brownell, said something similar in a letter he had sent to the ICC in July 1954 in support of a case on train travel that the NAACP had also filed at the ICC: *NAACP v. St. Louis–San Francisco Railway Company*. The ICC was considering that train case at the same time as *Sarah Keys v. Carolina Coach Company*. The ICC agreed to let Attorney General Brownell's comments be considered as part of its investigation of the Sarah Keys case, too. In his letter, the attorney general attacked the idea of "separate but equal" by quoting the only Supreme Court justice in 1896 who had disagreed with the other justices in the *Plessy v. Ferguson* case: Justice John Marshall Harlan (as noted in chapter 2). A passage in Justice Harlan's eloquent 1896 dissent had become famous for its clear defense of equal rights for all. Brownell realized that by quoting Justice Harlan in his letter, the ICC commissioners would understand that he was attacking the entire concept of "separate but equal" that had been a key feature of *Plessy v. Ferguson*, a policy the ICC had upheld for so long.[5]

Here are the words from Justice Harlan's *Plessy v. Ferguson* dissent that the attorney general included in his letter to the ICC: Harlan had written in 1896 that the "Constitution is color-blind, and neither knows nor tolerates classes among citizens." Attorney General Brownell, after quoting that phrase from Justice Harlan, then added his own conclusion: "So too is the Interstate Commerce Act. The time has come for this Commission, in administering that Act, to declare unequivocally that a Negro passenger is free to travel the length and breadth of the country in the same manner as any other passenger."[6]

Justice Harlan's 1896 quote had particular relevance given his personal history. Born and raised in Kentucky, his family had been slaveholders. He was in favor of slavery when the Civil War started, although he joined the Union Army because he didn't want to see the nation divided. After the war, at first he wasn't pleased with the three equal rights amendments added to the US Constitution, but he soon decided that those amendments were fair. After his appointment to the US Supreme Court in 1877, he defended those amendments.[7] Here's the full passage that is so often quoted from the dissent Justice Harlan wrote for the 1896 *Plessy* case: "In view of the Constitution, in the eye of the law, there is in this country no superior, dominant, ruling class of citizens. There is no caste here. Our Constitution is color-blind, and neither knows nor tolerates classes among citizens. In respect of civil rights, all citizens are equal before the law."[8] The language of Harlan's dissent would play an important role in Sarah Keys's quest for justice.

A New Decision

The ICC commissioners took more than a year to reach a new decision. At last, on November 7, 1955, nine ICC commissioners voted on *Sarah Keys v. Carolina Coach Company*. They didn't release their decision to the public for two weeks. Finally, on Friday morning, November 25, 1955—the day after Thanksgiving—Sarah at last received the phone call she had been waiting for. By then, she had graduated from beauty school and was working as a hairstylist and beauty consultant at Gold and Brown, a New York City beauty salon. She had also just moved to Brooklyn, starting a new chapter of her life there, where she would live for more than sixty years.

Dovey Roundtree phoned Sarah that morning at the beauty parlor and told her that the ICC had announced its decision. This time Sarah had won!

All but one of the nine ICC commissioners who voted on her case decided that forcing people to sit in certain seats on a bus because of skin color violated the 1887 law that had set up the ICC.[9] The ICC decision in *Sarah Keys v. Carolina Coach Company* stated that the bus company, by using segregated seating, was "subjecting Negro passengers to unjust discrimination and unreasonable prejudice and disadvantage, in violation of section 216 (d) of the Interstate Commerce Act. Order entered requiring defendant to cease and desist from such practices."[10]

The ICC commissioners reached the same decision in the NAACP's train case. From then on, segregation on a bus or train was officially illegal on state-to-state trips, whether caused by a state law or by rules a transportation company might make. The ICC also said segregation in bus and train stations had to end, too, although the ICC ruling didn't end segregation in station restaurants.[11]

Equally important, the commissioners took a stand against the whole idea of segregation. In explaining the rationale for their decision, the commissioners wrote in their ruling in *Sarah Keys v. Carolina Coach Company*: "We conclude that the assignment of seats in interstate buses, so designated as to imply the inherent inferiority of a traveler solely because of race or color, must be regarded as subjecting the traveler to unjust discrimination, and undue and unreasonable prejudice and disadvantage. In addition to the discrimination, prejudice, and disadvantage resulting from the mere fact of segregation, additional disadvantage to the passenger is always potentially present because the traveler is entitled to be free from the annoyances which inevitably accompany segregation and the variety and unevenness of methods of its enforcement."[12]

Sarah Keys v. Carolina Coach Company was a "first" in legal history and in civil rights history—the first time the ICC rejected the idea of segregation and the fiction of "separate but equal" which the ICC had supported for so long in its earlier rulings. The *Plessy v. Ferguson* legal underpinning of Jim Crow had now been officially rejected by two major governmental institutions: the US Supreme Court and the ICC. It would take more work to end segregation in other areas, but those decisions by the court and the ICC helped with future efforts to put an end to the Jim Crow era.[13]

"Never Been So Happy"

Sarah Keys was overjoyed when Dovey Roundtree phoned with the news about the ICC's decision. Sarah told people at the salon what had happened. "Everyone was so shocked," she recalled. "They said things like, 'How come you didn't tell us? Oh, that was so awful. We're so sorry.'" They couldn't believe that their quiet friend Sarah would be involved in anything like that.[14]

She had never told them about her arrest or about the ICC case for the same reason that she didn't share that information with many of those she had worked with in the army. She worried that some of them might not approve of what she had done, both being arrested and trying to fight for justice. The shock of her 1952 arrest in Roanoke Rapids still made her feel guarded and careful about what she said and to whom.

That is exactly the point NAACP lawyers had made in *Brown v. Board of Education*. It's also the point that her lawyers had emphasized in their comments to the ICC: Segregation is an insult that affects people's feelings about themselves. Worrying about whether you might be mistreated because of skin color is a stress that can wear people down.

Years later, Sarah wrote a letter to *Ebony* magazine, which, unfortunately, the magazine did not publish. But in that letter, a copy of which she kept for many years, she described her feelings about what she had accomplished and the personal stress that waging that battle against segregation had caused: "I fought the three and one half year battle as a matter of moral decency. There were many trials before triumphs. I learned firsthand about mental and physical fear. I am aware of the strain involved when fighting for one's freedom or human rights."[15]

On the day her ICC victory was announced, Sarah shared the good news not only with her coworkers but with reporters, too. "The phones were ringing, and the television people were at the door," she recalled, describing what happened that day at the salon. "The place was inundated with news people."[16] Reporters wanted to talk with the brave young woman who stood up for her rights and the rights of all people of color. "They wanted to know how I felt about the ruling," she said. "My first comment I made to them was that 'I feel free at long last.'"[17]

The next day articles about her victory appeared in newspapers around the country. In addition to describing the decision in the case, the articles explained that the ICC had issued an order that in about six weeks—on January 10, 1956—segregation had to end on interstate buses and trains, as well as in the waiting rooms at bus stations and railroad terminals, although not yet in restaurants in those stations and terminals.[18]

Reporters realized the momentous nature of this decision and of the January 10 deadline. Max Lerner wrote a column in the *New York Post* titled "We Ride Together," in which he noted, "These freedoms are now added to the slowly accumulating list of other hard-won freedoms. . . . I light a candle in my heart with the knowledge that, white and black alike, we can now ride together. . . . Now the name of Sarah Keys is added to that of Mitchell and Mrs. Morgan, as symbols of the movement that cannot be held back."[19] Black newspapers were especially pleased. The Pittsburgh

Courier noted that transportation segregation was particularly painful because it "flaunted the humiliation of a third of the South's population, with every train, bus, railroad station, ticket office and lunchroom a symbol of their subjugation."[20]

The New York *Herald Tribune* described Sarah's reaction to the decision, quoting her as saying, "I've never been so happy in my life. This is just the greatest thing for me and my people. It's a wonderful thing for the whole American people as well. It will show the other people in the world about Americans."[21] The *New York Times* also quoted Sarah, who told its reporter, "It is a big relief to have it behind me. It is a great occasion for me and my father, for it took more than three years for a decision. My father encouraged me when I needed encouragement."[22]

When she phoned her parents to tell them the good news, "they were excited," she said, although she felt that her father was more excited than her mother. Her mother was pleased, but Sarah always had the feeling her mother felt "that I had called a lot of attention that would not have been there if I had just followed directions and moved to the back of the bus."[23]

Fearing that others might feel the way her mother did made Sarah reluctant to put herself forward, even after the ICC victory. "It was an uneasy feeling all of a sudden to have your picture in the newspaper," noted Sarah. "I was a very private person. I was living in Brooklyn. I had no family with me. I didn't broadcast it in the neighborhood. I did not want anyone in the neighborhood to identify me. I didn't want that attention."[24]

She explained years later that "there were times I felt like I was being followed. I wasn't. But after the decision, I really felt like I was being followed. If I had not always been a strongly independent individual, I would probably have gone underground for a while. But I had always maintained my independence, taking care of myself, not having to depend on anyone to do that." Before long, she quit the job at the Manhattan salon and started working at a salon in Brooklyn so she wouldn't have to take the subway every day but could walk to work.[25]

More Battles to Fight

As important as Sarah's victory was, Jim Crow didn't suddenly end everywhere, even in interstate travel. Most parts of the country obeyed the new ICC rules for state-to-state travel on buses and trains, but some Southern states and bus companies did not comply. On the day after the ICC decision was announced publicly, South Carolina's attorney general was quoted in the *New York Times* as saying that the ICC ruling "'really means nothing' without backing of the courts." The same edition of the newspaper reported that Louisiana's Public Service Commissioner had "no intention" of changing its policies "merely because the I.C.C. has made such a revision." An editorial in a Mississippi newspaper declared that "Mississippi will not obey the order of the Interstate Commerce Commission."[26] In areas that obeyed the ICC's rules, some Black passengers continued to sit in the back of a bus, not wanting to risk confrontations with segregationist white drivers and passengers.[27]

Making matters worse, the ICC did nothing to force Southern companies to obey the new rules. This likely stemmed from the attitude of one ICC commissioner, J. Monroe Johnson, age seventy-seven, from South Carolina, the only commissioner who didn't vote in favor of the *Sarah Keys v. Carolina Coach Company* decision.[28] A *New York Times* article on the ICC decision quoted Johnson's explanation for his dissent: "It is my opinion that the Commission should not undertake to anticipate the Court and itself become a pioneer in the sociological field."[29]

Unfortunately, he became the chairman of the ICC right after the *Sarah Keys* decision was announced. The former ICC chairman had to resign because he was accused of doing something illegal. The ICC always chose its oldest member as its chairman, and so Johnson took control. Roundtree noted in her memoir that, in her opinion, he would "do everything in his power" to keep the ICC from taking the kind of bold action that would be needed to enforce *Sarah Keys v. Carolina Coach Company* and make Southern bus companies end Jim Crow on interstate trips.[30]

"I thought that was terrible," Sarah recalled. "The ICC never did work on enforcing it and training the drivers about what the law really was. The *Morgan* decision was not enforced either. That's what got people like me arrested."[31]

Major change takes time. Even the Supreme Court's momentous 1954 *Brown v. Board of Education* decision didn't result in automatic change. A few Southern cities made an effort to desegregate their schools during the next school term, but others delayed for many years. Some Southern cities even closed all their public schools for a while rather than have Black and white students go to school together. In North Carolina and other Southern states, some white families sent their children to all-white private schools to avoid using desegregated public schools. Three of North Carolina's big cities began integrating their public schools in 1957, and a few other areas in the state followed in 1959. But at the start of the 1958–59 school year, only 10 out of the state's more than 322,000 school-age students of color were attending schools that had previously been whites-only. Schools in most parts of North Carolina didn't integrate until more than ten years after the *Brown v. Board of Education* decision. Desegregation in all the state's schools did not occur until the 1970s.[32]

Desegregation, however, led to the end of the Mother of Mercy School that Sarah Keys had attended. In 1953, Catholic churches and schools in North Carolina began to desegregate. In 1963, the separate Black and white parochial schools in Washington, North Carolina, were combined, creating the first integrated school in that city. The two parish churches in Washington—the whites-only St. Agnes Church and the chapel in the Mother of Mercy School—also combined to form one church, called Mother of Mercy Church. When whites-only public schools integrated there five years later in 1968, fewer Black students enrolled in the Mother of Mercy School. It reached its highest enrollment level in 1968 with 113 students, but enrollment dropped the following year. Its high school closed in 1969, and its elementary school shut down in 1973. The school building is now a community building for the Mother of Mercy church, open to all.[33] The school that Sarah's father helped create played an important role in the lives of Sarah, her siblings, and their many classmates, but now students had other options for receiving an academic curriculum education.

In Halifax County, where Roanoke Rapids is located, integrated schooling didn't occur until a federal lawsuit was filed in 1969. Even today, despite every city, state, and county in the United States having officially ended school segregation, many schools in both North and South do not have diverse student populations. How to achieve truly equitable educational opportunity is an issue still being discussed and debated around the nation.[34]

It took six years before the ICC decided to enforce the rules it had set forth in *Sarah Keys v. Carolina Coach Company*.[35] The move toward enforcement resulted from the introduction of attention-getting nonviolent strategies that created enough of a sense of crisis to finally force the federal government to take firm action.

In addition, there was another transportation problem that the *Sarah Keys v. Carolina Coach Company* decision didn't cover: segregation on local buses that don't travel state-to-state. One week after Sarah's ICC victory was announced and reported on in newspapers around the country, thousands of Black people in Alabama found a different kind of headline-grabbing way to protest against Jim Crow on local city buses.[36]

11

Winning a Wider Victory

ON DECEMBER 1, 1955—ONE WEEK AFTER the ICC publicly announced its decision in *Sarah Keys v. Carolina Coach Company*—Rosa Parks was arrested for refusing to move to the back of a local city bus in Montgomery, Alabama, the kind of bus trip not covered by the ICC'S new interstate bus ruling. Her arrest led to the use of a dramatic weapon in the battle against transportation segregation that made headlines in newspapers and on TVs around the country. Four days after her arrest, 90 percent of Montgomery's Black community showed support for her courage by refusing to ride the city's buses. This marked the start of a boycott that would last for more than a year. Thousands were willing to walk to work or find ways to carpool instead of paying to ride a bus.

A young Baptist minister helped lead this long, peaceful boycott: Rev. Dr. Martin Luther King Jr., then age twenty-six, in his debut as a civil rights leader.[1] A Montgomery women's group, the Women's Political Council, led by local college professor Jo Ann Robinson, had already been trying to improve conditions for the city's Black bus riders. In 1954, this group suggested some changes for the city to make. When that effort failed, she warned the mayor that a bus boycott might occur. Rosa Parks's arrest provided the fuel needed to get a boycott going.[2]

The boycotters gained national news attention because they were doing something bold, peaceful, and persistent. They had found a way to refuse to support a bus system that had denied them their rights as American citizens, while also letting more people across the nation gain a view of the injustice of Jim Crow via national news coverage.[3]

A central element in the boycott's success was a carpool system involving about 300 cars. The Montgomery organizers had learned about such a system from a similar boycott two years earlier in Baton Rouge, Louisiana. The earlier boycott lasted only eight days and yielded only a limited victory, but its carpool strategy was needed in Montgomery because Alabama officials tried to prevent boycotters from taking taxis. Both boycotts had something else in common: a determined Black woman. On June 15, 1953, Martha White boarded a Baton Rouge bus and sat in a seat for white riders because all the other seats were filled. Police were called, but a Black pastor, Rev. T. J. Jemison, reminded them of a new local law that let Black riders take an empty seat for white passengers if there were no more seats for Black riders. Martha White wasn't arrested, but three days later, the Black community boycotted the buses to demand better treatment, traveling instead by carpooling. The bus company lost so much money without Black riders that after eight days, a compromise was reached: a few rows in the front were for whites, a bench at the back was for Blacks, and seats in between were for anyone. In 1955, shortly after Parks's arrest, Dr. King phoned Rev. Jemison to learn exactly how he had organized the Baton Rouge carpool.[4]

A boycott of segregated transportation, however, was not a new form of protest in Montgomery. Just over fifty years earlier, in 1900, Montgomery's Black citizens organized a boycott of the city's segregated streetcars, one of many boycotts that occurred in Southern cities at the time, as noted in chapter 2. A similar boycott occurred in 1902 in Mobile. Both efforts came to an end in 1903 when Alabama passed an anti-boycott law that outlawed boycotts against any business and criminalized anyone who helped with a boycott.

Streetcar boycotts occurred in several other Southern cities during the early 1900s. None succeeded in permanently ending streetcar segregation, although in the mid-1860s, at the start of the post–Civil War Reconstruction period, spontaneous protests against segregated streetcars did succeed in ending that form of transportation segregation for a while in New Orleans, Richmond, and other cities. Those 1860s protests often involved using the daring strategy of civil disobedience, with Black riders taking seats in whites-only streetcars. Sadly, those gains were undone after Reconstruction ended, as chapter 2 explains.[5]

However, something did survive from the early 1900s Alabama streetcar boycotts: the 1903 anti-boycott law. That law resurfaced in an updated 1921 version during the 1955–56 Montgomery bus boycott. It's the law that was used in February 1956 to arrest Dr. King and more than eighty others involved in the Montgomery bus boycott. Despite those arrests, the boycott continued and ultimately achieved its goal because civil rights leaders in Montgomery made use of the same weapon that helped Sarah Keys: filing a legal complaint.[6]

While the Montgomery bus boycott was going on, NAACP lawyers filed a lawsuit in the name of four Black women who had been arrested on a bus or mistreated by a bus driver in Montgomery: Aurelia S. Browder, Claudette Colvin, Susie McDonald, and Mary Louise Smith. Rosa Parks was not included in this court case because she had become a famous symbol of the boycott and of the struggle for equal rights, so NAACP lawyers feared that an Alabama court might delay hearing a complaint that included her name.[7] The lawyer who filed the complaint, Fred Gray, noted that he "wanted the court to have only one issue to decide—the constitutionality of the laws requiring segregation on the buses."[8] The lawyers built a case around the other women, filing charges against Montgomery's mayor, William A. Gayle, in a case called *Browder v. Gayle*.

A federal court in Alabama ruled on this case in June 1956, deciding that Alabama's bus segregation law was unconstitutional. The city and state appealed that decision, but the US Supreme Court supported the earlier court's ruling and announced on December 20, 1956, that segregation had to end on all of Montgomery's city buses.[9]

The 1956 Supreme Court *Browder v. Gayle* decision extended to local buses the prohibition against transportation segregation issued by the ICC in *Sarah Keys v. Carolina Coach Company*. The *Browder* ruling framed the prohibition in constitutional terms when it said that Montgomery's bus segregation laws "violate the due process and equal protection of the law clauses of the Fourteenth Amendment to the Constitution of the United States."[10]

Although tailored to Montgomery, the *Browder* ruling had a broader impact. In a few cities in the upper South, that court decision led to some bus companies desegregating, although segregated seating persisted farther south. The *Browder* decision had a significant impact in Tallahassee, Florida. A bus boycott had started there in May 1956 when two college students—Carrie Patterson and Wilhelmina Jakes—were arrested for sitting in the whites-only section of a local bus. When the Supreme Court issued its *Browder* decision that December, the Tallahassee boycott organizers officially ended their boycott, but threats of violence from those opposed to integrated seating led the state's governor to stop all the city's buses on December 31, 1956. A few days later, on January 7, 1957, the Tallahassee City Commission repealed the segregation clause in the city's bus-franchise rules for local buses; it also passed a new rule that let bus drivers assign seats. This let segregated seating continue for a while, leading to the arrest of three additional Black students who refused to sit in the rear seats assigned to them by the driver. Gradually, the situation improved, spurred partly by some officials' reluctance to have a lot of news coverage about segregation in the city. Also, a Black candidate for the city commission, though defeated, received more Black votes than had been expected. Gradually, the assigned seating rule "was quietly ignored," according to a book on Tallahassee civil rights by Glenda Alice Rabby. By the summer of 1957, Tallahassee's buses were effectively integrated, although some Black citizens never returned to riding the buses.

Lawsuits supported by the NAACP ended local bus segregation in a few cities, including New Orleans, where a lawsuit against bus and streetcar segregation in that city resulted in a federal circuit court decision in 1958, *Morrison v. Davis*, that cited the *Browder* precedent in calling for an end to streetcar and bus segregation there. An end to transportation segregation throughout the South would require additional strategies.[11]

Sarah Keys never met Rosa Parks but called her "my friend," seeing her as someone who shared the experience of putting herself on the line in standing up for justice.[12] "It was time to move in Alabama. Rosa Parks took on that responsibility, which I commend her for," Sarah noted many years later. "The Alabama bus boycott added to more integration and making people aware of their travel rights." She also noted that "my case was in all the papers. It was well publicized." So Sarah felt sure the Montgomery bus boycott "did not take place without the knowledge of the ICC decisions." As she noted in a news article shortly after Rosa Parks's death in October 2005, "I was always a little sad that we had never met."[13]

These two women were quite different. Rosa Parks was forty-two years old when she was arrested on that Alabama bus. She had been volunteering with the Montgomery branch of the NAACP since she was in her early thirties. The summer before her arrest, she attended a two-week workshop at the Highlander Folk School in Tennessee. There she took part in an interracial discussion on issues of segregation and the Supreme Court's *Brown v. Board of Education* decision.[14] Sarah Keys was twenty-three when she was arrested and had never been involved in civil rights activities. Yet they both had something in common. Both showed quiet, dignified courage while facing a dangerous situation when their rights as citizens were denied.

Additional Weapons

On February 1, 1960, four Black college students in Greensboro, North Carolina, used an especially effective strategy to strike a fresh blow at Jim Crow. They sat down at a Woolworth's lunch counter that wouldn't serve Black customers and refused to move. The protestors stayed in their seats at the lunch counter all day, even though the store wouldn't give them food. Other students joined the sit-in the next day, and even more in the days that followed. By March, newspaper and TV stories about the Greensboro sit-in had inspired thousands of people to hold sit-ins like that in more than fifty-five cities in thirteen states.

In some cities, sit-in protestors were arrested. That didn't keep others from continuing the protests. They were willing to break the law and risk arrest by engaging in these acts of nonviolent civil disobedience to show the unfairness of the laws they were breaking. Civil disobedience as a strategy became popular in the 1960s partly because of reports about its successful use by Mohandas Gandhi during two decades of nonviolent protests in India. His followers' civil disobedience, which often led to arrests, helped his country gain independence from Great Britain in 1947.[15]

Nonviolent civil disobedience as a protest strategy had been used in the United States many years earlier, going back to the mid-1800s, as described in chapter 2. Among the first to do this were those who followed up on Elizabeth Jennings's 1854 court victory against streetcar segregation in New York City, heeding the request of the newly formed Legal Rights Association to try to claim seats on whites-only streetcars. A similar sit-in strategy proved effective at the start of Reconstruction in temporarily ending streetcar segregation in several Southern cities.[16]

A more recent nonviolent civil disobedience sit-in that preceded the Greensboro protest took place in 1939 in Alexandria, Virginia, at the city's whites-only public library. Samuel Wilbert Tucker, a Black civil rights lawyer, rounded up five young Black men, ages eighteen to twenty-two, to apply for library cards at that library. He told them they would likely be denied a library card. If so, they should take a book off a shelf, sit quietly at a table, and read. The young men were indeed denied library cards, read quietly, and were then arrested for disorderly conduct. A local judge ruled that the five men did not seem to have been disorderly, but he didn't reach a decision in the case, which was postponed for further consideration. It was never officially resolved. Instead, the city created a separate library for Black people.[17]

The Congress of Racial Equality (CORE), a civil rights organization founded in 1942, was committed to the idea of nonviolent direct action as a form of protest. A book by August Meier and Elliott Rudwick on the history of CORE reports that, in 1943, it used the sit-in strategy at a Chicago restaurant. The organization's members in Chicago had been trying to educate patrons of restaurants about the unfairness of segregation by passing out flyers. When the restaurants refused to change, an interracial group of twenty-one CORE members showed up to eat at a restaurant in May 1943. At first, the restaurant manager called the police. But when the police declined to press charges, the sit-in participants were allowed to place orders and have a meal. Meier and Rudwick also report that Howard University students who were NAACP members held a successful sit-in at a DC restaurant in 1943.[18]

Of course, CORE was also one of the organizers of the 1947 Journey of Reconciliation (described in chapter 3), which used a modified version of nonviolent direct action by having pairs of Black and white travelers try to take seats in the front of interstate buses to test whether the *Morgan v. Virginia* court ruling was being enforced.[19] Its Chicago restaurant sit-in successes prompted CORE's new interracial chapter in Baltimore, Maryland, to use the same strategy. In 1953, Baltimore CORE teamed up with Black students at Morgan State College (now Morgan State University) to successfully use the sit-in strategy at lunch counters in local drug and variety stores. Even earlier, during the 1930s before CORE had been founded, Baltimore's Black community had used a different type of nonviolent protest strategy by boycotting white-owned businesses in the Black community that refused to hire people of color in responsible positions. As a result of this boycott, those stores opened up job opportunities for Black people, although discriminatory hiring continued in the city's main business area downtown.[20]

However, none of those earlier examples of direct-action nonviolent protest gained the impressive follow-up by others around the country that the 1960 student-led lunch counter sit-ins in Greensboro achieved. That wider reach happened partly because of more effective news coverage. After the Montgomery bus boycott, reporters began to realize the news value of such protests. Also, a new communication outlet was finding a place in US homes: the nightly TV news program.

Many of the stores targeted in 1960 with lunch counter sit-ins wound up dropping their segregation practices. The power of this strategy helped lead to the creation of a new organization made up primarily of young people, the Student Nonviolent Coordinating Committee (SNCC). It and other civil rights groups would continue to use nonviolent direct-action strategies throughout the 1960s.[21]

One of those follow-up sit-ins resulted in a significant 1961 US Supreme Court decision, *Garner v. Louisiana*, which protected the rights of individuals taking part in a peaceful nonviolent demonstration. This case involved college students who peacefully took seats at a segregated lunch counter in a drugstore in Baton Rouge, Louisiana, and were arrested for disturbing the peace, although they had remained peaceful throughout, made no speeches, and carried no posters. Thurgood Marshall argued their case at the Supreme Court, which ruled that Louisiana could not use its state law about those who disturb the peace to arrest peaceful protestors who were not disturbing the peace.

A follow-up Supreme Court case in 1965, *Cox v. Louisiana*, went farther and upheld the rights of people to gather peacefully in protest in a public place. This case was based on another incident in Baton Rouge when students and others gathered to protest lunch counter segregation. The leader of the demonstration was arrested when he failed to obey an order from the police to disband the protest. The justices ruled that such an arrest deprived him of his rights of free speech and assembly, thus violating both the First and Fourteenth Amendments to the US Constitution.[22]

Some of the lunch counter sit-ins and protests spurred by the Greensboro Woolworth's sit-in occurred at Southern bus stations. The *Sarah Keys v. Carolina Coach Company* decision didn't cover bus station restaurants, but a new lawsuit filed by Bruce Boynton, a law student, managed to extend that ICC decision to restaurants. By 1960, *Boynton v. Virginia* had made its way to the US Supreme Court, where NAACP lawyers argued on his behalf. News that the Supreme Court was considering his case caused a few bus depot restaurants in Virginia and Texas to desegregate when sit-in protestors showed up, perhaps to avoid becoming involved in a lawsuit like *Boynton*.

This case began when Bruce Boynton was arrested in December 1958 at a bus station in Richmond, Virginia, while traveling from Washington, DC, where he attended Howard University's law school, to his Alabama home for the Christmas holidays. The bus stopped briefly in Richmond so passengers could get something to eat. The restaurant for Black passengers looked dirty. So he sat in the area for white travelers and ordered a cheeseburger. He was arrested and spent the night in jail for refusing to move to the section for Black customers.

He filed a lawsuit to have the charges against him dropped, partly because an arrest might make it difficult for him to become a lawyer. The NAACP's lawyers defended him when his case reached the US Supreme Court in 1960. Thurgood Marshall used many of the same arguments used in *Sarah Keys v. Carolina Coach Company* and in the NAACP's ICC train case. In December 1960, the US Supreme Court ruled that if a bus station restaurant was "an integral part of the bus carrier's transportation service for interstate passengers," then the Interstate Commerce Act required that a Black passenger "has a right to be served without discrimination." Arrest charges against Boynton were dismissed. Alabama still delayed granting him a law license for six years, but he went on to become a prominent civil rights lawyer in Alabama and Tennessee.[23]

Some bus companies obeyed the new Supreme Court order in *Boynton v. Virginia*, but many did not. It took a massive campaign of nonviolent civil disobedience by young people organized in part by SNCC (the Student Nonviolent Coordinating Committee) from 1961 onward to make the ICC enforce the Supreme Court's *Boynton* and *Morgan* decisions as well as its own rules from *Sarah Keys v. Carolina Coach Company*.

Civil disobedience is what the bus company lawyers had accused Sarah Keys of doing when they badgered her with questions during her ICC testimony in 1954. They kept asking her who had "planted" her on that bus, implying that a civil rights group must have arranged for her to take that bus ride so she would be arrested.

It should have made no difference to the ICC vote whether or not she had been engaged in civil disobedience. But the fact that she was not part of any organized protest highlights the nature of the courage she showed in pursuing justice, supported only by her family, her two lawyers, and her conviction that "I believe in people being treated right and treated fairly no matter what the situation."[24]

The Freedom Rides

In 1961, CORE organized a new type of civil disobedience that targeted bus stations. It used a different strategy than it had in 1947 with its Journey of Reconciliation's test rides across the upper South to assess the effectiveness of *Morgan v. Virginia*. In early May 1961, CORE, assisted by SNCC, motivated hundreds of college students and other young people—both Black and white—to take bus rides through Virginia, North Carolina, South Carolina, Georgia, Alabama, and Mississippi to test whether bus stations were obeying the *Boynton v. Virginia* decision.

Calling themselves Freedom Riders, these young people were willing to be arrested and endure the beatings many would receive for breaking local segregation rules about what areas of a bus station people of color could use. One Freedom Rider who was seriously injured, John Lewis, later became a congressman from Georgia and dedicated his life to ending discrimination of all kinds.[25]

The protestors also used a new protest strategy: "Jail no bail." They refused to pay bail to get out of jail, choosing instead to stay in jail, despite dreadful conditions, in order to overload the prisons and the local court systems. According to James Farmer, CORE's leader at that time, change comes only "when the heat is on." He said CORE's goal was "to continue to create crises like the Freedom Rides."[26]

Reports on the mistreatment and arrest of nonviolent Freedom Riders appeared in newspapers and on TV screens around the world. These news reports did indeed create a crisis, shocking the nation and embarrassing the US government, which was in a fierce competition to show the world that democracy was better than the Communist form of government used in the Soviet Union. Television news stories about young people being beaten up for trying to use a bus station restaurant did not bolster democracy's image and reputation. The federal government realized it had to take firm action to end transportation segregation.

On May 29, 1961, US Attorney General Robert F. Kennedy sent a detailed legal document to the ICC, directing it to finally enforce rules to end transportation segregation, including the regulations it had already issued in *Sarah Keys v. Carolina Coach Company*.[27] An article in the *New York Times* about Kennedy's directive to the ICC noted that in the six years since the Sarah Keys ICC decision, "the ICC has brought only one complaint against bus segregation," although it was well known that there had been many more violations of that case's ruling.[28]

Kennedy specifically mentioned *Sarah Keys v. Carolina Coach Company* in the order he sent to the ICC. He also included the famous comment Justice John Marshall Harlan had used in 1896 to disagree with the Supreme Court's *Plessy v. Ferguson* decision, the language that Attorney General Brownell had also quoted in his letter to the ICC in 1954. By including these statements in his directive to the ICC, Kennedy was striking a firm blow against the *Plessy v. Ferguson* idea of "separate but equal." In addition, Kennedy included another remark from Brownell's letter. Here's how Kennedy wove those comments together in the forceful order he sent to the ICC: "Just as our Constitution is color blind, and neither knows nor tolerates classes among citizens, so too is the Interstate Commerce Act. The time has come for this commission, in administering that act, to declare unequivocally by regulation that a Negro passenger is free to travel the length and breadth of this country in the same manner as any other passenger."[29]

This time, the ICC took action. On September 22, 1961, all eleven ICC commissioners issued a unanimous decree to end transportation segregation. The ICC ordered interstate bus companies to end segregation on all bus trips, even ones that didn't cross into another state. Companies had to put signs inside all buses and train cars stating that segregated seating was forbidden. The ICC also outlawed segregation in bus and train stations as well as in their restaurants, waiting rooms, restrooms, and water fountains. All Jim Crow signs inside stations had to be removed. The new regulations would go into effect in less than two months, on November 1, 1961.

Members of CORE made sure that transportation companies obeyed. During November 1961, CORE members checked about two hundred bus stations across the South. By the end of the month, they found that most stations and bus companies had obeyed the ICC's orders. For the few stations in Mississippi and Louisiana that didn't, the Justice Department filed and won court cases against them. The ICC followed up on complaints from travelers to make sure its orders were obeyed. The following year, the Justice Department also took action against segregation in airports. By June 1963, the Justice Department reported that train, bus, and airline segregation had come to an end.[30]

"It was people like Kennedy speaking out that made people aware of their rights. That's what it took in order for people to realize that things had changed," said Sarah many years later, commenting on the changes that happened once the federal government decided to enforce the rules the ICC had established in *Sarah Keys v. Carolina Coach Company*.[31]

The ICC itself would come to an end just over thirty years later in 1995, when its responsibilities for monitoring interstate transportation were transferred to the newly created Surface Transportation Board (STB) and the Department of Transportation.[32]

New Laws

These transportation victories helped in the wider effort to end more forms of Jim Crow segregation, inspiring protests against other unjust policies, such as those that made it hard for members of the Black community to vote, find good jobs, and feel welcome at parks, restaurants, and other public places. In addition, civil rights lawyers kept filing lawsuits when individuals felt they were arrested unfairly and were denied service at a public place. Fair-minded legislators kept trying to pass laws to create a country where all would be treated justly.

A huge protest against segregation took place in Washington, DC, on August 28, 1963: the March on Washington for Jobs and Freedom, where Rev. Dr. Martin Luther King Jr. delivered his "I Have a Dream" speech. An interracial crowd of more than 200,000 people came to support Dr. King's call for an end to segregation everywhere. The main organizer for this huge gathering was Bayard Rustin, who got his first experience organizing a major civil rights project with the 1947 Journey of Reconciliation. This time he partnered with A. Philip Randolph, founder of the Brotherhood of Sleeping Car Porters, as well as with the leaders of five major rights organizations: the Southern Christian Leadership Conference, NAACP, National Urban League, Congress of Racial Equality, and SNCC.[33]

Following up on the enthusiasm generated by the March on Washington, protests against Jim Crow segregation continued around the nation until the US Congress passed the Civil Rights Act of 1964. This law prohibited discrimination on the basis of race, color, religion, sex, or national origin in public places or in employment, including in public schools. From then on, any business that served the public had to be open to all.[34]

By mentioning schools, the Civil Rights Act of 1964 helped prod states to begin taking action if they hadn't already begun desegregating their public schools. To encourage compliance, the follow-up legislation enacted—the 1965 Elementary and Secondary Education Act (ESEA)—contained provisions that linked federal funding for schools to effective desegregation efforts.[35]

Congressional supporters of the Civil Rights Act of 1964 made sure that it didn't suffer the same fate as a similar law passed during Reconstruction, the Civil Rights Act of 1875. That law was overturned after Reconstruction ended, when the US Supreme Court ruled in 1883 that the Fourteenth Amendment to the US Constitution gave Congress only the right to regulate the actions of states, not of businesses and individuals. Those who wrote the new 1964 Civil Rights Act didn't rely on the Fourteenth Amendment for permission to create this law. They cited a different part of the Constitution: the Commerce Clause. When two whites-only businesses challenged the law—a motel in Georgia and a restaurant in Alabama—defenders of the new law showed that both businesses were engaged in interstate commerce. That let the Supreme Court dismiss those businesses' complaints and declare that the Civil Rights Act of 1964 "is a valid exercise of Congress' power under the Commerce Clause."

The official account of this Supreme Court case notes that before reaching its conclusion, the court explored how the Civil Rights Act of 1964 had been created and found that "the Senate Commerce Committee made it quite clear" that its objective of ensuring equal access to public businesses could be met "by congressional action based on the commerce power of the Constitution."[36]

Another new federal law, the Voting Rights Act of 1965, sought to end unfair laws that made it hard for Black people to register to vote. The Voting Rights Act outlawed poll taxes, literacy tests, grandfather clauses, and other unjust obstacles. In recent years, however, new attacks on voting rights have emerged, prompting new responses from those concerned with safeguarding the right to vote.[37]

North Carolina students played a role in helping to start this new wave of reform with the lunch counter sit-ins they held in 1960. That same year, North Carolina elected Terry Sanford governor. He tried a different kind of strategy to bring about change by involving young people. Sanford was a new kind of Democrat in the state. He had defeated a rival who was intent on keeping schools segregated. Governor Sanford, a white lawyer, campaigned on improving schools and is thought to have won the election because of support from Black voters.[38] In a speech he gave in January 1963 marking the hundredth anniversary of the Emancipation Proclamation, he said it was time "to quit unfair discrimination" and give people of color "a full chance to earn a decent living . . . recognizing the urgent need for opening new economic opportunities. . . . We also recognize that in doing so we shall be adding new economic growth for everybody."[39] Economic growth was greatly needed in North Carolina at the time, as more than a third of the state's population lived below the poverty level, with Black sharecroppers suffering severely.

Governor Sanford decided it would be hard to persuade the legislature to fund programs aimed at helping people of color, so he established the North Carolina Fund, a private effort with money from the Ford Foundation and two North Carolina groups: the Z. Smith Reynolds Foundation and the Mary Reynolds Babcock Foundation.

The North Carolina Fund's young interracial workers launched community programs during the 1960s to improve schools and housing, provide job training and early childhood education, repair infrastructure, and help with voter registration. Although this fund's projects had mixed results and came under attack, they served as a model for President Lyndon Johnson's 1964 War on Poverty.[40]

One of the North Carolina Fund's main financial supporters, the Z. Smith Reynolds Foundation, would play a role many years later in spreading the word about what Sarah Keys Evans had accomplished.

Long Time Coming

The battle against segregation has gone on for many years and is still being waged today, as additional examples of unjust discrimination continue to arise and negatively impact people's lives. It has been a step-by-step journey, with many along the way standing up for what's right, using an array of strategies: legal complaints, civil disobedience, boycotts, sit-ins, protest demonstrations, and new legislation.

In the area of transportation segregation, many fought for change long before Sarah Louise Keys and Rosa Parks faced arrest and stepped up to put an end to that type of discrimination. Brief accounts of other early transportation warriors—from the North and the South—can be found at the end of this book in the appendix. It shines a light on people who sought to make it possible for people of any skin color or ethnicity to be "free to travel the length and breadth of this country in the same manner as any other passenger."[41]

The next two chapters describe how the courage and persistence shown by Sarah Keys Evans is helping now to recruit even more foot soldiers in the battle for equal rights.

12

Moving On

AFTER HER ICC VICTORY, SARAH KEYS kept doing what she loved most—creating wonderful hairstyles for those who came to the beauty salons where she worked as a hairstylist and beauty consultant. Shortly after the ICC decision, she took a job at the House of Beauty salon in Brooklyn, near where she was living then. She loved working in a salon because it gave her a chance to "be creative and give the clients what they want, to create the best hairstyle for your face. I loved that," she said. "I was very good at it. I was fast and I was creative." At the House of Beauty, she also created hairstyles for professional models who promoted the salon's hair products. In addition, she also "did modeling for a brochure for a beauty school one year. I was a beauty consultant. I worked with beauty product companies."[1]

For someone as reserved as Sarah, working in a beauty parlor was especially interesting because it let her meet "so many different people from all walks of life. In beauty salons, people sit around and they visit. You can 'go to school' if you're a good listener. They come in, and you get to hear things that most people in the community don't hear."[2]

She had always been a good listener. It kept her safe when she was arrested in Roanoke Rapids, as she tried to figure out what was going on during that frightening late-night encounter. She was never a big talker, however, not on that terrible night, and not for the rest of her life.

12.1 Sarah Keys Evans (*right*) and her younger sister Cornelia Keys Hargrave in Prospect Park, Brooklyn, New York, during the summer of 1955. Courtesy Sarah Keys Evans.

She never shared the story of her ICC victory with her clients in the salons where she worked. She always worried that some people might not approve of what she had done.

"In the late 1950s, I didn't have conversations with my clients about it," she recalled. "The Alabama bus boycott was going on. I had customers who sat down and expressed opinions on that. And school integration was going on at the same time. Many whose parents had migrated north during the war, or before the war, really thought that Blacks should make themselves comfortable and accept things as they were and not try to change things. Some of those people were angry that the ones they have left down there are being treated with the fire hoses and things of that sort"—the harsh techniques police were using to try to stop civil rights protests. "Imagine all the conversations going on day after day, people talking to me and I not revealing to them who I am. So that gave me a bit of fear sometimes. I was in a very delicate position. I had to keep quiet. I knew it was not good for me to do otherwise because of who I was and what had happened to me. I didn't broadcast that."[3]

After the civil rights victories of the 1960s, when people's opinions changed and many approved of what the civil rights struggle had achieved, she still kept quiet about what she had done. She didn't want to seem boastful or stir up painful memories for herself by having to tell again and again the story of that scary night at the Roanoke Rapids police station.

Not too long after her ICC victory, she met a man who was also a good listener but who wasn't shy about being a talker: George Evans. He became her husband. This tall, handsome Texan came to New York City to be a singer. He was a cousin of her best girlfriend in New York, who arranged for them to meet. Sarah loved the nickname he liked to use for her, calling her "Keys." Through him, she entered a whole new world.[4]

"He was a star football player at high school in Beaumont, Texas," she explained. "He was either valedictorian or salutatorian. His friends were going into the military." He signed up, too, during World War II. "When he got out of the army, he went to Fisk a couple of years. When he left Fisk, he came to New York. He wanted to be a singer and an actor. He always had a great voice to sing. He was in that environment for a few years before he met me," she said.

When they met, he was still struggling to make it in show business. He would sing in clubs late at night and go to parties to connect with other performers. "He was an absolutely wonderful singer," she said. "He even made a demo. It was beautiful. He had his spotlight at the Theresa Hotel for the coming out of his album." *Jet* magazine had an article about it. The Theresa Hotel was a major social and cultural center in Harlem until it closed in the late 1960s. "One party he took me to was for Langston Hughes's birthday," recalled Sarah, who was thrilled to meet the famous poet. They were having an exciting time, but after a while it was clear that a performing career for her husband wasn't likely to happen. As she observed, "You had to know somebody to get any place" in the theater and music world. He began to consider other options. When he saw how successful Sarah was by working in a salon, he enrolled in beauty school to give that profession a try.

After they married in Brooklyn in 1958 and Sarah became Sarah Keys Evans, they decided to go into business on their own. At first, she rented space in other salons to see clients privately. So did George. Before long, they opened their own salon in Brooklyn, the Glamour Nook. "He was dead set on owning his own business," she explained. "He came from a

12.2 Sarah Keys Evans and George Evans on their wedding day in 1958 in Brooklyn, New York. Courtesy Sarah Keys Evans.

family in Beaumont, Texas, where they made their living by owning their own businesses."[5]

Of course, Sarah also came from a family of independent-minded business owners, including the grandmother for whom she was named, who ran a successful boardinghouse and backyard farm stand. Sarah's father, also a savvy businessman, had sold the family farm in 1958 and moved with his wife and younger children to Washington, DC. There he could concentrate on his increasing success with construction jobs without having to keep commuting between the two Washingtons.[6]

Sarah noted that her husband "had a good knack of being able to give advice to folks." The women clients who came to their salon loved to tell him their personal problems and hear what he would advise. "Many of them depended on him for that, saying, 'Ask Mr. Evans.' He was a great talker," she said. That gave him a new career idea. "He decided after a while that he would go back to school and get his degree. He became a counselor and therapist," working at a Brooklyn clinic. Sometimes he still came to the salon in the evenings, to style someone's hair and give some free advice. That continued even after they closed their own salon and went back to renting space in other salons. "He would come in after his job and

12.3 Sarah Keys Evans at the Glamour Nook, the beauty salon in Brooklyn, New York, that she and her husband owned during the 1960s. Courtesy Sarah Keys Evans.

do some clients," Sarah recalled. "It was good that we had him there even though it was a few hours in the evening. His willingness to help others was bottomless. I was so proud of him. He often told how proud he was of me for many reasons, especially for unlocking another door of freedom for Blacks in November 1955."[7]

Sarah still had run-ins with Jim Crow, including on her wedding day in 1958. This problem didn't happen down south but way up north in Pennsylvania. Jim Crow rules could pop up anywhere until Congress passed the Civil Rights Act of 1964. After a lovely wedding ceremony in Brooklyn, Sarah and George drove off on what they thought would be a wonderful honeymoon trip.

"We were going to spend our honeymoon at a Pennsylvania honeymoon village. But we didn't know until we got there that they had never accepted Blacks before. We couldn't stay there. We stayed at a little inn next door that Blacks owned. We spent the night, and the next day we left," said Sarah. "We talked to a lawyer there and he said he would look into it, but we were unable to institute a lawsuit." Apparently, the problem involved an upcoming election. "They weren't going to touch anything like that with a ten-foot pole. They didn't want something like that to stand in their way. They might be looking down the line to being elected to the next highest post. After that, I didn't like to stay any place unless I knew for sure you could stay there," she explained.

"A few years later, the honeymoon village integrated," said Sarah. "Things were gradually integrated. It was people speaking out that made people aware of their rights, to realize that things had changed. Blacks began to know their rights and not be so fearful of traveling. You no longer had to be afraid to sit here and sit there. You didn't have to go into a restaurant and whisper, 'Can I get a Coke?' You [didn't] have to say 'Should I sit here or take it outside?' I remember fears like that." She had such an experience during one of the trips she made to DC by train to meet with her lawyers. "I remember being so fearful when I came out of the train. I had to get a cab to meet my dad, and I wanted something to drink." She went into a store that had a restaurant, or a counter. "I said quietly to the waiter, 'Could I get something to drink, and should I drink it in here or should I drink it outside?' I wanted to be sure. I didn't want to have policemen come and drag me to jail and I'm coming down there to fight a case. I didn't have to drink it outside."[8]

Overlooked by History

Sadly, George Evans died of heart disease in 1991. By then Sarah had retired as a hairstylist. She was in her sixties and suffered from painful bouts of rheumatoid arthritis that made it hard to stand up for a long time. She continued to stay active in her church, St. Peter Claver, part of the St. Martin DePorres Parish in the Bedford-Stuyvesant area of Brooklyn. She also visited a nearby nursing home on Sundays to meet with elderly people being cared for there. She never had children of her own, but she was close to her many nieces and nephews, and to other family members, now spread across the country.[9]

Her father had died a decade earlier, in 1980, after he and Sarah's mother had moved to Washington, DC. "He helped build the cathedral in Washington. The day he died, I was told by a few people, there was a Catholic convention happening at the cathedral, and when they heard he had died, they gave him a minute of silence," she recalled. She and other family members joined her mother and many of her father's friends and colleagues at a funeral service in DC. The tribute to him, written by his children, included this statement: "He was strong and taught us to be strong while impressing upon us the importance of accepting each other's weaknesses. Through his strength and prayers, we found support in every way." At a reception afterward at her parents' house, conversation turned to his early days in DC, and some of his friends were surprised to hear that he had attended Dunbar High School. "He didn't spend his time talking about that," said Sarah. "If you asked him questions about it, he would have the answers. We always did things in a low-key, quiet way. That's how he handled his life. You don't know what an impact all of us have on people, or who those people are, little things in a person's life that can have an impact on them. I really miss him and his stories."

She would continue to travel often to DC after her father's death to visit with her mother, especially once her mother had a stroke.[10]

A number of awards have come Sarah's way over the years to honor her contribution to civil rights history, including one from the New York State Beauty Culturalists Association in 1955 and a positive mention in *Travel Guide* magazine in 1956.[11] Shortly after the ICC decision, some people told her they were interested in making a movie about her. Nothing ever came of that, but NBC News taped an interview with her in December 1955 for a pilot episode of a new NBC TV series, *Outlook*. But she never saw the interview. She worked long hours at the salon and didn't get home until after the TV broadcast. Back then, there was no way to record a show to view later. She finally saw it more than fifty years later in 2007, when this author obtained a tape of the interview from NBC News Archives and sent it to her. It shows young Sarah Keys describing her arrest, the legal efforts to protest that arrest, and the victory at the ICC. The reporter who followed up on her presentation with commentary on segregation was Chet Huntley, who would soon co-host the popular *Huntley-Brinkley Report*.[12]

She didn't want to be in the spotlight, but one time she did speak up. In 1975, she was disappointed when *Ebony* magazine didn't include her ICC case in a special issue that was part of the magazine's celebration of the nation's bicentennial taking place the following year. That issue was titled "200 Years of Black Trials and Triumphs." She wrote a letter to the magazine to remind them of the significance of her ICC decision. They never wrote back. Nor did they cover her ICC victory in later issues.[13]

None of the major books on the civil rights movement mentioned her case. Most focused on the big protests that occurred just after her ICC victory: the Montgomery bus boycott, the Freedom Rides, the big protest marches. Those events were dramatic, involved many people, and were featured widely in newspaper and TV coverage. Sarah's more quiet contribution was overlooked. Also, her ICC victory was mainly the result of two women working together, without supervision by or collaboration with a famous male lawyer. That may have played a role in their case being overlooked during an era when the legal profession and the civil rights movement were still male dominated.

In 1983, Catherine Barnes, a graduate student at Columbia University, wrote an excellent legal history published by its university press about the struggle to end Jim Crow in public transportation, *Journey from Jim Crow*. Chapter 3, titled "A Legal Breakthrough," includes an account of *Sarah Keys v. Carolina Coach Company* that provides a long discussion of the case, with follow-up sections in the book on its delayed enforcement until after the Freedom Rides. Despite this fascinating account published by a respected university press, major books on civil rights history still didn't pick up on the strong case that Catherine Barnes had made for the role of the Sarah Keys ICC case in civil rights history. However, some law schools do teach law students about *Sarah Keys v. Carolina Coach Company* because of its contribution to overturning the *Plessy v. Ferguson* decision.[14]

It wasn't until the 1990s that a major breakthrough let more people know about Sarah Keys Evans, thanks to the institution that had been so important to her: the US military.

"The Army's Rosa Parks"

On October 18, 1997, women who had served in the military dedicated a new museum at the entrance to Arlington National Cemetery, across the Potomac River from Washington, DC—the Women in Military Service for America Memorial, known as the Military Women's Memorial. Female veterans raised the money for this museum, the first memorial to honor the nearly three million women who have volunteered to serve with the US armed forces throughout the nation's history. The founders set up an archive to collect stories from servicewomen and veterans and put out a call for veterans to send in accounts of their military service.[15]

"I had been given information by my oldest brother," explained Sarah. "Living in Washington, he got news that the memorial was in the process of being built. He said, 'They're asking for veterans to send information.' I wasn't so sure that I was going to do that. Then out of the blue Mrs. Roundtree called me. She had been looking for me so she could let me know about the dedication and how they wanted to create a plaque about us. I was shocked and surprised to hear from her after so many years. She told me all the things that would be happening at the memorial and why it had been established."

Then magazine writer Katie McCabe contacted Sarah and interviewed her for an article she was writing about Dovey Roundtree for *Washingtonian* magazine. McCabe explained about the plaque that Roundtree wanted to donate to the Military Women's Memorial, describing their ICC victory. "That's when I realized that I really was involved in this," recalled Sarah. She registered with the Military Women's Memorial archives and gave them news clippings about her case.[16]

"There was a lot of stress in the family then," she explained. "My oldest brother, David, took very ill and died, and my mother had a stroke the same week that we buried him." Sarah told some relatives about the Military Women's Memorial and the dedication ceremony planned for October 1997 and about the plaque that would be installed the following year. Word spread rapidly among the family. "Each one found out from another," said Sarah. Nearly all her relatives said they wanted to come to the dedication ceremony. "Younger people in my family traveled from all over the country to be there with me that day. They took time off from their jobs in Wisconsin, North Carolina, all over. I felt very happy. Some friends also attended." Sarah went to the dedication and also to a special ceremony of remembrance at Arlington National Cemetery. "It was quite moving. The children have never forgotten. They talk about it. They've read about it."[17]

In 2000, a big photo of Sarah appeared in the calendar that the Military Women's Memorial created for that year. This photo and a description of the ICC victory accompanied the page for February, in honor of Black History Month. February's calendar page also had this quote from Roundtree: "This was the great case of my life. And Sarah Keys (Evans) is its heroine."[18]

Dr. Judith Bellafaire, the Military Women's Memorial's historian in 1997, wrote an article about the ICC victory that was posted on the memorial's website. Air Force Brigadier General Wilma L. Vaught, the memorial's first president, often mentioned Sarah Keys Evans in talks she gave around the country, calling her "the Army's Rosa Parks" and noting that this young soldier's courage proved that "justice can be there for each of us."[19]

For some of Sarah's younger relatives, it was the dedication ceremony, the calendar, and other Military Women's Memorial events that let them know for the first time about their family member's role in civil rights history. "I didn't find out about it until she was awarded a plaque," said Michelle McComb, a daughter of Sarah's oldest sister, Marie. "I was in college, and I was like, 'What's going on?' Nobody ever told me. We had no Black history education until I got to college. I didn't realize the significance until about halfway through college. My mother didn't tell us anything. My grandparents never said anything about it either. I was surprised." She felt others in the family hadn't talked about her aunt's case earlier because "I don't think people like to tell the hardship stories." Now she and other family members are thrilled to share the story with their children and grandchildren to help them realize, as she explained, that "even someone in our own family had a part in helping all the people in the United States have privileges that serve everyone. Somebody had to go through the hardship of being the one who breaks the barrier. This is your family member. That's how close it is."[20]

Sarah's sister Connie had shared the story with her son. "I spoke about this with my son Bradley when he was growing up," said this retired elementary schoolteacher. "It was spoken about with pride. I wanted him to be aware of that so that when times came when he was faced with having to be courageous, he would have recollection of this having been something in the family. During my teaching years, I always shared information with my students about how brave my sister was. I always had a picture of her on the bulletin board during Black History Month."[21]

The Military Women's Memorial had another impact on Keys family relations. During one of Sarah's visits to DC, Dr. Bellafaire, the memorial's historian, came to Sarah's mother's house, where Sarah was staying. "She came to pick me up," said Sarah, for a meeting about the calendar. When Dr. Bellafaire came into the house, "she met my mother, in recovery there at the house, managing her stroke quite well. It made feel very proud," said Sarah, when Dr. Bellafaire told her mother, "Your daughter is a hero." Her mother's response surprised Sarah. "My mother looked up and smiled,

'Yes, my daughter is a hero.' From then on, something happened with her thinking," said Sarah. They began to have conversations about aspects of their mother-daughter relationship that they hadn't talked about before. Sarah recalled, "One time when I was visiting, she said, 'You had actions that I really did not know how to handle at times. I really didn't know what you were up to or what you wanted.'" Sarah began to realize that "I used to make my mother not very happy when I would be passive." By "passive" she meant not speaking up when someone said or did something that annoyed her, not explaining how she felt.

From then on, when she went for visits, Sarah said, "We talked like adults. We talked about any and everything." These new kinds of conversations between mother and daughter continued until her mother's death in 2002.[22]

Spreading the Word

Because of all the attention from the Military Women's Memorial, more people decided that Sarah Keys Evans's role in civil rights history deserved celebration. In 2006, she received the Trailblazer Award from the US Department of Justice at a ceremony at its office in Brooklyn, New York. Family members and friends came to the ceremony, with several relatives traveling from other states to share this special moment. Dressed elegantly with a stylish head wrap and a classic silk scarf, Sarah spoke confidently to the distinguished audience, which included the US attorney for the Eastern District of New York and other Justice Department officials. Among the friends she had invited were several who had been her neighbors for decades, living in the same Brooklyn apartment building where she resided, but who never knew of her ICC victory before receiving the invitation for the ceremony. She continued to be reluctant to call attention to herself and put herself forward.

Other honors followed, including official proclamations saluting her that were issued by her US congressman and the New York State district attorney. She was the keynote speaker at Brooklyn's 2007 Black History Month celebration. In 2014, she spoke at the public library in Wyandanch, New York, whose librarian came from her hometown of Washington, North Carolina. In addition, the New York Center for Minority Veterans hosted a Women's History Month celebration honoring her.[23]

In 2006, Sarah Keys Evans and I collaborated on self-publishing a slim book about her for young readers, after I had learned about her for the first

12.4 Sarah Keys Evans at the Brooklyn, New York, office of the U.S. Department of Justice on February 16, 2006, where she received the department's Trailblazer Award, presented by Roslynn R. Mauskopf, U.S. Attorney for the Eastern District of New York. Photograph by Amy Nathan.

time in 2001 when I saw the plaque about her at the Military Women's Memorial. The staff there put us in touch, which led to many conversations, by phone and in person, leading to our working together to create that 2006 children's book, *Take a Seat—Make a Stand*. It describes a true event: a school assignment given to a grandchild of Sarah's sister Connie. In 2000, that fifth grader was asked to report on a hero. Grandmother Connie suggested telling about Aunt Sarah. In the book, *Take a Seat—Make a Stand*, the young student learns from family members about what Aunt Sarah did—and so do the book's young readers.[24]

Gradually others began finding out about Sarah, partly from that children's book as well as from Katie McCabe's 2002 magazine article, another article in *Our Heritage* magazine in 2011, and an article posted in 2014 on the army's website. When Barack Obama became president, a copy of *Take a Seat—Make a Stand* was mailed to the White House. In 2009, Michelle Obama sent Sarah an eightieth birthday greeting. In

2014, both President Obama and the First Lady sent eighty-fifth birthday congratulations.[25]

Sarah isn't alone in having been overlooked by historians. For many years, others who also helped end transportation segregation didn't receive much coverage in major history books either. They include several heroes already mentioned in this book, such as Irene Morgan, Arthur Mitchell, Elmer Henderson, Rev. William Heard, William Councill, Sergeant Isaac Woodard, Elizabeth Whiteside, Martha White, and Bruce Boynton as well as Aurelia Browder, Claudette Colvin, Susie McDonald, Mary Louise Smith, and many others. Gradually, the stories of some of these overlooked heroes are being told in books, articles, and documentaries and on historical markers, as is happening now also with Sarah Keys Evans.[26]

A Family Cheering Section

Family members have played a role in spreading the word. In 2007, nephew Rodney Waters, the son of Sarah's youngest sister, Angela Keys Waters, wrote an article about his Aunt Sarah for *The Catholic Review*. Relatives who are teachers share Sarah's story with their students. Niece Joan Dudley has spread the story far and wide, including with students in schools on Native American reservations in New Mexico and other western states. "They fell in love with Aunt Sarah and the whole family," she said of her students' reactions.[27]

Krys Hargrave, who was the featured fifth grader in *Take a Seat—Make a Stand*, started teaching others about the Sarah Keys story even before becoming a teacher, explaining that "as a student in middle school or high school, I found ways to tell my peers or tell my teachers, regardless of whether it was for an assignment or for Black History Month or for a getting-to-know-you kind of thing, or to talk about someone who inspired you. There are always people to look up to, but this was on a totally different level. It's not just a family thing. It really is a nationwide thing, a worldwide thing. It has always had this kind of influence on my heart. I always found a way to mention it. Especially in high school, my teachers always embraced it, saying, 'Do you mind if I share that with my other class? Do you mind coming to tell my class?'"

It's no surprise that Krys became a teacher and later an assistant principal for humanities at a high school in Newark, New Jersey. Even though the book about Sarah was for younger students, Krys has shared it with high school classes. "I used it to tell the story. Some asked to read it on their own, probably interested in seeing the old pictures of me in the book. I've been filled with pride to share the story."

In 2017, Krys was teaching literature at the Academy for Urban Leadership Charter School in Perth Amboy, New Jersey. The school's mission focuses on issues of social and economic justice. "The demographics of that school were mostly Latino, and the students sometimes find it hard to find the relevancy of Black History Month to their own history and culture," explained Krys, who suggested to the school's principal that Sarah Keys Evans speak at an assembly for the whole school during Black History Month. "The principal, vice principal, and even superintendent were not only accepting but ecstatic and eager for my aunt to visit. I saw it as an opportunity to expand the students' perceptions. Students learn best when things become personal. I thought my aunt with her awesome, unique spirit can open their eyes a bit to their own experience in America."[28]

Sarah had given only a few speeches in recent years to large groups. Recounting the events from 1952 always upset her, causing her to experience again the fear of her arrest in Roanoke Rapids. Also, her worsening arthritis made travel difficult. She turned down many speaking engagements. But Krys had a special place in her heart. Krys's maternal grandmother died in the 9/11 World Trade Center attack, and Sarah was impressed with how the family faced the challenge of recovering from that loss. She was very proud of Krys—"a go-getter, very determined," said Sarah. Krys has also noticed their special connection: "In my family people are always saying, you and your aunt, you're so much alike. You're both always standing up for what you believe."

Krys phoned to ask if Sarah would be willing to come and talk with the students. "Only for you," said Sarah. She planned carefully for this visit, especially how to manage the trip physically. The day before the school visit family members drove her to her sister Connie's home in New Jersey to spend the night there. "I really pushed myself to do it. I ordered a new back brace because the pain in the lower back was getting really bad," said Sarah.

Perth Amboy, where the high school was located, was where Sarah Keys lived when she left home after her high school graduation in 1948. She had come to New Jersey because her older sister lived there and was working in a hospital that had the nursing school Sarah attended briefly. "It was a bit overwhelming to be back in a place where I first landed when I got out of high school," she recalled. "The nursing school is in the same town. It brought back so many memories. Many of the old buildings and the churches were still standing. I was quite in awe of all of the changes."

She had good memories of the people she had known there so many years before. "Everyone was always very friendly in Perth Amboy." But nursing school wasn't the right fit for her, something the director of the school quickly realized. "I had the problem of staying awake in class," said Sarah, a problem she struggled with all her life, even during high school and also years later when she attended beauty school. She had thought nursing might be a good career for her, or being a dietitian. "I loved home economics in high school. I got an award for being the best in home economics," she said. But a career in nursing was not to be.

"The director of the nursing school was a wonderful woman," she explained. "I was already alerted to the fact that I was going to be called into the office. But she didn't just say, 'You're being deleted. Your time is up here.' She had arranged my next step for me if I wanted to accept it. She had called the Handmaids of Mary convent in Harlem that had rooms for working girls." The convent allowed Sarah to live there while she looked for jobs in New York City and made plans for her future. Her father talked with a Black priest who knew about the Handmaids of Mary and assured him that that it was a good choice. Sarah lived there for more than a year until she joined the Women's Army Corps. In fact, a young woman who lived at that convent became her best friend and introduced her years later to the man who became her husband.

For this visit to Perth Amboy to speak with high school students, Sarah planned her outfit carefully. Thanks to her years as a beauty consultant, she has always been aware of fashion trends and how to fit an outfit to the occasion. Instead of choosing a flowing silk scarf as she did for the Justice Department event, she chose a different look to help the teenagers feel more comfortable hearing her story. She wound up looking very hip—an eighty-seven-year-old in slacks, a stylish tweed jacket, and a baseball cap. "I wore it to fit in. I knew how the kids dress in high school," she explained.

She talked to the entire high school, giving a brief account of her arrest and her pursuit of justice. "You could hear a pin drop," said Krys Hargrave. "The students were super interested. She was giving a perspective on the rights we take for granted. I think it had a pretty large impact on them. It's hitting close to home. It's their teacher's family. They got to hear her spirit. She sang to them, too. She caught all their vibrations. After the assembly, students were running up on stage asking her more questions. They were interested in telling about their families' experience in America, as immigrants in this crazy time, this political climate."

12.5 Sarah Keys Evans with family members and staff of the Academy for Urban Leadership (AUL) Charter School in Perth Amboy, New Jersey, on February 21, 2017, when she gave a presentation for the school's students. *From left to right* are Roberto Reyes, principal; John Hargrave, Sarah's brother-in-law; Cornelia Keys Hargrave, Sarah's sister; Dr. Nestor Collazzo, administrator; Sarah; Krys Hargrave, teacher and grandchild of Cornelia Hargrave; Robert Fink, president, AUL Board of Trustees; and Shanesia Davis-Clyburn, vice principal. Photograph by Katherine Massopust, *Amboy Guardian.*

"Another generation catching up with the past," said Sarah. "I felt great. It was something I had never imagined doing. The students were being introduced verbally to history, and I was the person that was standing in those shoes. They came up on stage and wanted a hug. They had books and wanted my autograph."

What song did she sing to the students? "For you my dear, I would do anything. I would do anything, for you."[29]

She also gave the students advice for the future: "Never ever stop fighting for our rights and for our freedom." She acknowledged that doing so could be difficult, explaining that the emotional toll of experiencing injustice may linger long after an incident has been dealt with, as had been true for her all her life. She used a metaphor to convey this idea to the students: "If you live long enough, all of us, at some point in time will come through a storm. It might be a day, it might be a week. Some things can hang onto you for years."

She urged the students, despite the difficulties, to stand up for what's right: "Losing our freedom is never but one generation away. You are a generation that can help keep us free, and stay free. Because when you lose it, it can take many years and generations to win it back. Never ever let anyone tell you that you don't deserve it. I like to think that we all have our steps. We all have many miles to go. I knew how to walk fast, and I knew how to walk slow. Each time you challenge a wrong, that news travels."[30]

Onward to North Carolina

Before long, that news traveled to her hometown of Washington, North Carolina. In 2016, an event there celebrated the history of the Catholic church in that area of the state. The event's organizer, Larry McDaniel, made Sarah Keys Evans's story a major focus of the celebration. He had been frustrated that her story was not more widely known and was doing his best to correct that. A street corner there has been named in her honor, and in 2021 there was a citywide celebration of her birthday. In 2024, the city officially declared that August 2 would be Sarah Keys Evans Day, honoring the date when she was arrested in Roanoke Rapids in 1952.[31]

This North Carolina city has changed a lot since Sarah Keys Evans grew up there. Census statistics in 2022 provide this racial profile for the city's 9,759 residents: 44 percent white, 43 percent Black, and 7 percent Latino. This city gained its first Black public official in 1953, the year after Sarah Keys was arrested, when Walter H. Mayo was appointed to Washington's planning board. In 1991, the city elected its first Black mayor, Floyd G. Brothers, but before his election, Louis Randolph, a Black member of the city council, had served briefly as mayor pro tem. His grandfather was Louis R. Randolph, the principal of an early public school in this city for Black students. During the 1960s, many years before Mayor Brothers became the mayor, he was the band director at the city's first official state-sponsored public high school for Black students, which by then had a music program, unlike when Sarah was a teenager in the 1940s, when her Mother of Mercy band would perform for some of the public high school's events.

That public high school, which opened in 1924, was first called Washington Colored High School. In 1950, it was renamed the P. S. Jones School, in honor of the dynamic and much-beloved educator who served

12.6 Street sign in Washington, North Carolina.
Courtesy Leesa P. Jones.

as its principal from 1927 until his retirement in 1949, shortly before his death in 1950. During the 1930s, under Jones's leadership, the school began broadening its curriculum to include more academic and college preparatory courses in addition to vocational instruction.

The city's high school for white students officially desegregated in 1968. That year, students from P. S. Jones High School joined the white students at the city's formerly whites-only high school, which retained its name from the pre-integration era: Washington High School. Because P. S. Jones High School had been such an important part of the local Black community, there was strong interest within that community for preserving its name, leading to the city's junior high being named the P. S. Jones School.

Washington High School understandably faced a period of adjustment for all its students and staff, but there was a special feeling of loss in the Black community with the closing of P. S. Jones High School, as noted in the displays at the P. S. Jones African-American Education Museum, which aims to keep alive the memory and the spirit of that early Black high school. The signage in the museum reads, "P. S. Jones High School was a community gathering place . . . used for community activities that enriched the lives of Black students and families." The museum notes also the economic consequences resulting from the closing of that high school. In Washington and throughout North Carolina, school integration resulted in many Black principals and teachers losing jobs when the faculties of formerly Black and white schools merged.

Washington gained another Black mayor in 2020, when Donald Sadler rose to that position after having served as a city council member. His wife, retired educator Alice Mills Sadler, in 1992 became the first Black official elected to the Beaufort County Board of Commissioners, and she is now the curator of the P. S. Jones African-American Education Museum.[32]

Another local museum also helps preserve the city's history: the Washington Waterfront Underground Railroad Museum, founded by Sarah's cousin Leesa P. Jones along with her husband, Milton Jones, and friend Rebecca Clark. The only official Underground Railroad museum in North Carolina, it highlights the diverse ways that freedom seekers in that area of the state managed to gain their freedom, aided often by others in the local community. The museum was featured in a 2025 video produced by PBS, *The Underground Railroad: The Paths and Places of Refuge.*

Leesa Jones also brings history to life in another way: by giving Walking History Tours, sharing stories about slavery and those who helped freedom seekers. During these tours, she describes how black-eyed peas helped those trying to escape from slavery. The peas could be boiled until all liquid was removed and then put into burlap bags to serve as food for their flight. In addition, abolitionist supporters used uncooked peas as a warning for freedom seekers, placing peas along the waterfront as a signal to those thinking of escaping on a boat in the harbor not to try that day because there were too many slaveholders in town looking for escapees—"too many eyes watching."

In addition, she writes a column each week for the local newspaper in which she describes various aspects of her hometown's history as well as reminiscing about past events and festivals that were important to both the Black and white communities. "Slavery is a difficult story to tell," she noted in one of her columns, "but there is another side some aren't aware of. It's the celebration of the human spirit to overcome. Even a pancake has two sides. We want to show some of the ways people in this town offered hope and help."

She also worked with the local Black community to have Beaufort County's first North Carolina Historical Marker on Black history installed in 2016 to honor the roughly one hundred Black men who volunteered to help the Union Army prevent Confederate forces from gaining control in

Washington, North Carolina, in March and April 1863 during the Civil War (as described in chapter 5). Many of those Black recruits had only recently been freed from slavery after Union forces took control of the city the year before. At least two of these volunteers died in their defense of the city that spring, in what became known as the Siege of Washington. Survivors continued fighting with the Union Army in other areas, and some settled later in Northern states.

Another historical marker was installed in 2021 to honor Hull Anderson, a formerly enslaved shipbuilder who ran a successful shipyard in the local harbor during the mid-1800s. He had gained his freedom in 1826 and by 1830 was operating his own shipyard along the town's waterfront, becoming one of the area's most successful businessmen. In 1841, he sold his business and moved with his wife and son to the African country of Liberia, perhaps driven away by the mounting restrictions placed on free people of color or maybe simply looking for new opportunities.

Planning is ongoing for a marker that will "designate the bus station where Sarah Keys Evans arrived after her historic stance in Roanoke Rapids," said Leesa Jones, who never learned during high school about the stories she presents in her museum and on her walking tours. She cites an old proverb to explain why she only recently learned about that history: "Until the lion can talk, you will always hear the hunter's version of what happened."[33]

By 2019, the story of Sarah Keys Evans's arrest and her ICC victory had also become the talk of the town in another North Carolina city, the one where she had been arrested more than sixty years earlier: Roanoke Rapids.

13

Closing the Circle

NEWS ABOUT SARAH KEYS EVANS BEGAN TO reach contemporary residents of Roanoke Rapids in 2010 because of a small exhibit in the Roanoke Rapids Canal Museum. This museum usually focuses on the history of the more than two-hundred-year-old Roanoke Rapids Canal. Built in 1823, the canal was used at first to transport goods down the Roanoke River. In the 1880s, after railroads began providing more reliable service, the canal switched to being a source of hydroelectric power, turning Roanoke Rapids into a manufacturing area. Soon better sources of power replaced the canal, which was then drained. Its dry canal bed serves now as a seven-mile hiking trail.[1]

In 2010, Lance Jenkins took over as the museum's director. He hoped to bring in more visitors by "making the museum about the community in the Roanoke Valley as a whole rather than just about the canal," he explained. "I've always been fascinated with the 1960s and thought it would be interesting to see how the 1960s impacted Roanoke Rapids."

He searched through the archives of the local newspaper. "I ran across this story and was absolutely blown away and could not figure out why I had never heard of it before." The story was about the arrest of Sarah Keys in 1952. He included a small panel about her as part of the museum's 1960s exhibit. Even though those events occurred in the 1950s, her ICC case paved the way for much that happened in the 1960s. He also wanted to feature her story because "it was a notable part of history that had been left out and not told for so long."

As a white man who grew up in that part of North Carolina, Lance Jenkins realized that "there are a number of reasons why her story didn't get a ton of attention early on. There has been a history of hiding the negative. People didn't want to talk about the negative things. They don't want to acknowledge that this period of history occurred. When the exhibit came out in 2010, there were some people who would not talk to me about it. But the exhibit was well received by others. I thought that maybe the tide could change. I didn't know that it would, but I think we're seeing it now."[2]

The change he hoped would happen in Roanoke Rapids got a boost when his assistant, Rodney Pierce, became fascinated with Sarah's story and decided it deserved more than a small exhibit. Having grown up in Roanoke Rapids, he too was astonished that he had never heard about her. He was a Cultural Resources Leader at the museum, the first Black man hired to give tours there. He loved telling visitors about Sarah Keys Evans's bravery. Other civil rights stories he had heard about or learned about in school always seemed to happen somewhere else. This one happened in his own hometown. He set out to learn more.

He saw an article about Sarah in *Our Heritage* magazine, which also mentioned the children's book about Sarah, *Take a Seat—Make a Stand.* He reached out to me and to Sarah to describe his goal of having his city honor her. In an August 17, 2013, email to us, he wrote, "I would like the city to issue a proclamation in honor of Mrs. Evans along with an official apology." He acknowledged that achieving these goals would be difficult. "But I'm not giving up hope, just like Mrs. Evans didn't give up." At his request, we sent copies of *Take a Seat—Make a Stand* to local officials to help them learn more about the woman he wanted to honor.

He began speaking with members of the local Black community about his goal. Among those he contacted was Rev. Dr. Charles C. McCollum Sr., president of Eastern Carolina Christian College, located in Roanoke Rapids. He also contacted members of the local chapter of a civil rights group, the Southern Christian Leadership Conference. That led to their giving Sarah Keys Evans their Drum Major of Justice Award in 2017. By then Rodney Pierce had left the museum staff and become an award-winning social studies teacher in the local schools, regularly teaching students about what Sarah Keys Evans had done. Learning about her story made him wonder, "What else do I not know that happened here?" He began doing research to learn about other Black heroes from Halifax County. He had a historical marker installed to honor Black newspaper publisher Louis Austin, born in the neighboring town of Enfield, who published an important newspaper in Durham during the mid-1900s, *The Carolina Times* (see chapter 8). Later, Rodney Pierce would also find a way to honor Sarah Keys Evans with an official North Carolina historical marker, even though those markers are not supposed to celebrate heroes while they are still alive.[3]

In 2018, Rev. Dr. McCollum of Eastern Carolina Christian College heard about a contest that might provide a way to honor Sarah Keys Evans. This contest was sponsored by the Z. Smith Reynolds Foundation, which is dedicated to improving the quality of life for people in North Carolina. As noted in chapter 11, it had been a major source of funds for the North Carolina Fund, started in 1960, which initiated anti-poverty programs. The 2018 contest would award $50,000 each to ten North Carolina communities if they could come up with a good idea for creating a monument or other public art that would celebrate "the achievements of a North Carolina person or group, especially women and people of color, whose story . . . has not been or is not often told."

The Sarah Keys Evans story was exactly what the foundation was looking for, thought Rev. Dr. McCollum. If Roanoke Rapids could win this contest, the city could afford to put up a wonderful monument about her. Rev. Dr. McCollum formed a committee to plan how to win the contest, with three other local Black educators as committee members: Dr. Ervin Griffin Sr., president emeritus of Halifax Community College; Dr. Georgette Kimball, director of Programs for Special Needs Students at a local school; and Ophelia Gould-Faison, a retired schoolteacher. Eastern Carolina Christian College agreed to be the official sponsor of the project. Rev. Dr. McCollum and his committee contacted Sarah and me. We provided the committee with information, historical photographs, and letters of support for the contest application.[4]

More than eighty North Carolina communities entered the contest. After several months, the foundation named twenty semifinalists. Roanoke Rapids made it into the semifinals. Now Rev. Dr. McCollum's committee had to send in a detailed plan for the monument they would install. They persuaded a local Black artist, Napoleon Hill, to create art for the monument. The committee decided they would place the monument in the city's Martin Luther King Jr. Park.[5]

To help their entry win, they wanted to send a cameraman to Brooklyn, New York, to videotape an interview with Sarah in which she would explain about her arrest in Roanoke Rapids more than sixty years earlier. At first, she didn't want to do the interview. She always found it upsetting to describe what happened to her at the bus station and police station on that hot summer night in 1952. Talking about those events brought back the terror she felt back then.[6] This is a prime example of what historian Dr. Blair LM Kelley calls "Black trauma," the cumulative effect of instances of racial injustice experienced by Black people and "the toll that has on our psyches. We have to pause and honor the difficulty of telling this kind of story again—the sadness, the trauma, the shame. There are so many layers that she must have lived through and is still experiencing in this moment in retelling that story."[7]

However, Sarah's sister Connie encouraged her to do the video, as a way to have a permanent record of what had happened, told in her own words. Other family members also urged her to do the interview. Connie and her husband offered to be with Sarah in the room where the taping would take place, just as her father and brother had done when she testified before the ICC in 1954. Thanks to the support from her family, she agreed to the interview.

On March 13, 2019, one month before her ninetieth birthday, Sarah Keys Evans met with Les Atkins, the Roanoke Rapids committee's videographer, who set up his camera in a small room in a branch of the Brooklyn Public Library near her apartment building. She chose an outfit that fit the occasion perfectly—a video for posterity. Dressed elegantly in a wool pantsuit with a bright-yellow turtleneck and pearls, and wearing a stylish head wrap, she spoke for more than an hour about her experiences in Roanoke Rapids. Joining Sarah's sister and brother-in-law in the interview room were a few librarians and this author, all listening intently as she shared her story, telling it so well that our eyes were moist with tears as she described the fear she felt on that August 1952 night.[8]

Rev. Dr. McCollum's committee sent a powerful twelve-minute excerpt from the taping to the Z. Smith Reynolds Foundation. The committee also sent letters of support from many in the Black community in Roanoke Rapids as well as from the city's mayor and the mayors of nearby cities. Those mayors were white, as were some others who wrote letters of support. This project was starting to bring people together.[9]

Because the committee members were all educators, they decided that the monument should have an educational role. They proposed building two large, semicircular brick walls set a few feet apart. On the inside wall of each brick arc would be mural paintings telling Sarah Keys Evans's story

13.1 Sarah Keys Evans at the March 13, 2019, video-recording session at a branch library in Brooklyn, New York. She described being arrested in Roanoke Rapids, North Carolina, in August 1952 and the impact that experience had on her. A committee of Black educators in Roanoke Rapids sent an excerpt from the video to the Z. Smith Reynolds Foundation, which helped to win funding from the foundation for the monument in Roanoke Rapids, installed in 2020, that honors her. Photograph by Amy Nathan.

so that future generations could learn in detail about her courage and persistence. "We wanted it to be something that anybody that would look at it, regardless of your age, could follow it," explained Dr. Griffin, describing the committee's planning process. He didn't want people to "be saying in 2050, they never heard of Sarah Keys Evans. We were trying to close that circle so that people would know about her. Whether you want to discuss the issues, that's up to you. But we wanted to make sure it was there."[10]

The committee marshaled local support by holding community forums at which they told her story and explained its importance. At one forum in the local library, Dr. Kelley gave a presentation that placed Sarah's story in historical context, noting that "when she boarded the bus that day, she did not know she would be making history." Dr. Kelley, whose book *Right to Ride* describes the long struggle that had been waged by many other transportation heroes who came before Sarah, pointed out that these protests "have deep roots. Generation after generation fought segregation," going back as far as the 1840s, when Frederick Douglass protested segregation on a train in Massachusetts. She explained how years of earlier protests set the stage for the stand for justice that Sarah Keys Evans would take.[11]

The committee's forums earned the project widespread support. All four members of the Roanoke Rapids City Council—one Black and three white—voted to support the project. This was important because the committee needed the city council's permission to put the monument in the city's Martin Luther King Jr. Park.

A lot had changed in Roanoke Rapids since that summer night in 1952, when nobody was there to support Sarah Keys. Now there were many people eager to honor her. Members of the Black community held important positions in the city's government. In addition to the representative on the city council, there were Black officers on the police force. Members of the white community had also begun to acknowledge what the Black community had known for so long—that segregation was unjust. Of course, there were still problems in this community, as there are everywhere. However, filing the application for this contest brought out a spirit of coming together in this city of 15,000—about 50 percent white and 35 percent Black.[12]

"As we went along, we got more and more support," said Dr. Griffin. This was particularly remarkable because some of the people on the city council and in the local community may have known the man who was the chief of police in 1952, T. J. Davis, now deceased. He was regarded as an important part of the city's history, with a local recreation center named for him. Dr. Griffin noted, however, that although the city council approved the installation of the monument, "It wasn't, 'Yay! Tell the story.' There's a certain level of shame that goes along with it. Because you want to think that, 'We couldn't have done that.' The reality is 'Yes, you did.' That's the hard part." That's why he and the others on the committee wanted to have a monument tell the facts of the story so that all could know what had happened all those years ago. "Because if we don't talk about it now," said Dr. Griffin, "it may be shameful for generations."[13]

In June 2019, the Z. Smith Reynolds Foundation announced the results of the contest. The Sarah Keys Evans Project was one of the winners. When she heard the good news, Sarah told a Roanoke Rapids newspaper reporter, "I am rather elated that the city is doing this. It's a great honor that the city wants to tell my story."[14]

She had written a letter to Rev. Dr. McCollum the month before, on May 12, 2019, in which she said, "The mural is a splendid idea." She explained that it was "a great honor to have this mural installed in Martin Luther King, Jr., Park." She wanted to make sure that "the mural should represent the truth of my journey," adding that she felt "each generation should have a view of the past."[15]

The committee members and the artist, Napoleon Hill, got busy creating the monument. The committee sent Sarah a copy of the text about her case that would be placed on the monument. They also let her see drawings of the illustrations Napoleon Hill was creating so she could make sure they presented her story accurately. She told the committee that she wanted to be remembered as a Trailblazer for Justice, which the committee then included in the text to be placed on the monument.[16]

The committee planned to dedicate the monument on Sarah's ninety-first birthday, April 18, 2020. The monument was ready by then, but the nation was then battling the deadly COVID-19 virus, and health officials advised against large group gatherings. The committee revised their dedication plans and decided to hold a small ceremony that would involve only a few people gathering in person in Roanoke Rapids while others could join online via Zoom. They found another significant day for this slimmed-down ceremony—August 1, 2020—exactly sixty-eight years after a young Private First Class Sarah Louise Keys boarded the bus in New Jersey that brought her to their city.[17]

Closing the Circle

Several dozen people gathered in Martin Luther King Jr. Park in Roanoke Rapids on the morning of the dedication day, sitting on folding chairs next to Sarah Keys Evans Plaza, the name emblazoned in bold silver letters on the outside wall of one of the monument's two brick arcs.

On the inside wall of each arc are four large mural paintings created by artist Napoleon Hill, for a total of eight paintings. They depict the story of the unjust arrest and impressive legal victory of "Trailblazer for Justice—Sarah Louise Keys Evans," as she is called in a text panel with historical information on one wall.

The two arcs do not touch, allowing people to enter the space between them from either side to view the murals. These open entrances suggest an openness to change, a break in the long chain of attitudes that led to the historic injustices portrayed on the murals. Above the murals is the title "Closing the Circle," an appropriate name. This permanent outdoor art exhibit is in the city where Sarah Keys Evans experienced a great injustice but which has now circled around to honor her for helping bring an official end to that kind of injustice.

Sarah, then ninety-one and with rheumatoid arthritis, was unable to travel from her home in Brooklyn to North Carolina for the ceremony. She connected to the event online. So did many family members and friends around the country. Sadly, her husband and parents hadn't lived to see this monument, nor had her lawyer Dovey Johnson Roundtree.

Seated at the front of those taking part in the dedication ceremony were Rev. Dr. McCollum and the other members of the organizing committee. One of Sarah's nieces, Julie Waters Graves, was in the audience representing the family. A schoolteacher, Graves lives fairly near Roanoke Rapids, in Chapel Hill, North Carolina. She is the daughter of Sarah's youngest sister, Angela Keys Waters, a retired librarian. Also in the audience were elected officials and local supporters, including one of Sarah's first Roanoke Rapids defenders, Rodney Pierce.[18]

Early in the ceremony, Rev. Dr. McCollum delivered a prayer. Another member of the organizing committee, Dr. Griffin, then gave a poetry reading, offering this statement about the purpose for the monument: "The essential element we are saluting is sheer bravery above and beyond the call of duty. . . . We are here to express our respect, appreciation, and faith in an outstanding individual whom we call a trailblazer for justice." Rev. Dr. McCollum added that Sarah Keys Evans's accomplishment was all the

13.2 The Sarah Keys Evans Plaza monument in the Rev. Dr. Martin Luther King, Jr., Park in Roanoke Rapids, North Carolina, with a view of some of the mural paintings by Napoleon Hill on the interior walls of the two brick arcs. Photograph by Les Atkins.

more impressive because she took a stand for justice "in an era when it was not safe to do so—she already had two strikes against her."

A statement was read from Michael Wray, a North Carolina state representative who was not able to be there in person but who said that Sarah Keys Evans's courage "set the tone for the civil rights movement that lay ahead."

Then Representative G. K. Butterfield Jr., a US congressman from North Carolina, gave a short history lesson to help the audience appreciate the significance of what Sarah had accomplished in terms of both legal history and civil rights history. A political science major in college who worked as a civil rights lawyer after law school, Congressman Butterfield had participated in civil rights protests himself in the early 1960s and was well aware of the role his father had played in the 1940s and 1950s in encouraging Black voting. Congressman Butterfield spoke with authority when he said: "Rosa Parks in Montgomery, Alabama, took a clue from Sarah Louise Keys. . . . Rosa Parks got the energy and the will with what she did partly because of what happened here in Roanoke Rapids. That just catapulted Martin Luther King, Jr., to the national stage. . . . It was all interconnected. It must be said that Sarah Louise Keys Evans was very much part of that history. You are commended for recognizing her today."[19]

Dr. Griffin thanked the many people who had helped make the monument possible, including two who got the ball rolling by being the first to alert the local community to Sarah's role in history: Lance Jenkins and Rodney Pierce. Several official proclamations honoring Sarah were then read aloud, with framed copies given to Julie Waters Graves to send to her aunt, including one in which the Board of Commissioners of Halifax County declared that August 1, 2020, would be known as Sarah Louise Keys Evans Day. One of the other proclamations is the one Rodney Pierce had been waiting for ever since he first learned about Sarah: a proclamation honoring her issued by the mayor of Roanoke Rapids, Emery G. Doughtie. This white mayor spoke to those at the ceremony, praising Sarah Keys Evans for having had "a positive impact on something that could have been very negative" and, as a result, had helped bring about "change."[20]

Julie Waters Graves then read aloud a message that her Aunt Sarah asked her to share: "This mural is a splendid idea. It's to represent the truth of my journey, not a fiction of it. I feel that each generation should have a view of the past—the good, the bad and the indifferent. I hope this mural will represent just that. It is a great honor to have this mural in Martin Luther King, Jr., Park." Sarah's niece added that she and her family hoped the monument "will uplift and empower future generations" and help them see her aunt "as one of the many trailblazers that took a stand against injustice." She added that what her aunt did "holds continued relevance"—and can serve as an example for today.[21]

Sarah then spoke by phone from her apartment in Brooklyn, sharing her thoughts with those in attendance in Roanoke Rapids, along with those watching online. She said: "Hello, everyone! This is a glorious day for me. This dedication and celebration makes me very, very happy. I believe we all have a kinship. I wish I could have been there in person, but from what I've heard it is marvelous and I am very, very happy and very proud of everyone. I am very happy to know that I am being honored there today."

After she spoke, Dr. Georgette Kimball, one of the committee members, told Sarah, "We send you so much love." She then gave Sarah's niece a bouquet of flowers, explaining that Sarah had told the committee not to send flowers to New York but to instead give them to Julie. Dr. Kimball noted that many of the flowers in the bouquet were yellow, the official color of the ceremony because of the uplifting shade of yellow that Sarah had worn when she recorded the video for the committee. "That's my favorite color," Sarah told her.[22]

After an official ribbon-cutting for the monument, everyone present was invited to enter the open space between the two brick arcs to explore the artwork and learn more. One arc, in addition to mural paintings, also has a plaque with a brief description of Sarah's arrest and ICC victory. The eight paintings on the two arcs show

- Sarah Keys at age twenty-three, in her Women's Army Corps uniform.
- A bus at the old Roanoke Rapids bus station.
- Police officers arresting her.
- Sarah Keys standing alone in a jail cell.
- A portrait of her father, David A. Keys Sr.
- A painting of the scales of justice, with a large "NO," symbolizing the first defeat at the ICC.
- A portrait of Dovey Roundtree and Representative Adam Clayton Powell Jr.
- A bus with a rainbow in the background, symbolizing the 1955 ICC victory.

Opening Minds

During the planning process for the monument, Rev. Dr. McCollum noted that he felt a personal connection to Sarah's story. He remembers having to sit in the back of a bus and is grateful that she helped put an end to people of color being treated that way. He hopes the monument will inspire young people and give them new ideas, letting them learn from the courage and persistence she showed. He also hopes the monument will deliver an important message that can help young people cope if they should experience unfairness: "Don't be afraid to challenge it, no matter how tough it might be."[23]

Dr. Eric Cunningham, superintendent of schools for Halifax County, noted in a conversation before the monument was installed that he had plans for teachers "to discuss Mrs. Keys in our history classes and then go to the monument to reinforce the lesson, so our children can know that there were courageous people here."[24]

For several years, Rodney Pierce had already been teaching his North Carolina middle school students about Sarah Keys Evans. He would sometimes arrange for her to connect to his classroom via speakerphone from her Brooklyn apartment so she could talk with his students about her experiences and share words of advice for them. He said that learning her story had "empowered me. My hope and prayer is when I bring these stories into the classroom, that it will empower my students." He hopes also that her story might now become an official part of the curriculum in all local schools. "You can't change what has already happened," he told a *Time* magazine reporter. "You've got to embrace it and try to make it right. And this is an ideal time to do it."[25]

"None of the young people we are teaching today are responsible for these things of the past," observed Professor Kelley, while taking part in a 2022 online discussion for teachers about Sarah Keys Evans, hosted by Carolina K–12, one of UNC–Chapel Hill's Carolina Public Humanities programs. "But what they are responsible for is what happens next, making sure that the freedom we all believe in is a reality for everybody."[26]

Even those who don't live in Roanoke Rapids can learn about Sarah from the monument because the committee that installed the monument has created an interactive website. Visitors to the website can hear the lecture Professor Kelley gave in one of the community forums that the committee held.

In April 2022, Rev. Dr. McCollum and the other members of the committee that created the Sarah Keys Evans monument received an award from the State of North Carolina, the Governor's Medallion Award for Volunteer Service, honoring them for helping tell the story of a North Carolina hero.[27]

Rodney Pierce has also spread Sarah's story by finding a way to have a historical marker about the ICC decision approved by the State of North Carolina and installed a year and a half after the monument was dedicated. The marker stands directly in front of the building that used to be the Roanoke Rapids bus station where the young Sarah Keys arrived just after midnight so many years ago. At the ceremony dedicating the historical marker in January 2022, Rev. Dr. McCollum said, "If anyone's story needs to be made known to the world, it is that of Sarah Keys Evans, especially in the very community where her story has great significance." Pierce also

13.3 The historical marker installed on January 15, 2022, in front of the building in Roanoke Rapids, North Carolina, that was the bus station where Sarah Keys was arrested in 1952. Courtesy Rodney Pierce.

spoke at the ceremony, explaining, "I have done my best to keep her story alive. It's been a labor of love."

The historical marker focuses only on the ICC's decision and doesn't mention Sarah's name. On the marker, the decision is called "Keys v. Carolina Coach Company," leaving off the name "Sarah." Ansley Herring Wegner, then the head of the North Carolina Highway Historical Marker Program, explained at the ceremony that the modification in the ICC decision's title was made in order to allow this historical marker to be installed. "One of our major rules for our program is that a person has to have been dead for 25 years before they can be named on a marker," she said. They removed Sarah's name from the title of the ICC's decision because "we didn't want to not be able to tell the story now. From our shared past, from a shared place, here we tell this important story to all who pass by . . . one small but true important act of community."[28]

Rodney Pierce tried to help his community come together in another way—by writing a letter to a local newspaper in June 2020, shortly before the Sarah Keys Evans monument was dedicated. In this letter, he commented on a plaque on the grounds of the Halifax County Historic Courthouse that honored a Confederate general, Junius Daniel. In his letter, he urged the Halifax County Board of Commissioners to remove the plaque, noting that in a county where more than 50 percent of the residents are Black, "the message sent by this marker is outright disrespectful, racially insensitive and racially inflammatory." It had been installed in 1929 by the United Daughters of the Confederacy, a group that is no longer in existence in Halifax County. On October 5, 2020, the Halifax County Board of Commissioners voted four to one to remove the plaque and move it to an undisclosed location until a private organization steps forward to take ownership. County officials followed up on that vote and did indeed have the plaque removed.

It is remarkable that just two months after the dedication ceremony for the Sarah Keys Evans monument in Roanoke Rapids—where leaders of Halifax County honored her as a trailblazer for justice—those same leaders showed that they were willing to take another step toward reconciling with the area's divisive past by removing a plaque celebrating a Confederate general. Perhaps this signals the possibility of community discussions on what kinds of plaques should be displayed on public property, along with explorations of ways to bridge divides that still exist.[29]

The following year, on April 18, 2021, both Roanoke Rapids and Washington, North Carolina, celebrated Sarah's ninety-second birthday. That summer, there was also a celebration at the monument in Roanoke Rapids to mark the first anniversary of its dedication. The following summer, on July 30, 2022, the annual observance of the monument's dedication featured a new way of celebrating the courage of Sarah Keys Evans by honoring two others who have also stood up for justice by giving them a new award, which the committee hopes to give annually: the Sarah Keys Evans Trailblazer Award. One of the 2022 recipients was Elijah Lee, age fourteen, who has raised awareness about the issue of child abuse by holding a yearly march in the Roanoke Rapids area. He had also started a nonprofit organization, Hear Our Voices, that raised funds to help the local hospital deal with this issue. On receiving the Trailblazer Award, he told Rev. Dr. McCollum, "As I go out and speak and advocate for our young people, I want you to know I stand on your shoulders." This teenager added that "the current generation will not stop. . . . We will prevail. In the words of the great Dr. Martin Luther King Jr., 'We shall overcome.'"

The other award presented that day was a posthumous one, given to honor the legacy of the lawyer who represented Sarah Keys Evans at the ICC in 1955, Dovey Johnson Roundtree. Her goddaughter Charlene Pritchard was there to receive the award. She thanked the committee and urged young people to "continue to pass the torch on. You be the change-maker in this world."

The committee has continued to hold ceremonies to present Sarah Keys Evans Trailblazer Awards to others who are helping to create a better and more just world. At the ceremony on August 10, 2024, in addition to honoring many health care workers who are expanding opportunities and services in their communities, an award went to one of Sarah's first supporters in Roanoke Rapids—Rodney Pierce, the social studies teacher who was soon to become the local community's representative in the North Carolina General Assembly.[30]

"We've taken a step with the monument and the tribute to Sarah Keys Evans," observed Lance Jenkins, former director of the Roanoke Rapids museum. "Nobody would have even believed it could happen ten years ago." But he also acknowledged that "there is still a sentiment in so many places in America of racial injustice and intolerance. Racial division is still there today. But this monument is indicative that things are changing—and that they can change. I think we're seeing it."[31]

The Army Remembers

On Veterans Day 2020, Lieutenant General Thomas James, commanding general of the First US Army—the branch of the army that Sarah Keys Evans served in as a WAC—delivered a special message about her. In a video message posted for his troops, he described her arrest and ICC victory. Then he added:

> This summer . . . Roanoke Rapids attempted to right the wrong that had been done to a brave American soldier. . . . A mural depicts her standing in jail, her hands clasped in prayer, her head held high. This year as we've watched our nation struggle with our painful legacy of racism and prejudice . . . I find myself deeply grateful for a change-maker like PFC Keys. . . . I'd often tell our troops that we stand on the shoulders of giants. But today on Veterans Day 2020, I remind myself and everyone at First Army, that we stand on the shoulders of a fearless

young soldier who refused to move, who changed the nation by taking a stand and fought a painful personal war right here at home. We stand on the shoulders of the indomitable and unbreakable Private First Class Sarah Keys. I had the honor of talking to her recently over the phone. . . . I told her we at First Army take great pride in sharing our lineage with her. But she asked me not to remember her for that night in 1952, but for the fight that came after. Hers, she said, was a story of perseverance, not persecution.[32]

The Military Women's Memorial also continues to remember Sarah Keys Evans by featuring her in an exhibit, the Color of Freedom, that highlights the achievements of women of color who have served in the US military. This exhibit was installed in 2021 at the memorial's main exhibit space, located at the entrance to Arlington National Cemetery, and was also on display at various locations around the nation as part of a traveling exhibit.[33]

Congressman Butterfield encouraged the US Congress to continue to remember Sarah. He entered into the *Congressional Record* the text of the speech he gave at the 2020 monument dedication ceremony. A year later, he joined with Congressman Mark Takano, chairman of the House Committee on Veterans Affairs, to introduce a bill on Veterans Day, November 11, 2021, nominating Sarah Keys Evans for the Congressional Gold Medal (H. R. 5922). "With this bill, we honor this North Carolina veteran for her tremendous contributions to the civil rights movement and the fight to end segregation," said Congressman Butterfield. His colleague Congressman Takano noted, "We are a better place today because of the courage, bravery, and sacrifice of Private First Class Keys and all those who followed in her footsteps." She was renominated for this honor by Representative Donald G. Davis during the next two congressional sessions in 2023 and 2025, after Representative Butterfield retired. There was no guarantee, of course, that she would receive this medal, but it was a great honor to be nominated.[34]

Looking Forward

Sarah Keys Evans died unexpectedly at age ninety-four on November 16, 2023, at a hospital in New Jersey, near the rehabilitation center where she had been convalescing for several months from a fall she had experienced the year before in her apartment. The rehab center is near the home of her sister Cornelia (Connie) Keys Hargrave, who was a big help to Sarah all her life, including during her final months. Connie was with her at the end.[35]

Just three months earlier, Sarah had received another honor. A celebration of her role in civil rights history was organized by that rehab center, Hampton Ridge Healthcare and Rehabilitation, for all its residents and staff to attend on August 1, 2023—a day they called "Sarah Evans Day." That was the seventy-first anniversary of the day she had boarded the bus in New Jersey that brought her to Roanoke Rapids. During her stay at the rehab center, although she used a wheelchair, she managed to wheel herself around and offer encouragement to other residents who were having a tough time, similar to what she did many years earlier when she would regularly visit a nursing home on Sundays near her apartment in Brooklyn.[36]

A funeral Mass celebrating her life was held on November 30, 2023, at St. Mary of the Lake Catholic Church in Lakewood, New Jersey. Many members of the family traveled from other states to be there to say farewell. Sarah Keys Evans was then laid to rest in Brooklyn's Evergreens Cemetery, next to the grave of her husband. A two-person uniformed detail provided military honors, playing taps and formally folding and presenting to her family the US flag that had covered her casket.

The spirit of Sarah Keys Evans lives on, in the memories of her family and friends as well as through the monument that honors her in Roanoke Rapids, and also in various exhibits about her in her own hometown, at the Military Women's Memorial, and elsewhere.

What advice might Sarah Keys Evans give to school groups and others who learn about her story if she could be there to meet with them as they visit the monument or exhibits about her? Perhaps she'd give the same advice she gave in 2017 to the students she spoke with at the high school in New Jersey, as described in chapter 12: "Never ever stop fighting for our rights and for our freedom."[37]

She might acknowledge, as she did at that high school, that standing up for justice isn't easy. To encourage others to give it a try, she might recommend that it isn't necessary to go it alone, making the same suggestion she offered at the end of the 2006 children's book *Take a Seat—Make a Stand*: "You have to be strong and remember that there's always that right person there to help you. It might be someone in your family. Or your family can tell you who can help. I had my father to help me, and then he found out who could help him to help me. As long as I had my father I would never give up. I'm glad I didn't give up. I'm glad I was able to help unlock another door of freedom."[38]

She gave similar advice in the video recorded for the Roanoke Rapids monument committee: "All the disparaging or things that I've seen happen in life, the mistreatment of people. If you don't have someone around to speak up for you, you're like a dead duck."

Perhaps she would also observe that sometimes it helps "to be a good listener," as she noted in the video for the monument committee, where she described the value of sometimes taking a quiet, thoughtful approach:

> I ran across a statement some time ago that says if you stop to throw rocks at every dog that barks, you'd never get to where you're going. There's some days you have to let some things go. You know, you don't forget about them. But now is not the time to handle it, not right now. Because you got to get to where you're going. If you remain on the negative side, you're not going to know when it's right there in front of you, help, if you need it. If it's nothing more than just to talk. You can sit down and take a rest on a park bench while waiting for a bus and strike up a conversation. It might give you some insight. Hey, there's a better way, a different way. You released a little bit of it to someone else. And that's a good thing.

She continued during that video to note that "there's a time and a place for everything. Who's to determine the time and who's to determine the place? It's determined by you, maybe one step, one measure of courage, a step that you had to make, or I had to make."[39]

Maybe she would advise all people—young and old—to be open to new ideas and possibilities, as she noted when she spoke to a reporter for *Time* magazine a few days before the 2020 dedication ceremony in Roanoke Rapids: "Keep on reading and keep on listening."[40]

Acknowledgments

Sarah Keys Evans had a huge team of supporters who helped us create this book, starting with her family, especially her sister Cornelia (Connie) Keys Hargrave, who was a loyal friend of Sarah's all her life and who helped enormously after Sarah suffered a terrible accident in 2022 and was severely injured. Connie found an excellent rehab center near her New Jersey home for Sarah, visiting her daily. Connie was also a wonderful support for me, too, agreeing to be interviewed multiple times, reading versions of the manuscript, answering innumerable questions, offering suggestions, and correcting errors. Her husband John Hargrave helped as well, especially during my visits to see Sarah at the rehab center. Other relatives helped Sarah throughout her life and also helped with the research for this book, including her sister Angela Keys Waters, nieces Joan Dudley, Michelle McComb, Sonya Keys, and Julie Ann Water Graves, as well as nephews Bradley Hargrave and Rodney Waters, who wrote a wonderful article about his Aunt Sarah for *Catholic Review*. Other relatives who helped with this book include Teresa Hargrave and Alexis Hargrave. In addition, Krys Hargrave was extremely helpful, both in being interviewed multiple times and for providing a tape of the presentation that Sarah Keys Evans gave at a Perth Amboy, New Jersey, school. Relatives Vernon Robinson, Jhade

Carney, and Cameron Carney also showed support for Sarah and helped with my earlier book on Baltimore civil rights history.

Sarah's cousin, Leesa Jones, provided essential historical information about Keysville and Washington, North Carolina, from research she has done for her Washington Waterfront Underground Railroad Museum, and then used her extraordinary research skills to scour local archives to answer questions about the school Sarah's father attended as a teen. Another excellent local researcher, Alice Sadler, provided important information from her P. S. Jones Museum and kindly fact-checked local education sections of the manuscript, as did Leesa Jones. Also helpful were James Smallwood for helping me locate John Wilson, whose late wife Agatha is in one of the photos in the book about the Mother of Mercy School.

Thanks also go to Stephen Farrell of the Brown Library in Washington, North Carolina, who provided important research suggestions, and to Richard Leach, who gave useful information about his grandmother. Larry McDaniel kindly shared his knowledge on the history of the Catholic Church in Washington, North Carolina, and Ray Midgett shared his insights and also wrote terrific articles that helped with the research. Thanks also to Ani Olivares for finding Sarah Keys's baptismal and confirmation records, and to Deacon Rick Fisher for providing fascinating information on St. Joseph's Church in New Bern.

Sarah's supporters in Roanoke Rapids helped enormously in multiple ways, including Rodney Pierce, Dr. Ervin Griffin, Rev. Dr. Charles C. McCollum Sr., Dr. Georgette Kimball, and Ophelia Gould-Faison, along with Lance Jenkins, Lori Medlin, Christina Caudle, Dr. Eric Cunningham, the wonderful artist Napoleon Hill, and the terrific photographer and videographer Les Atkins. Thanks also to Professor Blair LM Kelley for her excellent books and for providing valuable historical insights during a program we participated in for Carolina K–12 in May 2022, which Dr. Ervin Griffin and Rodney Pierce participated in as well, also offering important historical context. Ansley Herring Wegner was helpful both in explaining how Rodney Pierce created a historical marker and then in supporting the publication of a new book for young readers, *Sarah Keys Evans: The Power of Quiet Courage* (2025), with Sarah Keys Evans again my coauthor.

Also providing useful information was Carrie Thornhill of the Dunbar High School Alumni Association. Thanks go as well to Brenda Bentt-Peters of the Brooklyn Public Library for supporting Sarah Keys Evans during her years in Brooklyn.

I'm extremely grateful to Marilla Cushman, Britta Granrud, and Brigadier General USAF (retired) Wilma L. Vaught of the Military Women's Memorial for their support of Sarah Keys Evans as they continue to include her in their exhibits and make available the Oral History that the Memorial did, and most especially for the help they provided at the start of this research journey in helping me connect with Sarah Keys Evans.

Many thanks also go to Sister Beth Pearson, archivist of Sisters, Servants of the Immaculate Heart of Mary (IHM), Scranton, Pennsylvania, for locating wonderful photos of the Mother of Mercy School and for sharing useful information about the school and agreeing to let the photos appear in this book.

I'm glad I had the courage to approach Duke University Press with a proposal for a book about Sarah Keys Evans. I'm so grateful to Gisela Fosado for seeing the importance of sharing this story. Thanks also go to Alejandra Mejía, Miriam Angress, Lisa Lawley, and so many others at Duke University Press for shepherding it on its way.

Of course, this book would not have been possible without encouragement (and gentle editing) from my husband, who joined me on a trip to Roanoke Rapids on what was one of the hottest days of the summer of 2024 so we could see the impressive Sarah Keys Evans Monument, visit the bus station where she arrived in 1952, tour the Canal Museum, and attend that year's inspiring Sarah Keys Evans Trailblazer Award presentations. Thank you, Carl.

Appendix

TRANSPORTATION HEROES BRIGADE

Long before Sarah Keys Evans's 1955 ICC victory and also before Rosa Parks's defiance sparked a yearlong boycott, many other Black citizens had already protested against segregation on public transportation. A few have been mentioned in this book. This appendix presents brief accounts of additional courageous transportation heroes, along with more details about a few previously featured. Even so, this is a small sampling of the many who took a stand against the injustice of segregation in public transit. Some of those listed here are also noted for other roles they played in civil rights history. A resources section at the end of the appendix suggests books and articles where information about additional transportation heroes can be found.

David Ruggles: This free Black man was a major abolitionist and Underground Railroad activist in New York City who helped Frederick Douglass when he first arrived in New York after fleeing from slavery in Maryland. Like Douglass, Ruggles was forcibly ejected from train cars reserved for white passengers in Massachusetts. In 1841, he sued the employees of the Eastern Railroad, seeking damages for assault and battery. His suit was unsuccessful. Efforts to pass a state law in Massachusetts against train segregation failed, too, but in 1843 the state's train companies stopped using

Jim Crow cars when it was pointed out that they could lose their charters for violating the state constitution's guarantee of equal rights for all.[1]

Elizabeth Jennings Graham, Thomas L. Jennings, Rev. James W. C. Pennington, Dr. James McCune Smith, and Chester Arthur: On July 16, 1854, Elizabeth Jennings, a Black schoolteacher and church organist, was roughly thrown off a horse-drawn streetcar in New York City. Encouraged by her father, Thomas L. Jennings, she sued the Third Avenue Railway Company (see chapter 2). A young white lawyer and future US president, Chester Arthur, defended her successfully in a Brooklyn courtroom, where she won an award of $225 and a promise from the streetcar company to end its segregation policy. The judge did not specifically order the city's many other streetcar companies to end segregation. Some did, but not all. So her father and two other leaders of the local Black community—Reverend James W. C. Pennington and Dr. James McCune Smith—started the Legal Rights Association to encourage others to engage in civil disobedience by trying to ride streetcars and, if refused, to take legal action. Over the next few years, some lawsuits succeeded, but others did not. It took another brave woman (see next entry) to at last end segregation on all New York City streetcars.[2]

Ellen Anderson: Because of the 1863 Emancipation Proclamation, Black men were allowed to serve in the Union Army. Ellen Anderson, a widow of one of those soldiers who was killed in action in South Carolina, was denied a ride on a New York streetcar in 1864 and was dragged off the car by the conductor and a police officer. She was a friend of a Legal Rights Association member and knew her rights. Her lawyer sued the police department, protesting this mistreatment of a war widow. The police chief ruled in favor of Ellen Anderson, noting that "there was no law against these people riding in the cars." He scolded the officer for not using "common sense," noting that "it was rather his duty to have arrested the conductor than the woman." The company that denied her a ride dropped segregation, as did the other remaining holdout, marking the end of streetcar segregation in the city. Nine years later, New York State made it official with its 1873 law prohibiting race-based discrimination in all public businesses.[3]

Dr. Alexander Augusta: After earning his medical degree in Canada in the 1850s due to limited educational opportunities for Black students in the United States, Dr. Alexander Augusta returned home and volunteered to serve in the Union Army, becoming its first Black physician, starting as a major and rising to lieutenant colonel. In 1864, when he was denied a ride on a DC streetcar, he wrote a letter of complaint to an army official, which led to Congress passing legislation in 1865 that expanded its 1863 DC railroad charter so it would end segregation on all DC streetcars. After the war, Dr. Augusta became the first Black professor of medicine in the United States, teaching at the newly formed Howard University.[4]

Sojourner Truth: Not all conductors obeyed the DC charter that banned segregation on DC streetcars. Sojourner Truth helped change that. A staunch abolitionist who had freed herself from slavery in New York State in the 1820s, she moved to DC in 1864 to help newly freed people. She objected boisterously to being denied streetcar rides, yelling, "I want to ride!!" over and over one day as streetcars rolled by without stopping, until a crowd gathered and forced the next car to stop for her. In 1865, when a conductor ejected her roughly, she sued him. Her suit was dismissed, but the conductor lost his job. The publicity persuaded conductors from then on to abide by the DC streetcar antidiscrimination rules.[5]

Octavius Catto: This young Black teacher in Philadelphia helped Frederick Douglass recruit Black soldiers in 1863 for the Union Army. In 1865, Octavius Catto became a member of the Car Committee of Pennsylvania's chapter of the National Equal Rights League (founded by Douglass). The committee's goal was to have a law passed to end streetcar segregation. In 1866, to encourage the legislature to act, spontaneous protests sprang up in which Black Philadelphians rushed onto streetcars as whites were boarding. Catto gave a stirring speech urging more of these protests. In early 1867, the legislature passed the law that ended streetcar segregation. A statue of Catto was installed in Philadelphia in 2017, the first statue honoring a Black American to be installed in Philadelphia on public property.[6]

William Nicholls: The US Civil Rights Act of 1866 motivated people in New Orleans to put an end to their city's segregated streetcars, which let white riders use any streetcar but limited people of color to the few "star cars," marked with a large black star. The local Black-owned newspaper, the *Tribune*, had been writing articles calling for an end to the star car system, including a story on April 24, 1867. Four days later, on April 28, 1867, a Black rider, William Nicholls, was arrested for trying to ride in a whites-only car. Officials dropped the charges against him to avoid more disturbances and perhaps also to avoid lawsuits. But a week later, large numbers of Black people mobbed whites-only streetcars and refused to leave, bringing the streetcar system to a halt. Negotiations began between the mayor, the streetcar companies, the chief of police, and the army general in charge of federal forces in the city. The result: The star car system ended. A new constitution, which was written the next year by equal numbers of Black and white delegates, officially ended streetcar segregation, a policy that lasted until 1902, when the new white-dominated legislature segregated streetcars again, a situation that continued until 1958.[7]

Ellen Garrison Jackson Clark and **Mary J. C. Anderson:** The Civil Rights Act of 1866 inspired these two Black teachers to file suit in a Maryland court against a station master who rudely ejected them from the ladies' waiting room of a Baltimore train station. Ellen Garrison Jackson Clark said the goal of their lawsuit was "to ascertain whether respectable people have rights which are to be respected." They did not succeed, due to a legal maneuver that defeated other suits that had sought to benefit people of color, according to a 2004 article by David S. Bogen. The station master's lawyer tried to settle out of court. When that failed, he requested a jury trial because he knew Maryland's all-white juries would never rule in the women's favor. The case was dismissed in July 1866 because the women did not appear for the jury trial, whether from not having been informed of the court date or because they chose not to engage in this sham justice.[8] Their courage was honored recently when researchers discovered that Ellen Garrison Jackson Clark was buried in an unmarked grave in Altadena, California. Members of that community, both white and Black, had a headstone installed at her grave site, dedicated in 2021 on June 19—the Juneteenth federal holiday that commemorates the day in 1865 when the enslaved in Texas were at last informed that slavery had been abolished.[9]

Alexander Thompson, John W. Fields, Josephine Carr, and **the Stewart sisters (Martha, Mary, Lucy, and Winnie Stewart):** Also listed in David Bogen's article were cases involving Baltimore trolley cars and Maryland steamships. All had similar verdicts in the local federal court—that segregated accommodations were allowed, but their quality needed to be equal to those for white travelers. In each of the two trolley cases, a Black man was ejected from a car for white riders: Alexander Thompson in 1869 and

John W. Fields in 1871. The court ruled that separate cars for Black and white riders were permissible, but passengers paying the same fare should have the same-quality seating. This ruling wound up ending segregation on Baltimore's local transit because it would be too expensive for trolley companies to have separate good-quality cars for Black and white passengers. In the steamship cases, the court offered Josephine Carr $25 compensation for being denied a seat in a steamer's main cabin in 1872. The Stewart sisters were awarded $100 in damages after being given dirty sleeping cabins in 1884. Bogen concludes, "In Maryland, the insistence on real equality in conditions by the federal court and the costs of such treatment combined to produce substantial integration in transport." He notes, however, that after the 1896 *Plessy v. Ferguson* decision, Maryland's white legislators tried to pass new laws requiring segregation in public transportation. His article discusses the Black community's efforts—some successful and some not—to block those new segregation laws.[10]

Charlotte Brown and **Mary Ellen Pleasant:** In 1863, Charlotte Brown was roughly ejected from a horse-drawn streetcar in San Francisco. She sued the streetcar company. A judge awarded her only the price of her streetcar ticket. A few days later, another conductor forced her off a streetcar. She sued again and in 1864 won an award of $500. Streetcars continued to deny rides to Black travelers, leading to a suit filed by Mary Ellen Pleasant, a businesswoman and civil rights activist. Her case went to the California Supreme Court, which ruled in 1868 that refusing people rides based on skin color was unlawful. In 1893, the California legislature passed a law making streetcar segregation officially illegal.[11]

Josephine DeCuir: In 1872, this wealthy woman of color bought a first-class ticket for a riverboat ride from New Orleans to a point further up the Mississippi River. Denied access to one of the steamboat's better rooms, which were reserved for white passengers, Josephine DeCuir filed suit against the owner of the company for violating Louisiana's progressive 1868 constitution and the state's civil rights laws that prohibited segregation in public accommodations. She won in two Louisiana courts and was awarded $1,000. However, the steamboat company appealed to the US Supreme Court, which ruled against her, in a case called *Hall v. DeCuir*. The Supreme Court said that because the steamboat also traveled to Mississippi, it was engaged in interstate travel, which only Congress can regulate, so a state's regulations didn't apply.[12]

Jane Brown: In 1880, Jane Brown was not allowed into the ladies car on a train in Corinth, Tennessee, not simply because she was Black but also because railroad authorities claimed she was a "notorious courtesan" and thus not a suitable person for the ladies car. A Tennessee district court judge rejected that argument, saying that it "would put every woman purchasing a railroad ticket on trial for her virtue before the conductor as her judge," making all women reluctant to travel for fear of being subjected to such random and arbitrary judgment. The judge awarded Brown a settlement of $3,000.[13]

Ida B. Wells: Educator and journalist Ida B. Wells regularly traveled by train within Tennessee, where she was a teacher, buying first-class tickets and sitting with white passengers in the Ladies Car. In 1883, a conductor ordered her to move to the Jim Crow car. She refused. When the conductor tried to force her to move, she fought back, biting his hand. She was thrown off the train and sued the railroad company. She won in a local court, but the company appealed the decision to the Tennessee Supreme Court, which ruled against her. She later helped launch the NAACP in 1909 and used her skills as a journalist to focus public attention on the issue of lynching.[14]

Lola Houck: As noted briefly in chapter 2, this light-complexioned schoolteacher in Victoria, Texas, regularly traveled on trains within the state, buying first-class tickets and sitting in the first-class car. In 1886, while she was visibly pregnant, a train brakeman told Houck to go to the Jim Crow car for the ninety-mile trip to Rosenberg, Texas. She was going to visit her young child, who was sick and staying at the grandmother's home in Galveston. According to a description of her trip in *Right to Ride* by Blair LM Kelley, a Black bootblack who was shining shoes at the station had mentioned to the train's staff that Lola Houck was actually Black, which led the brakeman to ban her from the first-class car. Instead, she stood on the platform between cars for that long rainy journey rather than deal with the smoke-filled Jim Crow car. Each time the train stopped, she tried again to enter the first-class car. At one point she was shoved and almost fell off the platform. She suffered a miscarriage and sued the railroad company. A Texas circuit court awarded her a $7,500 settlement for personal injury (reduced to $2,500 on appeal). The court ruled that while segregation on trains may be legal, Black passengers who buy first-class tickets must be provided with cars that are comparable to those for white first-class passengers.[15]

John Mitchell Jr. and **Maggie Lena Walker:** In 1904, Virginia passed a law that not only allowed streetcars to segregate passengers by race but also made it dangerous to protest with sit-ins, as people in Richmond and other Southern cities had done in the mid-1860s. The new law gave streetcar conductors police powers, including the right to carry guns and make arrests. The only safe way to protest was by boycott, so as not to risk engaging with armed conductors. Maggie Lena Walker, a Richmond newspaper editor and the nation's first Black woman to own a bank, was one of the leaders of a streetcar boycott that started in Richmond in 1904. Also a leader was John Mitchell Jr., the editor of another local Black newspaper. The boycotters hoped to deprive the streetcar company of so much income that it would end segregation. The boycott continued for three years, but when the state passed a law in 1906 that *required* segregation on all streetcars, there was no chance of getting the streetcar company to change. Gradually the boycott came to end in Richmond and in other cities (as described in *Right to Ride* by Blair LM Kelley).[16]

Barbara Pope: In the summer of 1906, this Washington, DC, educator and short story writer sat in the main compartment of a train going from DC to a Virginia resort. When the train entered Virginia, a conductor told Barbara Pope to move to the Jim Crow car. She refused and was taken off the train. She was tried in a makeshift court in the train station and found guilty of breaking Virginia's separate train car law. She had to pay a fine of $10 plus court costs. She received help from a new civil rights organization, the Niagara Movement (precursor to the NAACP). It appealed her conviction, first in a local Virginia court (where she lost), and then in Virginia's Supreme Court of Appeals, where she won. W. E. B. Du Bois, one of the founders of the Niagara Movement and later of the NAACP, said her victory showed that "Virginia cannot fine an interstate passenger who refuses to be Jim-Crowed." The NAACP used that argument forty years later when Irene Morgan was "Jim-Crowed" on an interstate bus. In addition, the Niagara Movement filed a civil suit in 1907 in the Supreme Court of the District of Columbia to try to win $50,000 in damages for Barbara Pope. The jury in this court case ruled in her favor but "awarded her just one penny," according to a 2021 article in the *Washington Post*. Sadly, she experienced other problems in her life and committed suicide in 1908. Her legal victory faded from view, partly because it was thought at that time to be "impolite to discuss suicides," according to historian Jennifer Harris. In 2015, an article she wrote about Barbara Pope was published in *Legacy*, a journal about American women writers, to help others learn about the courage of this overlooked civil rights hero.[17]

Charlotte Hawkins Brown: As a result of the success of the Palmer Memorial Institute that she started in Sedalia, North Carolina, in 1902 (described in chapter 7), Charlotte Hawkins Brown became the president of the North Carolina Association of Colored Women's Clubs in 1912. At one of the association's meetings in the summer of 1920, two white women attended who were interested in starting interracial discussions. They invited Charlotte Hawkins Brown to speak that fall in Memphis at a gathering of white women taking part in the Woman's Missionary Convention. She traveled to Memphis by train but was pulled off the first-class car by a group of white men, who forced her to sit in the Jim Crow car. In her speech at the convention two days later, she described the insult she had experienced on that train, perhaps opening the eyes of these white church women to the fact that something like that could happen even to someone as accomplished as she was. She urged them to take action against lynching and work to help Black women. This meeting inspired women—both Black and white—in several states to start interracial women's committees for the new Commissions on Interracial Cooperation that were starting then. Brown served on the board of the committee that started in North Carolina. She also partnered with the North Carolina branch of the NAACP in 1920 to organize voter registration drives for Black women after the Nineteenth Amendment was ratified. Officials placed many obstacles in their way, but a few hundred Black women still managed to register to vote in North Carolina that year.[18]

William A. Roberts: Bus drivers in Northern states often asked Black customers to move to the rear, as happened in 1929 to William A. Roberts, who had bought a first-class ticket for a Greyhound bus from Chicago to St. Louis. When he complained about the driver's request to move to the rear, the station manager refunded the cost of the ticket but supported the driver's behavior. Roberts filed a complaint with the NAACP, but it didn't have funds at that time to fight every case in court. Instead, the NAACP used complaints from William A. Roberts and others as examples when it tried to negotiate with Greyhound and also in its planning for other legal efforts.[19]

Bessie Nelson and **Mamie Kinchlow:** These women didn't know each other when they boarded a Greyhound bus in the summer of 1932 to go to Virginia. Mamie Kinchlow started her trip in New York City; Bessie Nelson, in New Jersey. They wound up sitting next to each other in a back row when they had to change to a new bus in DC. The driver then asked them to give up their space for white passengers. They refused and were arrested and jailed when the bus reached Alexandria, Virginia. Both had to pay $25 fines. Kinchlow was released after two days. Nelson was found guilty of disorderly conduct and was forced to work at a city hospital for several days. Both sued the bus company, but a DC court rejected their lawsuits.[20]

Ellen Harris: On February 12, 1938, Ellen Harris took a ride home in Durham, North Carolina, on a local bus that had room for twenty-five passengers, with five rows of two seats each on either side of the bus and a rear seat for five passengers. She took a seat in one of the last rows in the back, just in front of the five-seater. At a later stop on the trip, a white couple, Mr. and Mrs. Jones, entered. There was only one empty seat in the rows of seats, other than the seat next to Ellen Harris. Mr. Jones demanded that she give up her seat and move to the five-seater. Harris refused but added that she'd leave the bus if the driver refunded her fare. Instead, this Black woman was arrested and found guilty of "willfully" violating segregation laws. She appealed her case with the help of two local Black lawyers. She lost in North Carolina's Superior Court but appealed that decision to North Carolina's Supreme Court, which overturned her conviction. The judge ruled that "we do not think the defendant intended to willfully violate the provisions" of the segregation act. She then filed a lawsuit against the Durham Public Services Company, the managers of the bus company, and won an undisclosed monetary award.[21]

Pauline Carth: In 1943, Pauline Carth, a teenager, tried to get on a local bus in Birmingham, Alabama. When the driver said there were no seats left for Black passengers, she forced her way onto the bus, was thrown off by the driver, and was then arrested, according to an article by Robin D. G. Kelley, which noted that working-class Black women in Birmingham were not shy about expressing their displeasure with Jim Crow seating.

The article also said that protesting bus segregation in court "was not a high-priority issue for Birmingham's black protest organizations" during World War II. Some people told the local NAACP about Carth's arrest, but no court case was filed.[22]

Jackie Robinson: Famous for integrating Major League Baseball in April 1947, Jackie Robinson took a different stand against Jim Crow during World War II. On July 6, 1944, as a second lieutenant in the US Army stationed at Fort Hood, Texas, he refused to move to the back of a bus. The army had decided to transport troops on its own non-segregated buses because of the rising number of incidents of mistreatment and violence against Black soldiers on segregated local buses near Southern army bases. Apparently, the driver of this Texas bus wasn't aware of the new regulation and had military policemen take Lieutenant Robinson to military police headquarters. He was charged with insubordination, conduct unbecoming an officer, and other charges, most of which were later dropped. But he still faced a court-martial for insubordination, which focused on his anger when an enlisted man referred to him with a racial slur. During the trial, the enlisted man said he had not used the slur, but a witness testified that he had. Lieutenant Robinson passionately explained why he found the slur insulting. The nine military judges found him not guilty. He spent the rest of his tour of duty at a base in Kentucky until his honorable discharge in November 1944. He wrote later about his acquittal: "It was a small victory, for I had learned that I was in two wars, one against the foreign enemy, the other against prejudice at home."[23]

Private First Class Booker T. Spicely: Drafted into the US Army during World War II, PFC Booker T. Spicely was stationed at Camp Butner, an army base near Durham, North Carolina. On July 8, 1944, PFC Spicely, age thirty-four, while on leave from the base, boarded a local bus in Durham and took a seat in the front row. The driver told him to move to the back of the bus. When two white soldiers got on the bus, PFC Spicely pointed out that he and the white soldiers were wearing the same uniform, so he questioned why he should have to move to the back. However, he did wind up moving to seats in the rear of the bus. He also used the rear exit to get off the bus. The bus driver, Herman Lee Council, pulled out a gun, got off the bus himself, walked along the side of the bus to approach PFC Spicely, and shot him twice. Military police officers took the wounded soldier to the nearest hospital, but it wouldn't treat him because he was

Black; it was a whites-only hospital. Officers then took him to another hospital that would treat Black patients, but by then it was too late and he died. A few hours later, a block of white-owned business burned down, perhaps set on fire by people angry about the shooting. The driver went on trial but was found not guilty by an all-white jury. In 2023, on December 1, Booker T. Spicely's birthday, an official North Carolina historical marker was installed in Durham to honor and remember him. Carolina K–12 (www.CarolinaK12.org) has created a lesson plan about his killing to teach students about the dangers Black military personnel faced during World War II in the South.[24]

Sarah Elizabeth Ray: In 1945, this young Black woman had just finished a secretarial course in Detroit. She and some white women classmates decided to celebrate at an amusement park on BobLo Island, fifteen miles up the Detroit River from the city of Detroit. The island, which is part of Canada, could be reached only by taking a short ride on a steamboat owned by the amusement park. When Ray entered the boat, one of the boat's employees made her leave because Black people weren't allowed. She contacted the NAACP. By 1948, her complaint had landed at the US Supreme Court, where Thurgood Marshall persuaded the court that the BobLo Company was guilty of breaking Michigan's civil rights law that prohibited racial discrimination on public transportation. Even though the boat traveled in Canadian waters, the court ruled that the park was such a big part of Detroit's social life that the Michigan law was applicable.[25]

William Chance: William Chance was the principal of a Black high school in Parmele, North Carolina, which he had started in 1909 in his own home as a private trade school. It merged two years later with the local Black public school, and by 1948 it had the highest percentage (70 percent) of graduating seniors entering college of any school in Martin County (the average was 50 percent). In June 1948, as he was returning home by train from a business trip in Pennsylvania, he was arrested when the train reached Richmond and he refused to move to the Jim Crow car. He was represented by NAACP lawyers, first in a Richmond court, where he lost, and then in the Fourth Circuit Court of Appeals, which ruled in 1951 that the train company's rule violated the Constitution's Commerce Clause. The *Chance v. Lambeth* decision cited the *Morgan v. Virginia* case; although Chance's complaint involved a train company's rule, rather than a state law, the judges decided that "we know of no principle of law which requires the courts to strike down a state statute which interferes with interstate commerce but to uphold a railroad regulation which is infected with the same vice." The judges noted also that they agreed with *Whiteside v. Southern Bus Lines*, a case that Sarah Keys's lawyers would cite at the ICC. In *Ebony* magazine, Langston Hughes made this comment on William Chance's court case: "The victory is not his alone. It is democracy." That statement was quoted in a 2003 *Baltimore Sun* obituary for his son, Edward Chance, who, inspired by his father, had become a civil rights activist and led a CORE protest in Baltimore in 1963 that ended segregation at an amusement park, which desegregated on the same day as the March on Washington for Jobs and Freedom.[26]

Reverend A. L. Davis, Dr. William R. Adams, A. P. Tureaud Sr., and **Judge J. Skelly Wright:** After the US Supreme Court in *Browder v. Gayle* declared Montgomery's bus segregation laws to be unconstitutional, Reverend Dr. Martin Luther King Jr. came to New Orleans in February 1957, where he founded and became president of the Southern Christian Leadership Conference (SCLC). Its vice president was a local Black pastor, Reverend A. L. (Abraham Lincoln) Davis, who with a local physician, Dr. William R. Adams, filed a lawsuit that year against Mayor deLesseps Morrison and other white New Orleans officials over the constitutionality of laws segregating the city's streetcars and buses. Arguing in support of Reverend Davis and Dr. Adams in court was the city's main NAACP lawyer, A. P. Tureaud Sr., who had been steadily filing lawsuits to chip away at Jim Crow. In this new case, called *Morrison v. Davis*, this Black Louisiana lawyer based his arguments on the *Browder* precedent, winning in a local court and again on appeal at the US Fifth Circuit Court of Appeals. Then, Judge J. Skelly Wright, a white opponent of segregation, issued a strong order on May 31, 1958, that declared Louisiana bus and streetcar segregation laws to be unconstitutional. The city promptly ended bus and streetcar segregation. In 1960, in response to another case filed by Tureaud, Judge Wright issued an order for New Orleans public schools to finally begin complying with the *Brown v. Board of Education* decision.[27]

Freedom Riders: The role of the Freedom Rides in ending transportation segregation is described briefly in chapter 11. The following sources (also listed in the bibliography) provide more information on the Freedom Rides and include vignettes about some of the Freedom Rider protestors: Raymond Arsenault, *Freedom Riders: 1961 and the Struggle for Racial*

Justice; Andrew Yawn, "Seven Women Who Helped Change the Nation Through Freedom Rides"; and "Meet the Players: Freedom Riders," *American Experience*, PBS.[28]

Transportation Heroes Resources

Books and articles in the bibliography by these authors provide additional examples of other heroes in the battle against transportation segregation.

Book authors: Raymond Arsenault, Catherine Barnes, Mia Bay, Daniel Biddle, John K. Bollard, Elaine Elinson, Richard Gergel, Glenda Gilmore, Phillip Hoose, Blair LM Kelley, Kate Masur, Keith Weldon Medley, August Meier, Jerry Mikorenda, Dovey Roundtree, Miriam Thaggert, and Jeanne Theoharis.

Article authors: David S. Bogen, Albert S. Broussard, Nina Cardona, Elaine Elinson, Allen Marcus Harter, John H. Hewitt, George Houser, Robin D. G. Kelley, Jeannette Marantos, Kate Masur, August Meier, Christina Melton, Aimee Ortiz, Chanel Stitt, and Barbara Y. Welke.

Timeline

1929 Sarah Louise Keys is born on April 18 in Washington, North Carolina.

1946 *Morgan v. Virginia*, a US Supreme Court decision, says states may not force interstate travelers to obey Jim Crow bus-seating *laws*; the court says nothing about *rules* a bus company makes.

1948 Sarah graduates from high school at Mother of Mercy School in Washington, North Carolina.

1951 On November 24, Sarah enters the US Army's Women's Army Corps (WAC).*

1952 On August 2, Sarah is arrested at a bus station in Roanoke Rapids, North Carolina, for not moving to the back of a bus on a trip that started hours earlier in New Jersey.

* According to SKE Military Women's Memorial registration.

Sarah and her father meet with lawyer Dovey Johnson Roundtree in Washington, DC.

1953 In February, the US District Court for the District of Columbia refuses to hear a lawsuit Sarah's lawyer filed against the bus company that had her arrested; the court says it doesn't have jurisdiction.

On September 1, Sarah's lawyer files a complaint called *Sarah Keys v. Carolina Coach Company* at the Interstate Commerce Commission (ICC).

On November 27, Sarah is honorably discharged from the WAC.*

1954 On May 12, the ICC holds a hearing on the Sarah Keys case; Sarah testifies.

On May 17, the Supreme Court issues its *Brown v. Board of Education* decision ending school segregation.

On September 30, the ICC rules against Sarah Keys.

On October 19, Sarah's lawyer files a document to have the ICC reconsider her case.

1955 On November 7, the ICC rules in favor of *Sarah Keys v. Carolina Coach Company*, ending discrimination in seating on interstate buses; it issues a similar decision on trains.

On November 25, the ICC decision is announced to the public.

On December 1, Rosa Parks is arrested in Montgomery, Alabama.

1958 Sarah Keys marries George Evans; she changes her name to Sarah Keys Evans.

1961 On May 4, the Freedom Rides begin.

On May 29, Attorney General Robert Kennedy urges the ICC to enforce the *Keys* decision.

1997 The Military Women's Memorial opens at the entrance to Arlington National Cemetery.

1998 The Military Women's Memorial displays a plaque about Sarah Keys Evans.

2000 Sarah Keys Evans is featured in the Military Women's Memorial calendar.

2006 Sarah Keys Evans receives a Trailblazer Award from the US Department of Justice.

2010 The Roanoke Rapids Canal Museum puts up a small poster about Sarah Keys Evans.

2016 Washington, North Carolina, celebrates Sarah Keys Evans in an event on the history of the Catholic church there; around that time, a street is named in her honor.

2017 Sarah Keys Evans speaks with students at Newark's Academy for Urban Leadership Charter School in Perth Amboy, New Jersey.

2019 Black educators in Roanoke Rapids win a contest sponsored by the Z. Smith Reynolds Foundation, providing funds to create a monument to honor Sarah Keys Evans.

2020 On August 1, a ceremony in Roanoke Rapids, North Carolina, dedicates a monument honoring Sarah Keys Evans in the city's Martin Luther King Jr. Park.

2022 A historical marker about the Sarah Keys ICC decision is installed in Roanoke Rapids.

2023 Sarah Keys Evans is honored with a celebration at Hampton Ridge Healthcare and Rehabilitation in Toms River, New Jersey, on August 1, 2023, the seventy-first anniversary of the day she boarded a bus in New Jersey that led to her arrest in North Carolina.

2023 On November 16, Sarah Keys Evans dies in New Jersey.

On November 30, after a funeral mass celebrating her life, she was laid to rest with military honors in Brooklyn's Evergreens Cemetery.

Notes

Chapter 1. Leading the Way

1 Sarah Keys Evans (hereafter SKE) interviews with author, January 20–22, 2004; C. A. Barnes, *Journey from Jim Crow*, 87–88, 96–107, 169, 177, 183; Bay, *Traveling Black*, 263–67; Roundtree and McCabe, *Mighty Justice: My Life*, 124–55, 177–79.

2 Fox, "Dovey Johnson Roundtree"; Roundtree and McCabe, *Mighty Justice: My Life*. Efforts to interview Dovey Johnson Roundtree in 2004, at the start of the author's research on Sarah Keys Evans, were unsuccessful; Roundtree's representative said she was very ill and was no longer giving interviews. By the time work began in 2019 on this book, Roundtree had died (in 2018). Her two memoirs, *Justice Older Than the Law* (2009) and *Mighty Justice: My Life* (2019), provide information about her life and her legal defense of Sarah Keys Evans.

3 SKE interview, January 22, 2004.

4 Martin, "Saluting Sheer Bravery."

5 Rice, *Jim Crow, American*; Bay, *Traveling Black*, 26–27; SKE interviews, January 20–22, 2004.

6 The discussion of more attention-getting strategies appears in chapter 11.

Chapter 2. A Glimmer of Hope

1 Evans, "Full Interview for Roanoke Rapids."

2 SKE interview, January 20, 2004; SKE personal document.

3 SKE interview, January 20, 2004.

4 SKE interview, January 20, 2004, and December 20, 2019.

5 C. A. Barnes, *Journey from Jim Crow*, 45–51; Bay, *Traveling Black*, 230–32; Arsenault, *Freedom Riders*, 11–23; Morgan v. Virginia, 328 U.S. 373 (1946).

6 SKE interview, January 20, 2004.

7 Murray, *States' Laws*, xxi–xxvii, 5–19; Lovett et al., *Profiles of African Americans*, 292–93; Bay, *Traveling Black*, 4–5, 170–72; C. A. Barnes, *Journey from Jim Crow*, 16.

8 Morgan v. Virginia, 328 U.S. 373 (1946).

9 Bay, *Traveling Black*, 2, 64; Du Bois, "On Being Black"; Du Bois, "Race Relations," 243; C. A. Barnes, *Journey from Jim Crow*, 18; B. LM Kelley, *Right to Ride*, 6–8; Alridge, "W. E. B. Du Bois in Georgia."

10 U.S. Constitution, art. 1, § 8, cl. 3; "Commerce Clause."

11 C. A. Barnes, *Journey from Jim Crow*, 45–51; Bay, *Traveling Black*, 230–32; Arsenault, *Freedom Riders*, 11–23; "Irene Morgan Kirkaldy (1917–2007)."

12 Morgan v. Virginia, 328 U.S. 373 (1946) at 381, 382, 386.

13 Bay, *Traveling Black*, 250; SKE interview, January 20, 2004.

14 B. LM Kelley, *Right to Ride*, 15–17; Bay, *Traveling Black*, 1, 11–12, 15, 25–32, 63–75, 78; C. A. Barnes, *Journey from Jim Crow*, 15; Luxenberg, "Jim Crow Car"; Rice, *Jim Crow, American.*

15 Blight, *Frederick Douglass*, 109–11.

16 Volk, *Moral Minorities*, 139.

17 Volk, *Moral Minorities*, 132–46; Bay, *Traveling Black*, 28; Archer, *Jim Crow North*, 197–203; Massachusetts Constitution of 1780, pt. 1, art. 1.

18 Bay, *Traveling Black*, 22–23.

19 Volk, *Moral Minorities*, 146–58, 163–66; B. LM Kelley, *Right to Ride*, 17–32; Mikorenda, *America's First Freedom Rider*, 113–40, 171; Hewitt, "Search for Elizabeth Jennings," 387–415.

20 B. LM Kelley, *Right to Ride*, 21; for more on Elizabeth Jennings, see the section about her in the appendix.

21 "Common Law."

22 Volk, *Moral Minorities*, 163–66; B. LM Kelley, *Right to Ride*, 21–32; McBride, "Fourteenth Amendment Idealism"; Biddle and Dubin,

Tasting Freedom, 2–3, 333–54; Elinson, "San Francisco's Own Rosa Parks"; Lowe, "Mary Ellen Pleasant (1814–1904)"; for more on Ellen Anderson, see entry about her in the appendix.

23 C. A. Barnes, *Journey from Jim Crow*, 2–5; Fourteenth Amendment to the U.S. Constitution, § 1; Fifteenth Amendment to the U.S. Constitution, § 1; Du Bois, *Black Reconstruction in America*, 166–81; Foner, *Reconstruction*, 198–216; Bay, *Traveling Black*, 35–36; Blow, "On Juneteenth"; Leloudis and Korstad, *Fragile Democracy*, 8–9; W. C. Harris, "Black Codes."

24 C. A. Barnes, *Journey from Jim Crow*, 2–5; Civil Rights Act of 1866, 14 Stat. 27 (1866); Medley, *We as Freemen*, 78–80; B. LM Kelley, *Right to Ride*, 51–54, 92–93, 142; Meier and Rudwick, *Along the Color Line*, 309–10; for more on William Nicholls, see the appendix entry about him.

25 Reconstruction Act of 1867, 14 Stat. 428 (1867); C. A. Barnes, *Journey from Jim Crow*, 2–3; Bay, *Traveling Black*, 20, 34–40, 49–56; Civil Rights Act of 1875, 18 Stat. 335 (1875); Mitchell et al., *Monumental*, 100–103; Avins, *Reconstruction Amendments' Debates*, 575–76.

26 Bay, *Traveling Black*, 18, 44–49; Welke, "When All the Women," 278, 292–93.

27 Welke, "When All the Women," 281; Masur, *Example for All the Land*, 87–88, 98, 101–2, 106–7; "Kate Brown Story"; Railroad Company v. Brown, 84 U.S. 445 (1873), at 446–53; "Supreme Court of the United States, Justices."

28 Welke, "When All the Women," 278–80; B. LM Kelley, *Right to Ride*, 46–47, 209; "Rare Victory for Texas Woman, 1888"; Robinson v. Memphis & Charleston Railroad Co., 109 U.S. 3 (1883); Houck v. Southern Pacific Railway Co., 38 Fed. 226 (W.D. Tex. 1888); for more on Lola Houck, see the appendix entry about her.

29 Welke, "When All the Women," 300–303; Gray v. Cincinnati Southern Railroad Co., 11 F. 683 (1882).

30 Welke, "When All the Women," 312–13.

31 Bay, *Traveling Black*, 56–60; Welke, "When All the Women," 301, 312.

32 Bay, *Traveling Black*, 79.

33 Bay, *Traveling Black*, 56–60, 78–80; Paschal, *Jim Crow in North Carolina*, 228–38.

34 Bay, *Traveling Black*, 88–97, 233–40; C. A. Barnes, *Journey from Jim Crow*, 1–3, 10, 13–15, 21–28; Kelly, "Rise and Fall"; "Pullman Car Shops."

35 Fourteenth Amendment to the U.S. Constitution, § 1; Lewis, "1873 Colfax Massacre"; Lane, *Day Freedom Died*, 2–6, 244–47, 251–54, 265–66; United States v. Cruikshank, 92 U.S. 542 (1875); Foner, *Reconstruction*, 530–31.

36 Foner, *Reconstruction*, 531.

37 C. A. Barnes, *Journey from Jim Crow*, 6; Foner, *Second Founding*, 150–54; Civil Rights Cases, 109 U.S. 3 (1883); Bay, *Traveling Black*, 49–53.

38 Civil Rights Cases, 109 U.S. 3 (1883) at 26; Bay, *Traveling Black*, 51; "Letter from Frederick Douglass."

39 Interstate Commerce Act, 24 Stat. 379 (1887) § 3.

40 Bay, *Traveling Black*, 53–56; C. A. Barnes, *Journey from Jim Crow*, 6–7; Dempsey, "Rise and Fall"; for more on the creation of the ICC, see chapter 9.

41 Medley, *We as Freemen*, 90–208; Nathan, *Together*, 37–81; C. A. Barnes, *Journey from Jim Crow*, 10; Bay, *Traveling Black*, 59–62; Luxenberg, *Separate*, 465–87.

42 Plessy v. Ferguson, 163 U.S. 537 (1896) at 544, 548, 551.

43 Medley, *We as Freemen*, 90–208; Nathan, *Together*, 37–81; C. A. Barnes, *Journey from Jim Crow*, 10; Bay, *Traveling Black*, 59–62; Luxenberg, *Separate*, 465–87; Plessy v. Ferguson, 163 U.S. 537 (1896) at 559.

44 C. A. Barnes, *Journey from Jim Crow*, 12, 52–53; Bay, *Traveling Black*, 101; Chiles v. Chesapeake & Ohio Railway Co., 218 U.S. 71 (1910).

45 Chiles v. Chesapeake & Ohio Railway Co., 218 U.S. 71 (1910) at 77.

46 B. LM Kelley, *Right to Ride*, 1–6; C. A. Barnes, *Journey from Jim Crow*, 11; Bay, *Traveling Black*, 155–58; Meier and Rudwick, "Boycott Movement Against Jim Crow"; Meier and Rudwick, "Negro Boycotts of Segregated Streetcars"; "Richmond Streetcar Boycott, 1904."

47 B. LM Kelley, *Right to Ride*, 124.

48 B. LM Kelley, *Right to Ride*, 121.

49 B. LM Kelley, *Right to Ride*, 118–63, 165–200.

50 Bay, *Traveling Black*, 155–58.

51 B. LM Kelley, *Right to Ride*, 158–59; Bay, *Traveling Black*, 151–52; Cardona, "50 Years Before Rosa Parks."

52 Terry, "When Cars Ran On Rails"; Bay, *Traveling Black*, 60, 156.

53 B. LM Kelley, *Right to Ride*, 198–200.

54 Bay, *Traveling Black*, 151–53, 158–61; Ford, "1920s Black-Owned Safe Bus"; "Safe Bus Company."

55 Ford, "1920s Black-Owned Safe Bus."

56 Bay, *Traveling Black*, 161–64; S. Smith, "One Hundred Years of Greyhound"; Walsh, "Tracing the Hound."

57 Bay, *Traveling Black*, 164–65; Gholson, "Constitutional Law"; "Citizens Fight Bus Boycott"; "N.C. Buses Must Carry Colored."

58 "N.C. Buses Must Carry Colored"; Gholson, "Constitutional Law."

59 Bay, *Traveling Black*, 164–65; Gholson, "Constitutional Law"; "Citizens Fight Bus Boycott"; "N.C. Buses Must Carry Colored"; Murray, *States' Laws*, 345.

60 Bay, *Traveling Black*, 165–66.

61 Bay, *Traveling Black*, 166.

62 Bay, *Traveling Black*, 166–77.

63 Bay, *Traveling Black*, 177.

64 Bay, *Traveling Black*, 177–79; Murray, "Excerpt from Oral History Interview"; Schulz, "Many Lives of Pauli Murray"; Gilmore, *Defying Dixie*, 315–29.

65 C. A. Barnes, *Journey from Jim Crow*, 5–7, 41–42; Bay, *Traveling Black*, 41–43; Medley, *We as Freemen*, 90; Beermann, *Journey to Separate but Equal*; Hall v. DeCuir, 95 U.S. 485 (1877); for more on Josephine DeCuir, see the entry about her in the appendix.

66 "Charles Evans Hughes Court (1930–1941)"; Frank, "United States Supreme Court"; "Landmark: *Smith v. Allwright*"; Smith v. Allwright, 321 U.S. 649 (1944); Mitchell v. United States, 313 U.S. 80 (1941).

Chapter 3. Test Rides

1 Arsenault, *Freedom Riders*, 22–55; C. A. Barnes, *Journey from Jim Crow*, 58–60; Bay, *Traveling Black*, 232, 253–57; Meier and Rudwick, *CORE*, 33–39; Crow et al., *History of African Americans*, 196–97; Hill, "Journey of Reconciliation"; Houser and Rustin, "We Challenged Jim Crow!," 1–15.

2 C. A. Barnes, *Journey from Jim Crow*, 37–40, 62; Bay, *Traveling Black*, 188–91; Harter, "Isaac Woodard"; Gergel, *Unexampled Courage*, 12–25, 31–34, 73–83, 114–32, 150–62; Price, "Documenting the History."

3 Arsenault, *Freedom Riders*, 22–55; C. A. Barnes, *Journey from Jim Crow*, 58–60; Bay, *Traveling Black*, 232, 253–57; Meier and Rudwick, *CORE*, 1–14, 33–39; Hill, "Journey of Reconciliation"; Houser and Rustin, "We Challenged Jim Crow!," 1–15.

4 Arsenault, *Freedom Riders*, 40–55; Houser and Rustin, "We Challenged Jim Crow!," 1–15.

5 Houser and Rustin, "We Challenged Jim Crow!," 3, 6, 10.

6 Arsenault, *Freedom Riders*, 44–48; Houser and Rustin, "We Challenged Jim Crow!," 5–6.

7 Houser and Rustin, "We Challenged Jim Crow!," 10.

8 Arsenault, *Freedom Riders*, 51–54; Houser and Rustin, "We Challenged Jim Crow!," 10–15; T. Branch, *Parting the Waters*, 846–87; Leland, "1963 March on Washington."

9 Houser and Rustin, "We Challenged Jim Crow!," 13.

10 Arsenault, *Freedom Riders*, 52.

11 Arsenault, *Freedom Riders*, 20–22; C. A. Barnes, *Journey from Jim Crow*, 51–53, 63; Bay, *Traveling Black*, 232, 250–53.

12 Shelley v. Kraemer, 334 U.S. 1 (1948); "Segregation by Design"; Silva, "Racial Restrictive Covenants."

13 C. A. Barnes, *Journey from Jim Crow*, 50.

14 Email from Cornelia Hargrave, January 26, 2021, that her father David Keys told the family he was born on September 22, 1896, although his draft card lists his birth year as 1897; Murray, *States' Laws*, 569–70; Executive Order No. 9808, 11 F.R. 14153 (1946); Gergel, *Unexampled Courage*, 72–75, 283n15.

15 Murray, *States' Laws*, 571–86; Executive Order No. 9981, 13 F.R. 4313 (1948); SKE personal document.

16 SKE interview, January 20, 2004.

17 SKE interview, January 20, 2004; T. A. Bell, "Quietly Defiant."

18 SKE interview, April 14, 2021, and December 20, 2019; Keys-Evans, "Sarah Keys-Evans," 16.

19 SKE interview, January 20, 2004; Keys-Evans, "Sarah Keys-Evans," 12.

20 SKE interview, January 20, 2004.

Chapter 4. Heading Home

1 SKE interview, January 20, 2004.

2 Evans, "Full Interview for Roanoke Rapids."

3 SKE interviews, January 20 and 21, 2004, February 11, 2019; T. A. Bell, "Quietly Defiant"; Evans, "Interview of Sarah Keys Evans"; Keys-Evans, "Sarah Keys-Evans"; "Black History Month: Local Hero"; "Black History Month Presentation"; Price, "New Focus"; Evans, "Full Interview for Roanoke Rapids."

4 A slightly different account of Sarah's arrest appears in the 2009 memoir of her future lawyer, Dovey Johnson Roundtree (McCabe and Roundtree, *Justice Older Than the Law*, 124–27). That account suggests the arresting officers and bus driver treated Sarah roughly and rudely, whereas Sarah recalled that the arrest, while terrifying, proceeded calmly, with no disturbance or rude words, leading to her not realizing the danger she faced until she was in a patrol car. Roundtree had experienced mistreatment on a bus in 1943 that was different than Sarah's mistreatment (65–66); perhaps Roundtree conflated the two incidents in writing her memoir more

than sixty-five years later. Sarah, after receiving a copy of Roundtree's memoir in 2009, said she was not pleased with some parts of it. The account in this chapter is how Sarah Keys Evans consistently described it in many settings over many years.

5 SKE interview, January 20, 2004.

6 T. A. Bell, "Quietly Defiant."

7 SKE interview, January 20, 2004.

8 Evans, "Full Interview for Roanoke Rapids."

9 "Black History Month Presentation."

10 SKE interview, January 20, 2004.

11 Evans, "Full Interview for Roanoke Rapids."

12 SKE interview, January 20, 2004.

13 "Black History Month Presentation."

14 "Black History Month: Local Hero"; T. A. Bell, "Quietly Defiant."

15 "Black History Month Presentation."

16 SKE interview, January 20, 2004.

17 "Keeping Your Seat."

18 SKE interviews, January 20 and 21, 2004.

19 Evans, "Full Interview for Roanoke Rapids."

20 SKE interview, January 20, 2004.

21 Evans, "Full Interview for Roanoke Rapids"; SKE interview, January 20, 2004.

22 SKE interview, January 20, 2004.

23 Evans, "Full Interview for Roanoke Rapids."

24 SKE interview, January 20, 2004.

25 Evans, "Full Interview for Roanoke Rapids."

26 "Black History Month Presentation."

27 SKE interviews, January 20 and 21, 2004, and February 11, 2019.

28 Bay, *Traveling Black*, 250–53; C. A. Barnes, *Journey from Jim Crow*, 51–53, 63.

Chapter 5. "The Quietest of Us All"

1 Cornelia Keys Hargrave interview, March 16, 2004; Waxman, "Years Before Rosa Parks."

2 SKE interview, January 20, 2004; Loy and Worthy, *Washington and the Pamlico*, 1–10; "History."

3 SKE interviews, January 20, 2004, January 23, 2019, and February 11, 2019; Joan Dudley interview, August 17, 2020; Cornelia Keys Hargrave, email to author, October 18, 2020.

4 SKE interview, January 20, 2004, and January 23, 2019; Sonya Keys interview, August 12, 2020; Michelle McComb interview, August 11, 2020; Joan Dudley interview, August 17, 2020; Cornelia Keys Hargrave, email to author, October 18, 2020.

5 SKE interviews, January 23, 2019, February 9, 2021, and January 27, 2022; Loy and Worthy, *Washington and the Pamlico*, 129–30; Abrams, "Works Progress Administration (WPA)." For a discussion of the identity of the white woman who helped David Keys Sr. work for the WPA, see chap. 7, n. 3.

6 Leloudis and Korstad, *Fragile Democracy*, 33–36; Abrams, "Works Progress Administration (WPA)."

7 SKE interviews, January 20 and 22, 2004, January 23, 2019, and February 11, 2019; Keys-Evans, "Sarah Keys-Evans," 5.

8 Cornelia Keys Hargrave, email to author, October 18, 2020.

9 SKE interviews, January 20, 2004, and August 20, 2020.

10 SKE interview, February 25, 2019; Keys-Evans, "Sarah Keys-Evans," 10.

11 SKE interviews, January 23, 2019, February 9, 2021, and December 9, 2021.

12 SKE interview, January 20, 2004.

13 Leesa P. Jones, email to author, August 18, 2020; Tabb, "For Some."

14 Leesa P. Jones, email to author, February 19, 2021; SKE interview February 9, 2021; Loy and Worthy, *Washington and the Pamlico*, foreword (n.p.); Joan Dudley interview, August 17, 2020.

15 Milteer, *North Carolina's Free People*, 154, 265–66; Franklin, *Free Negro in North Carolina*, 68, 122–30, 168–69.

16 Loy and Worthy, *Washington and the Pamlico*, 480–81.

17 Crow et al., "Slavery"; Milteer, *North Carolina's Free People*, 16–18, 20–21; Crow et al., *History of African Americans*, 7–11, 51; Franklin, *Free Negro in North Carolina*, 17–18.

18 Crow et al., *History of African Americans*, 1–69; Crow et al., "Slavery"; *Born in Slavery*.

19 Crow et al., *History of African Americans*, 1–30, 48–69; Jones, *Bright Ma*, 5; Loy and Worthy, *Washington and the Pamlico*, 8–14; "History"; Crow et al., "Slavery"; Anderson, *Education of Blacks*, 16–17; A Bill to Prevent All Persons from Teaching Slaves.

20 SKE interview, February 9, 2021.

21 Franklin, *Free Negro in North Carolina*, 166–68; A Bill to Prevent All Persons from Teaching Slaves; Crow et al., *History of African Americans*, 1–30, 48–69; Leesa P. Jones, email to author, August 18, 2020; Cutler, "Washington Museum Documents"; Crow et al., "Slavery"; Simpson, "Great Dismal Swamp"; Gilmore, *Gender and Jim Crow*, 7; Tabb, "For Some."

22 Loy and Worthy, *Washington and the Pamlico*, 478; Milteer, *North Carolina's Free People*, 27–52, 154–57; Crow et al., *History of African Americans*, 36, 48–69; Franklin, *Free Negro in North Carolina*, 23–30, 43, 48–57, 102; Manumission Society of North Carolina, *Address to the People*; *Official Inflation Data*; North Carolina General Assembly, *"Slaves and Free Persons"*; *"Thomas Day Website Timeline."*

23 Franklin, *Free Negro in North Carolina*, 5, 12–13, 43, 63–84, 105–6, 120, 160–61; Milteer, *North Carolina's Free People*, 12–14, 64–84, 107–130, 154; Crow et al., *History of African Americans*, 48–51; D. Rasmussen, *American Uprising*; Du Bois, *Souls of Black Folk*, 37–38.

24 Loy and Worthy, *Washington and the Pamlico*, 480–1; Franklin, *Free Negro in North Carolina*, 17–18, 133–50, 197–98; Milteer, *North Carolina's Free People*, 172–84, 187, 317; Midgett, "Pamlico River's Past: Hull Anderson."

25 Williard, "North Carolina in the Civil War."

26 Williard, "North Carolina in the Civil War"; Cecelski, *Fire of Freedom*, 58–65; Reid, *Freedom for Themselves*, 1–2, 8–12; "New Bern"; Crow et al., *History of African Americans*, 73; Coffey, "African Americans Defend Washington, N.C."; "African Americans Defend Washington"; P. Branch, "Washington N.C., Siege of"; Mariner, "African Americans Defend Washington"; Loy and Worthy, *Washington and the Pamlico*, 24–25, 37–42.

27 Cecelski, *Fire of Freedom*, 58–62, 65; Gilmore, *Gender and Jim Crow*, 6.

28 Cecelski, *Fire of Freedom*, 62–67, 72–77; Milteer, *North Carolina's Free People*, 328–33; Reid, *Freedom for Themselves*, 13–17, 30; Emancipation Proclamation (January 1, 1863); "African Americans Defend Washington."

29 Cecelski, *Fire of Freedom*, v–xvii, 61–4, 72–98; Reid, *Freedom for Themselves*, 15–17, 23–35, 41–49, 52–58, 73, 75–78; Miller, "This Month in New Bern"; "Prisoner Exchanges Halted"; "Black Soldiers in the U.S."; Bryant, *36th Infantry*, Kindle ed. Loc. 1054–55.

30 Reid, *Freedom for Themselves*, 155–60; Blair, "Plymouth, Battle of"; Cecelski, "'As Long as a Star'"; Jordan and Thomas, "Massacre at Plymouth"; "Ram Albemarle"; "Siege and Burning of Washington"; Midgett, "Burning of Washington"; Loy and Worthy, *Washington and the Pamlico*, 41–45; Thomas, "Former Slaves Turned Soldiers."

31 Bryant, *36th Infantry*, Kindle ed. loc. 3562–69; Reid, *Freedom for Themselves*, 308; Sonya Keys interview, August 12, 2020.

32 Cecelski, *Fire of Freedom*, 84.

33 SKE interview, March 16, 2021.

34 SKE interview, January 20, 2004; Crow et al., *History of African Americans*, 89.

Chapter 6. Education Backstory: North Carolina

1 Anderson, *Education of Blacks*, 4–25; Milteer, *Beyond Slavery's Shadow*, 204–5; Crow et al., *History of African Americans*, 81–83; Umfleet, *Day of Blood*, 3–4, 7, 9–10, 174, 195, vn. 33; Reaves, *Strength through Struggle*, 460–61; R. S. Alexander, "Freedmen's Bureau"; Sandifer and Renfer, "Schools for Freed Peoples"; Du Bois, *Black Reconstruction in America*, 637–50; Du Bois, *Souls of Black Folk*, 12–32.

2 Anderson, *Education of Blacks*, 15.

3 Crow et al., *History of African Americans*, 77–81; Cecelski, *Fire of Freedom*, 115–18, 160–89, 195; Leloudis and Korstad, *Fragile Democracy*, 8–9; Zucchino, *Wilmington's Lie*, 34–36; Anderson, *Education of Blacks*, 24–25.

4 Leloudis and Korstad, *Fragile Democracy*, 9–10; Crow et al., *History of African Americans*, 83–85; Umfleet, *Day of Blood*, 8–11; Zucchino, *Wilmington's Lie*, 38–40; Paschal, *Jim Crow in North Carolina*, 63–64; Colomb et al., "Public Education: Part 3"; Constitution of North Carolina of 1868.

5 Du Bois, *Black Reconstruction in America*, 638; Anderson, *Education of Blacks*, 6, 19.

6 Crow et al., *History of African Americans*, 84–88; Umfleet, *Day of Blood*, 11; Raper, "Holden, William Woods "; Elmore, "Hyman, John Adams"; "Reconstruction in North Carolina."

7 Anderson, *Education of Blacks*, 27–31; Colomb et al., "Public Education: Part 3"; Gilmore, *Gender and Jim Crow*, 10–14, 21, 33–34, 39–41; Crow et al., *History of African Americans*, 156–57.

8 Gilmore, *Gender and Jim Crow*, 1, 4, 7–22, 33, 101; Colomb et al., "Public Education: Part 3"; Paschal, *Jim Crow in North Carolina*, 135; Leloudis, *Schooling the New South*, 20–28, 107.

9 Gilmore, *Gender and Jim Crow*, 11, 12, 14, 21, 39–40, 45; "'What Are We Fighting For?'"; Michals, "Mary McLeod Bethune"; Crow et al., *History of African Americans*, 102, 127, 137, 155, 187, 200; Matthews, "What Is an HBCU?"

10 Gilmore, *Gender and Jim Crow*, 28–29; "Sharecropping"; Zipf, "Sharecropping"; Leloudis and Korstad, *Fragile Democracy*, 14–15.

11 Du Bois, *Black Reconstruction in America*, 532–34; Crow et al., *History of African Americans*, 88–91; Paschal, *Jim Crow in North Carolina*, 65–67; Leloudis and Korstad, *Fragile Democracy*, 11–12.

12 Du Bois, *Black Reconstruction in America*, 532.

13 Du Bois, *Black Reconstruction in America*, 532–34; Crow et al., *History of African Americans*, 89–92; Leloudis and Korstad, *Fragile Democracy*, 11–12; Paschal, *Jim Crow in North Carolina*, 65–67.

14 Crow et al., *History of African Americans*, 91.

15 Du Bois, *Black Reconstruction in America*, 532–36; Crow et al., *History of African Americans*, 91–94; Leloudis and Korstad, *Fragile Democracy*, 12–13; Paschal, *Jim Crow in North Carolina*, 67–74, 206, 214, 216.

16 See chap. 2, nn. 34–45.

17 Hunt, "Fusion of Republicans and Populists"; Crow et al., *History of African Americans*, 112–14; Leloudis and Korstad, *Fragile Democracy*, 14–19; Paschal, *Jim Crow in North Carolina*, 76–78; Zucchino, *Wilmington's Lie*, 67–68; Umfleet, *Day of Blood*, 21–34.

18 Crow et al., *History of African Americans*, 114–17; Leloudis and Korstad, *Fragile Democracy*, 19–22; Paschal, *Jim Crow in North Carolina*, 78–93; Umfleet, *Day of Blood*, 34–60; Zucchino, *Wilmington's Lie*, 65–76; Wormser, "Wilmington Riot (1898)."

19 Umfleet, *Day of Blood*, 37; Zucchino, *Wilmington's Lie*, 75.

20 Crow et al., *History of African Americans*, 114–17; Leloudis and Korstad, *Fragile Democracy*, 19–22; Paschal, *Jim Crow in North Carolina*, 78–93; Umfleet, *Day of Blood*, 34–60; Zucchino, *Wilmington's Lie*, 65–76.

21 Wormser, "Wilmington Riot (1898)."

22 Paschal, *Jim Crow in North Carolina*, 91–97; Zucchino, *Wilmington's Lie*, 46–51, 83–272; Leloudis and Korstad, *Fragile Democracy*, 20–22; Umfleet, *Day of Blood*, 21–128, 136–39; "Wilmington Coup"; Davis, "Wilmington Massacre November 1898."

23 Umfleet, *Day of Blood*, 49; Zucchino, *Wilmington's Lie*, 147.

24 Zucchino, *Wilmington's Lie*, 220–72; Umfleet, *Day of Blood*, 102–28.

25 Umfleet, *Day of Blood*, 125.

26 Paschal, *Jim Crow in North Carolina*, 204, 206, 210, 228, 230, 232, 234.

27 Paschal, *Jim Crow in North Carolina*, 236–37.

28 Paschal, *Jim Crow in North Carolina*, 104–7, 114–16, 118–20, 125–245; Murray, *States' Laws*, 329–48; Leloudis and Korstad, *Fragile Democracy*, 27–31; Cecelski, "Convict Labor Camp"; Spurr, "Prison Camps"; Mancini, "Convict Labor"; T. A. Bell, "Quietly Defiant"; Nathan, *Together*, 70–73; "Black Farmers FAQ"; Loy and Worthy, *Washington*

and the Pamlico, 363; SKE interview, February 9, 2021; Keys-Evans, "Sarah Keys-Evans," 15.

29 Crow et al., *History of African Americans*, 116–19; Gilmore, *Gender and Jim Crow*, 119–22; Hunt, "Disfranchisement"; Leloudis and Korstad, *Fragile Democracy*, 22–26; Paschal, *Jim Crow in North Carolina*, 97–101; Zucchino, *Wilmington's Lie*, 301–17; Baldino and Kreider, *Of the People*, 181, 194; Greenblatt, "Racial History"; Nathan, *Together*, 80; Jacobs, "Take the Intentionally Confusing Reading Test."

30 Zucchino, *Wilmington's Lie*, 314–17; Hunt, "Disfranchisement."

31 Zucchino, *Wilmington's Lie*, 317.

32 Zucchino, *Wilmington's Lie*, 313.

33 Paschal, *Jim Crow in North Carolina*, 149–56 (quotation on p. 156).

34 Connor and Poe, *Life and Speeches*, 162.

35 Greenblatt, "Racial History."

36 Fields and Fields, *Racecraft*, 154–59.

37 Fields and Fields, *Racecraft*, 155.

38 Connor and Poe, *Life and Speeches*, 163.

39 Leloudis and Korstad, *Fragile Democracy*, 29; Paschal, *Jim Crow in North Carolina*, 140–45; Colomb et al., "Public Education: Part 4."

40 Anderson, *Education of Blacks*, 33, 73–78, 102–6; Gilmore, *Gender and Jim Crow*, 25–26; "Booker T. Washington and the 'Atlanta Compromise'"; Brooks, "Booker T. Washington"; Crow et al., *History of African Americans*, 123, 159.

41 "Booker T. Washington Delivers."

42 Anderson, *Education of Blacks*, 20–29, 31–72; Brooks, "Booker T. Washington"; Engs, "Samuel Chapman Armstrong."

43 Anderson, *Education of Blacks*, 39.

44 Anderson, *Education of Blacks*, 39.

45 Anderson, *Education of Blacks*, 31–78, 102.

46 Anderson, *Education of Blacks*, 59.

47 Anderson, *Education of Blacks*, 31–78, 102.

48 Anderson, *Education of Blacks*, 73–75.

49 Washington, "Address Before the National Education Association."

50 Anderson, *Education of Blacks*, 60–69, 17–31, 102, 108–9; Gilmore, *Gender and Jim Crow*, 25–26.

51 Gilmore, *Gender and Jim Crow*, 11–12, 26, 242.

52 Anderson, *Education of Blacks*, 103–9; Du Bois, *Souls of Black Folk*, 33–46, 64–67.

53 Anderson, *Education of Blacks*, 105.

54 Anderson, *Education of Blacks*, 20–25, 81, 95–98.

55 Anderson, *Education of Blacks*, 96; Paschal, *Jim Crow in North Carolina*, 129.

56 Anderson, *Education of Blacks*, 79–185.

57 Anderson, *Education of Blacks*, 89.

58 Anderson, *Education of Blacks*, 79–89.

59 Anderson, *Education of Blacks*, 82.

60 Gilmore, *Gender and Jim Crow*, 138–42.

61 Du Bois, *Negro Artisan*; Gilmore, *Gender and Jim Crow*, 140.

62 Anderson, *Education of Blacks*, 137–237; Leloudis, *Schooling the New South*, 183–229; "Nathan Newbold."

63 Leloudis, *Schooling the New South*, 185.

64 Paschal, *Jim Crow in North Carolina*, 130.

65 Anderson, *Education of Blacks*, 137–41, 152–53; Leloudis, *Schooling the New South*, 182–91; "Jeanes Teachers."

66 Leloudis, *Schooling the New South*, 188.

67 Leloudis, *Schooling the New South*, 185–92.

68 Anderson, *Education of Blacks*, 156–79, 183; Leloudis, *Schooling the New South*, 213–29; Medlin and Putt, "Rosenwald Schools in North Carolina"; Spangler, "Rosenwald Schools"; "Robert R. Taylor"; Feiler, *Better Life for Their Children*, 17, 20; Harding, "Historical Account"; Schneider and Johnson, "Rosenwald Schools."

69 Anderson, *Education of Blacks*, 179; Schneider and Johnson, "Rosenwald Schools."

70 Medlin and Putt, "Rosenwald Schools in North Carolina"; Feiler, *Better Life for Their Children*, xiii.

71 Schneider and Johnson, "Rosenwald Schools in North Carolina"; Anderson, *Education of Blacks*, 203–35.

72 Anderson, *Education of Blacks*, 210.

73 Anderson, *Education of Blacks*, 199–231.

74 Crow et al., *History of African Americans*, 135–37, 157–61; Leloudis, *Schooling the New South*, 220–28.

75 Crow et al., *History of African Americans*, 135.

76 Crow et al., *History of African Americans*, 137; "Nathan Newbold."

77 Diploma certificate shared by Sonya Dudley; Alice Sadler, emails to author, January 22–23, 2022; Loy and Worthy, *Washington and the Pamlico*, 265–66; Stewart, *First Class*, 40–44, 84–88, 262.

Chapter 7. "Can Anything Be Done for My People?"

1 SKE interview, February 9, 2021.

2 Loy and Worthy, *Washington and the Pamlico*, 255–58; P. S. Jones Museum website, https://psjonesalumni.com/p-s-jones-museum; Jackson, "P. S. Jones Museum"; Barnes, "P. S. Jones"; David A. Keys Sr. diploma, courtesy of Joan Dudley; Leesa P. Jones, emails to author, August 28–31, 2024; Alice Sadler, interview, August 12, 2024; Alice Sadler, email to author, August 18, 2024.

3 Sarah Keys Evans reported in telephone interviews in 2004 that when she was a child, her father told her a woman in Washington, DC, hosted him there during the early 1900s. Sarah variously described this woman as a family member or daughter of a wealthy white woman in Washington, North Carolina, identified only as "Mrs. Leach." Sarah knew nothing about her but recalled her father saying she helped him get a job with the WPA. Her father told her that as a child he played with this woman's son. During research for this book, queries made to several people knowledgeable about the history of Washington, North Carolina—Leesa Jones, Alice Sadler, a local librarian and newspaper editor—yielded no confirmation of the woman's identity. The book *Washington and the Pamlico* notes a prominent Leach family in the town. Census records show a Julia Cox Leach, the wife of George T. Leach (owner of a lumber mill), with a son, George T. Leach Jr., who was about the same age as Sarah's father, but Julia Leach's daughters were too young (age four, eight, and eleven) to be married and living in DC in 1915 when David Keys moved there. One daughter later created a trust fund that, after her death, endowed a professorship at Duke University. Outreach to people mentioned in a news article on the endowment yielded no results. In a January 2022 phone interview with Julia Cox Leach's grandson, Richard Leach, he said his grandmother was influential and "could pull a lot of strings," but he never heard her talk about helping David Keys and doesn't know of relatives who lived in DC in the early 1900s. She died in 1950; her husband, in 1922. The then Secretary of the Navy, Josephus Daniels, was from North Carolina. Perhaps the husband of David Keys's hostess came to DC to work for the navy, but navy archives do not show such a person. Lee Craig, who wrote a biography of Daniels, emailed that he saw no reference to Keys during his research. Nor is there a mention of a young man like David Keys in a memoir by Daniels's wife.

4 SKE interview, January 23, 2019.

5 SKE interviews, January 23, 2019, August 20, 2020, and February 9, 2021.

6 Stewart, *First Class*, 40–44, 84–88, 262; Tabor, "Dunbar High School."

7 SKE interview, January 23, 2019.

8 Cornelia Keys Hargrave, email to author, October 18, 2020.

9 SKE interview, February 9, 2021; draft record courtesy of Joan Dudley; Carrie Thornhill, phone calls, December 2021.

10 SKE interview, February 9, 2021; "African American Sailors"; Goldenberg, "African-American Troops."

11 "African American Sailors."

12 "African American Sailors"; Aneja and Xu, "Costs of Employment Segregation"; Foy, "How Woodrow Wilson's Racist Policies"; MacLaury, "Federal Government."

13 "African American Sailors"; Zucchino, *Wilmington's Lie*, 69–76, 304–7; Umfleet, *Day of Blood*, 38, 40, 43; Craig, *Josephus Daniels*; Paschal, *Jim Crow in North Carolina*, 79–82. (See also chap. 6, n. 20.)

14 "African American Sailors."

15 SKE interview, December 9, 2021.

16 SKE interviews, September 20, 2020, February 9, 2021, and January 20, 2004; Keys-Evans, "Sarah Keys-Evans," 6.

17 "200 Years in Washington, NC"; Loy and Worthy, *Washington and the Pamlico*, 265–66; SKE interviews, January 20, 2004, and January 27, 2022; Hand, "St. Joseph's"; George, "Legacy of St. Joseph's"; Carbonneau, "Conflicting Images"; Deacon Rick Fisher interview, October 7, 2024, and personal documents.

18 Loy and Worthy, *Washington and the Pamlico*, 265–66.

19 Loy and Worthy, *Washington and the Pamlico*, 257, 265–67; Carbonneau, "Conflicting Images"; Hand, "St. Joseph's"; George, "Legacy of St. Joseph's"; Deacon Rick Fisher interview, October 7, 2024, and personal documents; SKE interview, January 20, 2004; Alice Sadler, emails to author, January 22–23, 2022; Leesa P. Jones, email to author, June 16, 2025; P. S. Jones Museum website, https://psjonesalumni.com/p-s-jones-museum.

20 SKE interviews, January 20, 2004, February 9, 2019, and February 9, 2021; Cornelia Keys Hargrave, email to author, October 18, 2020; Sister Beth Pearson, emails to author, December 20, 2023, and

September 23, 2024; Loy and Worthy, *Washington and the Pamlico*, 265–66; "200 Years in Washington, NC"; Bernard, "Legacy of St. Joseph's"; "Historical Marker B-59"; documents shared by Deacon Rick Fisher; Keenan, "Remembering Mother of Mercy School."

21 Cornelia Keys Hargrave, email to author, September 20, 2024.

22 SKE interview, January 20, 2004; Loy and Worthy, *Washington and the Pamlico*, 265–66; Sister Beth Pearson, emails to author, December 18, 2021, and December 20, 2023; SKE personal documents provided to author; "Mother of Mercy Church to Celebrate"; Keenan, "Remembering Mother of Mercy"; "200 Years in Washington, NC"; Carbonneau, "Conflicting Images."

23 Baptism and confirmation records courtesy of Anai Olivares, Mother of Mercy Church, September 20, 2024; SKE interviews, January 23, 2019, and January 20, 2004.

24 "200 Years in Washington, NC"; Rowe, "Church Spotlights Long Heritage"; "Mother of Mercy Catholic Church to Host Open House"; "History" ; "Historical Marker B-59."

25 SKE interview, December 9, 2021.

26 SKE interviews, February 11, 2019, February 9, 2021, and December 9, 2021; Cornelia Keys Hargrave, interview, February 25, 2023; Harding, "Historical Account."

27 SKE interview, January 23, 2019.

28 SKE interview, January 23, 2019.

29 SKE interview, January 23, 2019.

30 SKE interviews, January 23, 2019, February 9, 2021, and January 20, 2004.

31 Loy and Worthy, *Washington and the Pamlico*, 265–66; "Mother of Mercy Catholic Church to Host Open House."

32 Sister Beth Pearson, email, December 18, 2021; author visit to Mother of Mercy school building, August 11, 2024.

33 Crow et al., *History of African Americans*, 139; J. L. Bell, "Lawrence Augustus Oxley," 98–101, 107, 109.

34 Crow et al., *History of African Americans*, 140, 139.

35 Medlin and Putt, "Rosenwald Schools"; Harding, "Historical Account"; Anderson, *Education of Blacks*, 155.

36 SKE interview, February 9, 2021; note on SKE's photo of the nun; Keys-Evans, "Sarah Keys-Evans," 7.

37 SKE interview, November 24, 2020; "History of Home Economics"; Heggestad, "What Is Home Economics?""

38 SKE interviews, November 24, 2020, and February 9, 2021.

39 SKE interviews, February 9, 2021, and December 9, 2021.

40 SKE interview, January 23, 2019.

41 Anderson, *Education of Blacks*, 203–4; Gilmore, *Gender and Jim Crow*, 177–95, 199–201; Wormser, "Charlotte Hawkins Brown (1870–1924)"; for more on Charlotte Hawkins Brown, see the appendix entry about her.

42 Gilmore, *Gender and Jim Crow*, 184.

43 Leloudis and Korstad, *Fragile Democracy*, 60–63.

44 Leloudis and Korstad, *Fragile Democracy*, 62.

45 Leloudis and Korstad, *Fragile Democracy*, 62–64.

46 SKE interview, February 9, 2021; Cornelia Keys Hargrave interview, March 16, 2004.

47 Cornelia Keys Hargrave interview, March 16, 2004.

48 Leloudis and Korstad, *Fragile Democracy*, 49–52.

49 SKE interviews, February 11, 2019, and January 20, 2004.

50 SKE interviews, January 22, 2004, and February 11, 2019.

51 SKE interview, January 20, 2004.

52 SKE interview, January 22, 2004.

53 SKE interview, January 20, 2004.

54 T. A. Bell, "Quietly Defiant."

55 Evans, "Full Interview for Roanoke Rapids."

56 SKE interviews, January 20 and 22, 2004; Keys-Evans, "Sarah Keys-Evans," 23–24.

57 T. A. Bell, "Quietly Defiant."

58 SKE interview, January 20, 2004.

59 SKE interview, December 20, 2019.

60 Crow et al., *History of African Americans*, 132–34; Tippett, "Majority of NC-Born Adults."

61 SKE interview, January 20, 2004; Keys-Evans, "Sarah Keys-Evans," 4, 6, 9.

62 Evans, "Full Interview for Roanoke Rapids"; SKE interviews, January 20, 2024, and October 5, 2018.

63 SKE interview, January 20, 2004; Keys-Evans, "Sarah Keys-Evans," 9–11; Evans, "Full Interview for Roanoke Rapids."

64 SKE interview, January 20, 2004.

65 SKE personal documents given to the author.

Chapter 8. A Plan of Attack

1 SKE interview, January 21, 2004; Keys-Evans, "Sarah Keys-Evans," 22.

2 Evans, "Full Interview for Roanoke Rapids."

3 SKE interview, January 21, 2004; "Black History Month Presentation."

4 Evans, "Full Interview for Roanoke Rapids"; Keys-Evans, "Sarah Keys-Evans," 22–23.

5 SKE interview, January 20 and 21, 2004; Keys-Evans, "Sarah Keys-Evans," 23.

6 Leloudis and Korstad, *Fragile Democracy*, 34–36, 49–55; Gershenhorn, "Courageous Voice," 76–85.

7 SKE interviews, January 20–22, 2004.

8 Evans, "Full Interview for Roanoke Rapids."

9 T. A. Bell, "Quietly Defiant."

10 SKE interview, January 22, 2004.

11 Cornelia Keys Hargrave interview, March 16, 2004.

12 SKE interviews, January 20 and 21, 2004; Evans, "Full Interview for Roanoke Rapids."

13 SKE interviews, January 21 and 22, 2004.

14 Bay, *Traveling Black*, 249, 253.

15 SKE interviews, January 21 and 22, 2004; Keys-Evans, "Sarah Keys-Evans," 26.

16 SKE interview, January 22, 2004; Roundtree and McCabe, *Mighty Justice: My Life*, 95–111, 124–25.

17 SKE interview, January 21, 2004.

18 Fox, "Dovey Johnson Roundtree"; SKE interview, January 21, 2004.

19 Roundtree and McCabe, *Mighty Justice: My Life*, 64–67, 125–26; Fox, "Dovey Johnson Roundtree"; "Army Women"; "'What Are We Fighting For?'"; Michals, "Mary McLeod Bethune."

20 SKE interview, January 21, 2004.

21 SKE interview, January 21, 2004; Keys-Evans, "Sarah Keys-Evans," 33.

22 SKE interview, January 21, 2004.

23 Roundtree and McCabe, *Mighty Justice: My Life*, 127.

24 C. A. Barnes, *Journey from Jim Crow*, 52–53; Bay, *Traveling Black*, 250–52.

25 SKE interview, January 21, 2004.

Chapter 9. Finding a Strategy

1 SKE interviews, January 21 and 22, 2004, and December 9, 2021.

2 Evans, "Full Interview for Roanoke Rapids."

3 Roundtree and McCabe, *Mighty Justice: My Life*, 130–31; SKE interview, January 21, 2004.

4 B. LM Kelley, *Right to Ride*, 17–32; Volk, *Moral Minorities*, 147–58, 163–66; McBride, "Fourteenth Amendment Idealism."

5 Roundtree and McCabe, *Mighty Justice: My Life*, 130–38, 240–41.

6 U.S. Constitution, art. 1, § 8, cl. 3; "Commerce Clause"; Bay, *Traveling Black*, 53–56; C. A. Barnes, *Journey from Jim Crow*, 6–7, 87; Interstate Commerce Act, 24 Stat. 379 (1887).

7 Interstate Commerce Act, 24 Stat. 379 (1887) § 3.

8 Roundtree and McCabe, *Mighty Justice: My Life*, 110–11, 127–43; B. LM Kelley, *Right to Ride*, 38–42; C. A. Barnes, *Journey from Jim Crow*, 13–14, 19–34, 66–80; Bay, *Traveling Black*, 233–40, 257–60; Blue, "William Hooper Councill"; Bishop, "Plessy v. Ferguson," 130–31; Welke, "When All the Women," 284, 303; Mitchell v. United States, 313 U.S. 80 (1941); Henderson v. US, 339 U.S. 816 (1950).

9 Roundtree and McCabe, *Mighty Justice: My Life*, 132–37, 140–41.

10 Roundtree and McCabe, *Mighty Justice: My Life*, 142–43; C. A. Barnes, *Journey from Jim Crow*, 87–88, 96–107; Bay, *Traveling Black*, 263–64; SKE interview, January 21, 2004.

11 SKE interview, January 21, 2004.

12 Roundtree and McCabe, *Mighty Justice: My Life*, 91–92; SKE interviews, January 21, 2004, and February 25, 2019.

13 Roundtree and McCabe, *Mighty Justice: My Life*, 143; SKE interview, January 22, 2004.

14 SKE interviews, January 21 and 22, 2004, and December 9, 2021.

15 SKE interviews, January 21 and 22, 2004, and February 14, 2018.

16 T. A. Bell, "Quietly Defiant."

17 Roundtree and McCabe, *Mighty Justice: My Life*, 143.

18 SKE interview, January 22, 2004.

19 C. A. Barnes, *Journey from Jim Crow*, 92–94; Roundtree and McCabe, *Mighty Justice: My Life*, 144–47; Nathan, *Together*, 85–88; Clark and Clark, "Racial Identification and Preference"; "Revealing Experiment"; Brown v. Board of Education, 347 U.S. 483 (1954) at 492–95.

20 Roundtree and McCabe, *Mighty Justice: My Life*, 145–47.

21 Roundtree and McCabe, *Mighty Justice: My Life*, 147–48.

22 Roundtree and McCabe, *Mighty Justice: My Life*, 148–49.

23 Roundtree and McCabe, *Mighty Justice: My Life*, 149; SKE interview, January 21, 2004.

Chapter 10. Never Give Up

1 Roundtree and McCabe, *Mighty Justice*, 147–50; Bay, *Traveling Black*, 264; C. A. Barnes, *Journey from Jim Crow*, 96; "Isadore I. Freidson"; Brown v. Board of Education, 347 U.S. 483 (1954) at 492–95; "Seek Ouster of Official."

2 Roundtree and McCabe, *Mighty Justice: My Life*, 150–52; Bay, *Traveling Black*, 264; C. A. Barnes, *Journey from Jim Crow*, 64–65, 87–88, 96–107; Henderson v. United States, 339 U.S. 816 (1950); Mitchell v. United States, 313 U.S. 80 (1941); Whiteside v. Southern Bus Lines, 177 F.2d 949 (1949); Hirabayashi v. United States, 320 U.S. 81 (1943) at 100.

3 Roundtree and McCabe, *Mighty Justice: My Life*, 150–52.

4 Brown v. Board of Education, 347 U.S. 483 (1954) at 494; Roundtree and McCabe, *Mighty Justice: My Life*, 151–52.

5 C. A. Barnes, *Journey from Jim Crow*, 91, 96–107; National Association for the Advancement of Colored People v. St. Louis–San Francisco Railway Co. (1955). See chap. 2, n. 43 for sources referencing the *Plessy* case.

6 C. A. Barnes, *Journey from Jim Crow*, 98; Plessy v. Ferguson, 163 U.S. 537 (1896) at 559.

7 Luxenberg, *Separate*, 483–84.

8 Plessy v. Ferguson, 163 U.S. 537 (1896) at 559.

9 SKE interview, January 21, 2004; Roundtree and McCabe, *Mighty Justice: My Life*, 152–54; C. A. Barnes, *Journey from Jim Crow*, 98–100.

10 Sarah Keys v. Carolina Coach Company, 64 M.C.C. 769 (1955) at 769. When the Interstate Commerce Commission (ICC) was dissolved in 1995, many texts of its cases (including the *Keys* decision) were preserved by the Library of Congress, making them available to the Hathi Trust; other documents related to the *Keys* case (and others) were shredded. Access to the texts of ICC decisions is now via an official Hathi Trust link for each case, including *Keys* and an NAACP case, *National Association for the Advancement of Colored People v. St. Louis–San Francisco Railway Company* (1955) (Roundtree, and McCabe, *Mighty Justice: Untold Story*, 180). See page 238 for the Keys and NAACP cases' Hathi links.

11 C. A. Barnes, *Journey from Jim Crow*, 98–99; Roundtree and McCabe, *Mighty Justice: My Life*, 152–53; Sarah Keys v. Carolina Coach Company, 64 M.C.C. 769 (1955) at 772.

12 Sarah Keys v. Carolina Coach Company, 64 M.C.C. 769 (1955) at 772.

13 C. A. Barnes, *Journey from Jim Crow*, 99–100.

14 SKE interview, January 21, 2004.

15 Brown v. Board of Education, 347 U.S. 483 (1954) at 494; SKE personal document.

16 SKE interview, January 21, 2004.

17 T. A. Bell, "Quietly Defiant."

18 Huston, "I.C.C. Orders End of Segregation."

19 Roundtree and McCabe, *Mighty Justice: My Life*, 154; Lerner, "We Ride Together"; SKE personal document.

20 C. A. Barnes, *Journey from Jim Crow*, 101.

21 "Great Thing, Says Victor"; SKE personal document.

22 "Winner Acclaims Decision by I.C.C."; SKE personal document.

23 SKE interview, September 20, 2020.

24 SKE interview, September 20, 2020.

25 SKE interview, January 22, 2004.

26 "Ruling 'Means Nothing'"; "Louisiana Bars Change"; C. A. Barnes, *Journey from Jim Crow*, 101.

27 C. A. Barnes, *Journey from Jim Crow*, 102–7.

28 Roundtree and McCabe, *Mighty Justice: My Life*, 154–55; Huston, "I.C.C. Orders End of Segregation."

29 Huston, "I.C.C. Orders End of Segregation."

30 Roundtree and McCabe, *Mighty Justice: My Life*, 154–55.

31 SKE interview, January 22, 2004.

32 Leloudis and Korstad, *Fragile Democracy*, 64; Crow et al., *History of African Americans*, 165–76; Frankenberg and Taylor, "ESEA"; "Southern Manifesto and 'Massive Resistance.'"

33 Loy and Worthy, *Washington and the Pamlico*, 267; Crow et al., *History of African Americans*, 165; "200 Years in Washington, NC"; Keenan, "Remembering Mother of Mercy School"; "Historical Marker B-59"; P. S. Jones African-American Education Museum, https://psjonesalumni.com/p-s-jones-museum.

34 Strauss, "New Story"; Vaden, "Case for Forced School Merger"; Himmel, "NAACP Blasts Segregation"; United States v. Halifax County Board of Education, 314 F. Supp. 65 (E.D.N.C. 1970).

35 Roundtree and McCabe, *Mighty Justice: My Life*, 177–78.

36 C. A. Barnes, *Journey from Jim Crow*, 108.

Chapter 11. Winning a Wider Victory

1 C. A. Barnes, *Journey from Jim Crow*, 108–31; T. Branch, *Parting the Waters*, 128–96; Arsenault, *Freedom Riders*, 57–77; Theoharis, *Rebellious Life*, 46–132; "Montgomery Bus Boycott."

2 "Jo Ann Robinson"; C. A. Barnes, *Journey from Jim Crow*, 109; Theoharis, *Rebellious Life*, 50–57, 97–98; T. Branch, *Parting the Waters*, 131–32, 147, 159, 312; C. A. Barnes, *Journey from Jim Crow*, 108–9; "Montgomery Bus Boycott."

3 T. Branch, *Parting the Waters*, 185; Braden, "Montgomery Bus Boycott"; C. A. Barnes, *Journey from Jim Crow*, 115.

4 T. Branch, *Parting the Waters*, 145–46; C. A. Barnes, *Journey from Jim Crow*, 112; "Jemison, Theodore Judson"; Melton, "We'll Keep Walking"; Nicholson, "Martha White"; Melton, *Signpost to Freedom*.

5 "Alabama Senate Passes Boycott Bill"; "To Fight Anti-Boycott Law"; B. LM Kelley, *Right to Ride*, 1–13, 51–193.

6 B. LM Kelley, *Right to Ride*, 1, 201; "Montgomery Bus Boycott"; T. Branch, *Parting the Waters*, 173, 176–85; C. A. Barnes, *Journey from Jim Crow*, 115–16.

7 Martin Luther King, Jr. Research Institute, "*Browder v. Gayle*, 352 U.S. 903"; C. A. Barnes, *Journey from Jim Crow*, 116–25; Theoharis, *Rebellious Life*, 108–9, 114; Bay, *Traveling Black*, 268.

8 Martin Luther King, Jr. Research Institute, "*Browder v. Gayle*, 352 U.S. 903."

9 Martin Luther King, Jr. Research Institute, "*Browder v. Gayle*, 352 U.S. 903"; C. A. Barnes, *Journey from Jim Crow*, 120–25; Theoharis, *Rebellious Life*, 133–35; Bay, *Traveling Black*, 268.

10 Browder v. Gayle, 142 F. Supp. 707 (M.D. Ala. 1956).

11 "Tallahassee Bus Boycott"; Smith and Killian, *Tallahassee Bus Protest*, 1–23; Rabby, *Pain and the Promise*, 24–64; C. A. Barnes, *Journey from Jim Crow*, 124–31; Morrison v. Davis, 252 F.2d. 102 (1958); for more on *Morrison v. Davis*, see the appendix entry about Rev. A. L. Davis et al.

12 "Black History Month Presentation."

13 SKE interview, January 22, 2004; Richardson, "Like Parks, She Wouldn't Budge."

14 Theoharis, *Rebellious Life*, 1–45.

15 Arsenault, *Freedom Riders*, 84–90; C. A. Barnes, *Journey from Jim Crow*, 142–43; Crow et al., *History of African Americans*, 187–92; T. Branch, *Parting the Waters*, 207–8, 271–75; Stoesen, "Greensboro Sit-Ins"; Wilson, "Moment When Four Students Sat"; Meier and Rudwick, *CORE*, 4–8.

16 See chap. 2, nn. 19, 20, 22, and 24; for more on Elizabeth Jennings, see the entry about her in the appendix.

17 Wiegand and Wiegand, *Desegregation of Public Libraries*, 48–50; Knepler, "August 21, 1939."

18 Meier and Rudwick, *CORE*, 3–14.

19 See chap. 3, nn. 2–9.

20 Mills, *"Got My Mind Set,"* 134–35, 147–58; Nathan, *Round and Round*, 28–35, 49–51; Cassie, "And Service for All"; C. F. Smith, *Here Lies Jim Crow*, 81–88.

21 Arsenault, *Freedom Riders*, 87–90; "Student Nonviolent Coordinating Committee."

22 Girolimon, "Activist Joan Garner"; Garner v. Louisiana, 368 U.S. 157 (1961); Cox v. Louisiana, 379 U.S. 536 (1965).

23 C. A. Barnes, *Journey from Jim Crow*, 144–51; Bay, *Traveling Black*, 269; Arsenault, *Freedom Riders*, 93, 97, 106; Boynton v. Virginia, 364 U.S. 454 (1960) at 463–64; Gassiott, "Civil Rights Icon"; H. Smith, "Bruce Carver Boynton."

24 Student Nonviolent Coordinating Committee; T. A. Bell, "Quietly Defiant."

25 C. A. Barnes, *Journey from Jim Crow*, 157–205; Bay, *Traveling Black*, 270–84; Arsenault, *Freedom Riders*, 96–439; Meier and Rudwick, *CORE*, 135–58; "Meet the Players"; Yawn, "Seven Women"; "Student Nonviolent Coordinating Committee." (See chap. 3, n. 19.)

26 Arsenault, *Freedom Riders*, 26, 111–12; C. A. Barnes, *Journey from Jim Crow*, 187; for more on Freedom Riders, see the entry about them in the appendix.

27 C. A. Barnes, *Journey from Jim Crow*, 168–69; Roundtree and McCabe, *Mighty Justice: My Life*, 177–78.

28 "Excerpts from Bus Petition to I.C.C."; "Robert Kennedy Asks I.C.C."

29 Roundtree and McCabe, *Mighty Justice: My Life*, 177; "Excerpts from Bus Petition to I.C.C."

30 C. A. Barnes, *Journey from Jim Crow*, 176–92.

31 SKE interview, January 22, 2004.

32 Dempsey, "Rise and Fall." For more about the end of the ICC, see chap. 10, n. 10.

33 Meier and Rudwick, *CORE*, 223–25; T. Branch, *Parting the Waters*, 846–87; Leland, "1963 March on Washington"; "March on Washington."

34 Civil Rights Act of 1964, 78 Stat. 241 (1964).

35 Frankenberg and Taylor, "ESEA."

36 Foner, *Second Founding*, 172–73; Heart of Atlanta Motel, Inc. v. United States, 379 U.S. 241 (1964) at 250.

37 Voting Rights Act of 1965, 79 Stat. 437 (1965).

38 Leloudis and Korstad, *Fragile Democracy*, 66–75.

39 Leloudis and Korstad, *Fragile Democracy*, 72.

40 Leloudis and Korstad, *Fragile Democracy*, 73–80; Korstad and Leloudis, *To Right These Wrongs*.

41 "Z. Smith Reynolds Foundation Inclusive Public Art Project"; see note 29 of this chapter.

Chapter 12. Moving On

1 SKE interviews, February 25, 2019, and December 20, 2019.

2 SKE interview, February 26, 2019.

3 SKE interview, January 22, 2004.

4 SKE interview, February 25, 2019.

5 SKE interviews, February 25 and 26, 2019; "Hotel Theresa."

6 SKE interview, January 20, 2004.

7 SKE interviews, January 20, 2004, February 25 and 26, 2019, and December 20, 2019.

8 SKE interviews, January 22, 2004, and December 9, 2021.

9 SKE interviews, January 22, 2004, and February 11 and 26, 2019; Ella Whicker email; St. Martin DePorres Parish, https://stmartindeporresparish.org.

10 SKE interviews, January 20 and 22, 2004, January 23, 2019, February 11, 2019, and April 18, 2021.

11 SKE personal documents given to the author; Richardson, "Like Parks, She Wouldn't Budge."

12 SKE interviews, January 20, 2004, and February 25, 2019; video files of NBC TV programs from the 1950s are now part of the Getty Images collection, which says the Sarah Keys video is not easily accessible now to the public.

13 SKE personal documents given to the author.

14 C. A. Barnes, *Journey from Jim Crow*, 86–87, 96–107, 169, 177, 183; author's informal conversations with lawyers; UNC Law Library lists in its catalog Dovey Roundtree's memoir.

15 Military Women's Memorial website, https://womensmemorial.org/about/.

16 SKE interview, January 22, 2004; McCabe, "She Had a Dream"; SKE personal documents.

17 SKE interview, January 22, 2004.

18 SKE personal documents.

19 Nathan, *Take a Seat*, back cover; author's informal conversations with Military Women's Memorial staff, 2003 onward.

20 Michelle McComb interview, August 11, 2020.

21 Cornelia Keys Hargrave interview, March 16, 2004.

22 SKE interview, February 11, 2019; Evans, "Full Interview for Roanoke Rapids

23 Towns, "Tribute to Sarah Keys Evans"; Davis, "Alone but Not Afraid"; SKE personal documents and interviews.

24 Nathan, *Take a Seat*; Tousignant, "Book of the Week"; Smee, "Take a Seat."

25 McCabe, "She Had a Dream"; Bowman, "Sarah Louise Keys"; T. A. Bell, "Quietly Defiant"; SKE personal documents.

26 Gergel, *Unexampled Courage*; A. Clark, "Returning from War"; Hoose, *Claudette Colvin*; "Jo Ann Robinson"; "State Historical Marker 'The Irene Morgan Story'"; Mikorenda, *America's First Freedom Rider*.

27 Waters, "Hero in the Family"; Joan Dudley interview, August 17, 2020.

28 Krys Hargrave interview, August 20, 2018.

29 SKE interviews January 20, 2024, and October 5, 2018; Krys Hargrave interview, August 20, 2018.

30 "Black History Month Presentation."

31 Rowe, "Church Spotlights Long Heritage"; Jones, "Happy Birthday"; Leesa P. Jones, emails to author, July 23, 2024, and June 16, 2025.

32 Census Reporter, "Washington, NC"; P. S. Jones African-American Education Museum, https://psjonesalumni.com/p-s-jones-museum; Alice Sadler, emails to author, 2022–2024; Alice Sadler interview, August 12, 2024; author visit to P. S. Jones Museum, August 12, 2024; Loy and Worthy, *Washington and the Pamlico*, 256, 517; "Washington High School"; S. Barnes, "Conversation with Mayor Sadler"; Hudson, "PS Jones Museum"; Tabb, "For Some"; SKE interview, January 23, 2019.

33 Cutler, "Washington Museum Documents Underground Railroad"; "Washington Waterfront Underground Railroad Museum"; Leesa P. Jones, emails to author, 2020–2025; Leesa P. Jones interviews, August 11 and 12, 2024; author visit to Waterfront Underground Museum, August 11, 2024; Jones, "Underground Railroad Matriarch"; Jones, "Walking Tours Return"; Jones, "Local War Hero"; Mariner, "African Americans Defend Washington"; Mariner, "Hull Anderson"; *Underground Railroad*, PBS; see chap. 5, n. 26.

Chapter 13. Closing the Circle

1 Roanoke Rapids Canal Museum, https://roanokecanal.com/roanoke-canal-museum.html.

2 Lance Jenkins interview, August 21, 2020.

3 Rodney Pierce, multiple emails to author, August 17, 2013–February 11, 2025; Bowman, "Sarah Louise Keys"; Nathan, *Take a Seat*; Waxman, "Years Before Rosa Parks"; Childress, "Teacher Has Passion"; Martin, "Highway Marker"; Martin, "Marker Honoring Keys Unveiled"; "Keeping Your Seat." See also Leloudis and Korstad, *Fragile Democracy*, 34–36, 73–80.

4 Z. Smith Reynolds Foundation, "Inclusive Public Art Initiative"; Christina Caudle interview, October 9, 2018; Christina Caudle, emails to author, October 10, 2018, December 5, 2018, and June 12, 2019; Rev. Dr. Charles McCollum Sr. interview, February 25, 2019, and email to author, October 3, 2019; Dr. Georgette Kimball, interview, February 25, 2019; Ophelia Gould-Faison, interview, February 25, 2019; Dr. Ervin Griffin Sr., interview, February 25, 2019, and emails March 20, 2019, April 23, 2019, June 4, 2019, July 11, 2019, May 13, 2020, and July 16, 17, and 29, 2020; Leloudis and Korstad, *Fragile Democracy*, 73–74; Korstad and Leloudis, *To Right These Wrongs*.

5 Sarah Keys Evans Inclusive Public Art Project, https://sarahkevansproject.com; Z. Smith Reynolds Foundation, "Inclusive Public Art Initiative"; Martin, "Groups Support Push."

6 SKE interview, February 11, 2019.

7 "Keeping Your Seat."

8 For this videotaped oral history, see Evans, "Interview of Sarah Keys Evans."

9 Martin, "Groups Support Push."

10 "Keeping Your Seat"; "Sarah Keys Evans—Closing the Circle."

11 Evans, "Interview of Sarah Keys Evans."

12 Martin, "Council Backs Location"; "Minutes of the Roanoke Rapids City Council"; Roanoke Rapids, North Carolina, website, https://roanokerapidsnc.com; DATA USA, "Roanoke Rapids, NC."

13 "Keeping Your Seat."

14 Z. Smith Reynolds Foundation, "Inclusive Public Art Initiative"; Sayblack, "College Named as Grant Recipient."

15 SKE documents given to author.

16 SKE documents given to author; "Sarah Keys Evans—Closing the Circle."

17 Dr. Georgette Kimball, emails to author, March 3, 2019, May 13, 2020, and July 16, 17, 23, and 29, 2020; "Interim Guidance"; Weise, "'Not Out of the Woods.'"

18 SKE interviews, February 11 and 26, 2019; Fox, "Dovey Johnson Roundtree"; "Sarah Keys Evans—Closing the Circle."

19 Martin, "Committee Members Memorialize Keys"; Martin, "Saluting Sheer Bravery"; "Butterfield, George Kenneth (G. K.), Jr"; "Sarah Keys Evans—Closing the Circle."

20 Martin, "Saluting Sheer Bravery."

21 Martin, "Saluting Sheer Bravery"; "Sarah Keys Evans—Closing the Circle."

22 Zoom recording of 2020 SKE Roanoke Rapids monument dedication ceremony; "Sarah Keys Evans—Closing the Circle."

23 Rev. Dr. Charles McCollum Sr. interview, February 25, 2019.

24 Dr. Eric Cunningham interview, July 29, 2019.

25 Waxman, "Years Before Rosa Parks."

26 "Keeping Your Seat."

27 For the interactive website and video of Professor Blair LM Kelley and Sarah Keys Evans, see Sarah Keys Evans Inclusive Public Art Project, https://sarahkevansproject.com/; Evans, "Interview with Sarah Keys Evans," https://sarahkevansproject.com/who-is-sarah-keys-evans/; Martin, "Keys Plaza Committee."

28 Martin, "Marker Honoring Keys Unveiled."

29 Pierce, "Marker Honoring Confederate General"; Martin, "Confederate Memorial to Be Removed."

30 Jones, "Happy Birthday"; Martin, "Keys-Evans Birthday"; Martin, "Trailblazers"; "5th Sarah Keys Evans Day"; Wooten, "With Recounts Done"; author recollections of an event she attended.

31 Lance Jenkins interview, August 21, 2020.

32 Berogan, "Sarah Keys."

33 "Color of Freedom."

34 Sarah Keys Evans Congressional Gold Medal Act; Martin, "Bill Introduced Honoring Keys Evans"; Butterfield, "Sarah Keys Evans Plaza"; Gilkes, "Gold Medal."

35 Holm, "Trailblazer Sarah Keys Evans Passes"; Cornelia Keys Hargrave email and interviews, November 18 and 20, 2023.

36 Cornelia Keys Hargrave, interview (in person), August 14, 2023; author visit with SKE at rehab center, August 14, 2023.

37 "Black History Month Presentation."

38 Nathan, *Take a Seat*, 68.

39 Evans, "Full Interview for Roanoke Rapids"; "Sarah Keys Evans—Closing the Circle."

40 Waxman, "Years Before Rosa Parks."

Appendix. Transportation Heroes Brigade

1 B. LM Kelley, *Right to Ride*, 17; Masur, *Example for All the Land*, 106; Mikorenda, *America's First Freedom Rider*, 50–52; Volk, *Moral Minorities*, 141–46, 254.

2 Hewitt, "Search for Elizabeth Jennings"; B. LM Kelley, *Right to Ride*, 17–32; Mikorenda, *America's First Freedom Rider*, 111–40; Volk, *Moral Minorities*, 147–59, 163–66 (see chap. 2, n. 19).

3 McBride, "Fourteenth Amendment Idealism"; "Right of Colored People"; Mikorenda, *America's First Freedom Rider*, 171; Volk, *Moral Minorities*, 165–66 (see chap. 2, nn. 19–20, 22).

4 Masur, *Example for All the Land*, 101–9; Railroad Company v. Brown, 84 U.S. 445 (1873), at 446; Fenison, "Alexander T. Augusta (1825–1890)."

5 Masur, *Example for All the Land*, 106–9.

6 Salisbury, "Monument at Last"; Biddle and Dubin, *Tasting Freedom*, 2–3, 290–97, 310–12, 333–54.

7 B. LM Kelley, *Right to Ride*, 92–93, 102–4; Medley, *We as Freemen*, 78–80; Fischer, "Pioneer Protest"; Baker, *Second Battle*, 299–301; Perkins, "Streetcar Protests of 1867."

8 Bogen, "Precursors of Rosa Parks," 725–26; Marantos, "She Was the Rosa Parks of Her Day."

9 Marantos, "She Was the Rosa Parks of Her Day."

10 Bogen, "Precursors of Rosa Parks," 730–51.

11 Elinson, "San Francisco's Own"; Lowe, "Mary Ellen Pleasant (1814–1904)"; Harris and Cohen, *Women Trailblazers*; "Transportation Is for All."

12 Itkin, "Creating 'What Might Have Been'"; C. A. Barnes, *Journey from Jim Crow*, 5–6, 45–46; Medley, *We as Freemen*, 90; Hall v. DeCuir, 95 U.S. 485 (1877) at 488–89.

13 Welke, "When All the Women," 305–6.

14 Wormser, "Ida B. Wells"; B. LM Kelley, *Right to Ride*, 35, 45; The Chesapeake, Ohio and Southwestern Railroad Company vs. Ida B. Wells, Tennessee Supreme Court (March 31, 1885); Legal Brief for Ida B. Wells' Lawsuit.

15 Welke, "When All the Women," 278–80; B. LM Kelley, *Right to Ride*, 46–47; "Rare Victory for Texas Woman"; Houck v. Southern Pacific Railway Co., 38 Fed. 226 (W.D. Tex. 1888).

16 Meier and Rudwick, "Boycott Movement"; Meier and Rudwick, "Negro Boycotts"; B. LM Kelley, *Right to Ride*, 120–25, 145–58, 160–62, 198–200; Norwood, "Maggie Lena Walker (1864–1934)."

17 Taylor, "Rosa Parks of D.C."; J. Harris, "Barbara E. Pope (1854–1908)."

18 Gilmore, *Gender and Jim Crow*, 178–202, 212–24; Wormser, "Charlotte Hawkins Brown (1870–1924)"; "Civic Life of Dr. Charlotte Hawkins Brown."

19 Bay, *Traveling Black*, 170–76.

20 Bay, *Traveling Black*, 177.

21 Adams, "Dignified Defiance."

22 R. D. G. Kelley, "'We Are Not What We Seem.'"

23 Henry Louis Gates Jr., "Was Jackie Robinson Court-Martialed?"; Ortiz, "Jackie Robinson"; Tygiel, "Court-Martial."

24 Price, "In the Jim Crow Era"; "Pfc. Booker T. Spicely."

25 Stitt, "Learn About the Detroiter"; Stitt, "She Was Kicked Off"; Schillinger, "Sarah Elizabeth Ray"; C. A. Barnes, *Journey from Jim Crow*, 48–49; Bob-Lo Excursion Co. v. Michigan, 333 U.S. 28 (1948) at 40.

26 Chance v. Lambeth, 186 F.2d 879 (4th Cir. 1951); C. A. Barnes, *Journey from Jim Crow*, 80–85, 117; Leloudis, *Schooling the New South*, 194–99; Caldwell, "Chance, William Claudius, Sr."; Nathan, *Round and Round*, 149–50, 158, 168, 197, 202; F. N. Rasmussen, "Edward Chance."

27 "*Browder v. Gayle, 352 U.S. 903*"; Baker, *Second Battle*, 281–83, 300–301, 331, 363, 394; McLaughlin-Stonham, *From Slavery to Civil Rights*, 182–94; Morrison v. Davis, 252 F.2d. 102 (1958); Nathan, *Together*, 88–90.

28 See chap. 11, n. 25.

Sources

Primary Sources

Legal

Note: Links have been provided for cases and documents not readily available through a web search.

A Bill to Prevent All Persons from Teaching Slaves to Read or Write, the Use of Figures Excepted (1830). Legislative Papers, 1830–31 Session of the General Assembly, North Carolina

Bob-Lo Excursion Co. v. Michigan, 333 U.S. 28 (1948)

Boynton v. Virginia, 364 U.S. 454 (1960)

Browder v. Gayle, 142 F. Supp. 707 (M.D. Ala. 1956)

Brown v. Board of Education, 347 U.S. 483 (1954)

Chance v. Lambeth, 186 F.2d 879 (4th Cir. 1951)

Chesapeake, Ohio and Southwestern Railroad Company vs. Ida B. Wells, Tennessee Supreme Court (March 31, 1885). Tennessee Virtual Archive. https://teva.contentdm.oclc.org/digital/collection/p15138coll18/id/115

Chiles v. Chesapeake & Ohio Railway Co., 218 U.S. 71 (1910)

Civil Rights Act of 1866, 14 Stat. 27 (1866)

Civil Rights Act of 1875, 18 Stat. 335 (1875)

Civil Rights Act of 1964, 78 Stat. 241 (1964)

Civil Rights Cases, 109 U.S. 3 (1883)

Constitution of North Carolina of 1868

Cox v. Louisiana, 379 U.S. 536 (1965)

A Declaration of the Immediate Causes Which Induce and Justify the Secession of the State of Mississippi from the Federal Union (1861)

Emancipation Proclamation (January 1, 1863)

Executive Order No. 9808, 11 F.R. 14153 (1946) (creating the President's Committee on Civil Rights)

Executive Order No. 9981, 13 F.R. 4313 (1948) (desegregation of the armed forces)

Garner v. Louisiana, 368 U.S. 157 (1961)

Gray v. Cincinnati Southern Railroad Co., 11 F. 683 (1882)

Hall v. DeCuir, 95 U.S. 485 (1877)

Heart of Atlanta Motel, Inc. v. United States, 379 U.S. 241 (1964)

Henderson v. United States, 339 U.S. 816 (1950)

Hirabayashi v. United States, 320 U.S. 81 (1943)

Houck v. Southern Pacific Railway Co., 38 Fed. 226 (W.D. Tex. 1888)

Interstate Commerce Act, 24 Stat. 379 (1887)

Legal Brief for Ida B. Wells' Lawsuit Against the Chesapeake, Ohio, and Southwestern Railroad Company Before the State Supreme Court, 1885. Digital Public Library of America. https://dp.la/primary-source-sets/ida-b-wells-and-anti-lynching-activism/sources/1113.

Massachusetts Constitution of 1780

Mitchell v. United States, 313 U.S. 80 (1941)

Morgan v. Virginia, 328 U.S. 373 (1946)

Morrison v. Davis, 252 F.2d. 102 (1958)

National Association for the Advancement of Colored People v. St. Louis–San Francisco Railway Company (1955). Hathi Trust. https://hdl.handle.net/2027/uc1.b2911239?urlappend=%3Bseq=373%3Bownerid=9007199273784402-419.

Ohio & Southwestern Railroad v. Wells (Sept. 15, 1883)

Plessy v. Ferguson, 163 U.S. 537 (1896)

Railroad Company v. Brown, 84 U.S. 445 (1873)

Reconstruction Act of 1867, 14 Stat. 428 (1867)

Robinson v. Memphis & Charleston Railroad Co. (part of Civil Rights Cases, 109 U.S. 3 [1883])

Sarah Keys v. Carolina Coach Company, 64 M.C.C. 769 (1955). Hathi Trust. https://hdl.handle.net/2027/uc1.b2949044?urlappend=%3Bseq=815%3Bownerid=9007199273608329-873.

Shelley v. Kraemer, 334 U.S. 1 (1948)

Smith v. Allwright, 321 U.S. 649 (1944)

United States Constitution

United States v. Cruikshank, 92 U.S. 542 (1875)

United States v. Halifax County Board of Education, 314 F. Supp. 65 (E.D.N.C. 1970)

Voting Rights Act of 1965, 79 Stat. 437 (1965)

Whiteside v. Southern Bus Lines, 177 F.2d 949 (1949)

Author Interviews

All author interviews were conducted by phone unless indicated otherwise.

ATKINS, LES
2019: March 13 (in person)

BARRICELLA, JOE
2022: January 26 (email)

CAUDLE, CHRISTINA
2018: October 9, October 10 (email); December 5 (email)
2019: June 12 (email)

CRAIG, LEE A.
2022: June 28 (email)

CUNNINGHAM, DR. ERIC
2019: July 29

DUDLEY, JOAN
2020: August 17, October 11 (email)
2023: August (email)

EVANS, SARAH KEYS
2004–2023: multiple interviews between January 20, 2004, and August 14, 2023 (some email)

FARRELL, STEPHEN
2020: August 12 (email)

FISHER, DEACON RICK
2024: October 7

FOWLER, AUSTEEN

2023: December 6

GOULD-FAISON, OPHELIA

2019: February 25

GRAVES, JULIE ANN WATERS

2004: March

2020: July

GRIFFIN, SR., DR. ERVIN

2019: February 25, March 20, April 23, June 4, July 11 (email)

2020: May 13, July 16, July 17, July 29 (email)

HARDER, SPRUILL

2025: August 17, August 18 (email)

HARGRAVE, CORNELIA KEYS

2004: March 16

2020: October 18, November 3

2021: January 26, February 17 (email)

2023: February 25 (in person), August 14 (email and in person), November 18, November 20

2024: July 24, September 20 (email)

HARGRAVE, KRYS

2004: March 16

2018: August 20

HARGRAVE, TERESA

2004: March 16

JENKINS, LANCE

2020: August 21

JONES, LEESA P.

2020: August 18, October 30, November 10, November 12

2021: January 28, February 10

2023: December 6

2024: January 11 (email), August 11, August 12 (in person), August 28, August 29, August 30, August 31

2025: June 16 (email)

KEYS, SONYA

2020: August 12

KIMBALL, DR. GEORGETTE
2019: February 25, March 3, May 13
2020: July 16, July 17, July 29 (email)

LEACH, RICHARD
2022: February 7

MCCOLLUM, SR., REVEREND DR. CHARLES
2019: February 25, March 5, March 13, October 13 (email)

MCCOMB, MICHELLE
2020: August 11

MCDANIEL, LARRY
2019: January 22
2024: September 20

MEDLIN, LORI
2019: March 14, June 12 (email)

MIDGETT, RAY
2021: December 13

OLIVARES, ANAI
2024: September 20 (email)

O'SULLIVAN, TERRY
2022: February 16 (email)

PADGETT, ASHLEY
2020: August 25 (email)

PEARSON, SISTER BETH
2020: October 21, October 23, October 26
2021: December 18
2023: December 6, December 8, December 20
2024: January 5, January 15, January 18, September 23 (email)

PIERCE, RODNEY
2013: August 17 (phone and email), October 19, October 25, November 14
2014: January 3, June 26
2015: February 18, March 2
2017: October 3
2018: June 20
2019: February 12, February 27, March 15, March 20, March 26, April 17, December 19

2020: January 1, February 13, May 21, June 9
2023: January 1, April 18, November 18
2024: December 4
2025: February 11 (email)

SADLER, ALICE
2022: January 22, January 23 (email)
2024: August 12 (in person), August 18 (email), December 5 (email)

SKOWRONSKI, LAUREN
2007: April 10 (email)

SYAL, SHAHEEN R.
2019: June 14 (email)

THORNHILL, CARRIE
2021: December 2021

WEGNER, ANSLEY HERRING
2019: December 19 (email)

WHICKER, ELLA
2025: June 19 (email and phone)

ZWILLING, DIANA
2024: September 2024

Oral History

Evans, Sarah Keys. "Interview of Sarah Keys Evans." Video of a portion of interview by Les Atkins. March 31, 2019. Sarah K. Evans Inclusive Public Art Project. https://sarahkevansproject.com/who-is-sarah-keys-evans/.

Keys-Evans, Sarah. "Sarah Keys-Evans." Oral history interview. Conducted by Kate Scott. January 30, 2006. Military Women's Memorial. https://womensmemorial.starter1ua.preservica.com/index.php?name=SO_5cdf56c6-12fa-43e1-85af-b69eb75b46e4.

Video and Audio

Berogan, Aaron, videographer. "Sarah Keys: A First Army Trailblazer." Defense Visual Information Distribution Service, November 5, 2020. https://www.dvidshub.net/video/772014/sarah-keys-first-army-trailblazer. Lt. General Thomas James's 2020 tribute to Sarah Keys Evans includes video and audio from her.

"Black History Month: Local Hero." *The Brian Lehrer Show*, WNYC-FM, February 9, 2011. https://www.wnyc.org/story/113646-black-history-month-local-hero/.

"Black History Month Presentation." Academy for Urban Leadership Charter School, Perth Amboy, New Jersey, February 21, 2017. YouTube. https://www.youtube.com/watch?v=3WIoms1RiMU.

Evans, Sarah Keys. "Full Interview for Roanoke Rapids Sarah Keys Evans Project." Interview by Les Atkins. March 13, 2019. Provided to author by Atkins.

"HERstory Spotlight: Civil Rights Trailblazer." Military Women's Memorial. YouTube, March 3, 2022. https://www.youtube.com/watch?v=FLT7N9CUXFc.

"Keeping Your Seat to Take a Stand: Sarah Keys Evans and the Fight Against Jim Crow Transportation." Virtual workshop, Carolina Public Humanities, May 12, 2022. YouTube, May 17, 2022. https://www.youtube.com/watch?v=P_ImqNVUoB8.

Melton, Christina, dir. *Signpost to Freedom: The 1953 Baton Rouge Bus Boycott*. Louisiana Public Broadcasting, 2004. https://www.lpb.org/programs/signpost-to-freedom-the-1953-baton-rouge-bus-boycott.

Price, Jay. "Documenting the History of Mob Violence Against African-American Veterans." *Morning Edition*, NPR, September 20, 2018. https://www.npr.org/2018/09/20/649797847/documenting-the-history-of-mob-violence-against-african-american-veterans.

"Sarah Keys Evans—Closing the Circle." PBS North Carolina, Visibly Speaking: NC's Inclusive Public Art Project. YouTube, June 1, 2022. https://www.youtube.com/watch?v=SN22NOp30ZU.

Schillinger, Aaron. "Sarah Elizabeth Ray: Detroit's Other Rosa Parks." With Desiree Cooper. WDET, Detroit Public Radio, August 1, 2020. https://wdet.org/2020/08/01/watch-a-short-film-on-the-black-woman-who-integrated-the-boblo-boats/.

Schneider, Quinn, and Jake Johnson. "The Rosenwald Schools." QE Adventures. YouTube, June 19, 2014. https://www.youtube.com/watch?v=kfxfxSgSlGM.

Underground Railroad, The: The Paths and Places of Refuge. PBS, May 30, 2025. https://www.pbs.org/video/the-underground-railroad-the-paths-places-of-refuge-awapxj/.

Video recording of Roanoke Rapids historical marker ceremony, January 15, 2022. Provided to author by Rodney Pierce.

"Virtual Tour." Sarah K. Evans Inclusive Public Art Project. Accessed April 2025. http://sarahkevansproject.com/virtualtour/.

"Women's History Month Celebration, Mrs. Sarah Keys Evans." Center for Military Veterans, March 14, 2014. YouTube. https://www.youtube.com/watch?v=tygy-DebmC4&.

Other Sources

Copies of Sarah Keys Evans's personal documents shared with author
Documents and photographs shared by interviewees

Secondary Sources

"5th Sarah Keys Evans Day Scheduled." *Washington (NC) Daily News*, July 16, 2024.

"1948: Shelley v. Kraemer." Fair Housing Center of Greater Boston. Accessed August 14, 2025. https://www.bostonfairhousing.org/timeline/1948-Shelley-v-Kramer.html.

"200 Years in Washington, NC: Celebrating Our Bicentennial/1820–2020." Mother of Mercy Roman Catholic Church. Accessed August 14, 2025. https://www.motherofmercync.com/about-us.

Abrams, Douglas Carl. "Works Progress Administration (WPA): One Failure to End the Great Depression." North Carolina History Project. Accessed August 14, 2025. https://northcarolinahistory.org/commentary/works-progress-administration-wpa-one-failure-to-end-the-great-depression/.

Adams, Stella J. "Dignified Defiance: The Ellen Harris Story." Social Science Research Network (SSRN), February 22, 2021. https://ssrn.com/abstract=3790182.

"African American Sailors in the U.S. Navy." U.S. Navy Naval History and Heritage Command. Accessed August 14, 2025. https://www.history.navy.mil/content/history/nhhc/browse-by-topic/diversity/african-americans/chronology.html (page removed).

"African Americans Defend Washington." American Battlefield Trust. Accessed August 14, 2025. https://www.battlefields.org/visit/heritage-sites/african-americans-defend-washington.

"Alabama Senate Passes Boycott Bill." *New York Times*, September 27, 1903.

Alexander, Leslie M. *African or American? Black Identity and Political Activism in New York City, 1784–1861*. Urbana: University of Illinois Press, 2012.

Alexander, Roberta Sue. "Freedmen's Bureau." *NCpedia*, State Library of North Carolina, 2006. Accessed August 17, 2025. https://www.ncpedia.org/freedmens-bureau.

Alridge, Derrick P. "W. E. B. Du Bois in Georgia." *New Georgia Encyclopedia*, May 14, 2003. https://www.georgiaencyclopedia.org/articles/history-archaeology/w-e-b-du-bois-in-georgia/.

Anderson, James D. *The Education of Blacks in the South, 1860–1935*. Chapel Hill: University of North Carolina Press, 1988.

Aneja, Abhay, and Guo Xu. "The Costs of Employment Segregation: Evidence from the Federal Government Under Woodrow Wilson."

Quarterly Journal of Economics 137, no. 2 (May 2022): 911–58. https://doi.org/10.1093/qje/qjab040.

Archer, Richard. *Jim Crow North: The Struggle for Equal Rights in Antebellum New England*. New York: Oxford University Press, 2017.

"Army Women: World War II and Beyond." Women's Army Corps Veterans' Association. Accessed August 17, 2025. https://www.armywomen.org/history.

Arsenault, Raymond. *Freedom Riders: 1961 and the Struggle for Racial Justice*. New York: Oxford University Press, 2006.

Avins, Alfred, comp. *The Reconstruction Amendments' Debates: The Legislative History and Contemporary Debates in Congress on the 13th, 14th, and 15th Amendments*. Richmond: Virginia Commission on Constitutional Government, 1967.

Baker, Liva. *The Second Battle of New Orleans: The Hundred-Year Struggle to Integrate the Schools*. New York: HarperCollins, 1996.

Baldino, Thomas J., and Kyle L. Kreider. *Of the People, by the People, for the People: A Documentary Record of Voting Rights and Electoral Reform*. Santa Barbara, CA: Greenwood, 2010.

Barnes, Catherine A. *Journey from Jim Crow: The Desegregation of Southern Transit*. New York: Columbia University Press, 1983.

Barnes, Steve. "A Conversation with Mayor Sadler." *Washington (NC) Daily News*, December 11, 2020.

Bay, Mia. *Traveling Black: A Story of Race and Resistance*. Cambridge, MA: Harvard University Press, 2021.

Beermann, Jack M. *The Journey to Separate but Equal: Madame DeCuir's Quest for Racial Justice in the Reconstruction Era*. Lawrence: University Press of Kansas, 2021.

Bell, John L. "Lawrence Augustus Oxley: The Beginnings of Social Work Among Blacks in North Carolina Counties." *Journal of the Appalachian Studies Association* 3 (1991): 98–109. https://www.jstor.org/stable/41445604.

Bell, T. Anthony. "The Quietly Defiant, Unlikely Fighter: PFC Sarah Keys and the Fight for Justice and Humanity." U.S. Army, February 25, 2014. Accessed August 2016. http://www.army.mil/article/120456/The_quietly_defiant_unlikely_fighter_Pfc_Sarah_Keys (page removed).

Bellafaire, Judith. "Challenging the System: Two Army Women Fight for Equality." Military Women's Memorial. Accessed 2003. https://www.womensmemorial.org/challenging-the-system (no longer available).

Biddle, Daniel R., and Murray Dubin. *Tasting Freedom: Octavius Catto and the Battle for Equality in Civil War America*. Philadelphia: Temple University Press, 2010.

Bishop, David W. "Plessy v. Ferguson: A Reinterpretation." *Journal of Negro History* 62, no. 2 (April 1977): 125–33.

"Black Farmers FAQ: The History of Discrimination Against Black Farmers and Policy Initiatives to Remedy These Inequities." NAACP Legal Defense Fund. Accessed August 14, 2025. https://www.naacpldf.org/case-issue/black-farmers-faq/.

"Black Soldiers in the U.S. Military During the Civil War." National Archives. Last reviewed October 4, 2023. https://www.archives.gov/education/lessons/blacks-civil-war.

Blair, Dan. "Plymouth, Battle of." *NCpedia*, State Library of North Carolina (SLNC), 2006. Revised by SLNC Government and Heritage Library, October 2023. https://www.ncpedia.org/plymouth-battle.

Blight, David W. *Frederick Douglass: Prophet of Freedom*. New York: Simon and Schuster, 2018.

Blow, Charles M. "On Juneteenth, Freedom Came with Strings Attached." *New York Times*, June 18, 2024.

Blue, Christopher. "William Hooper Councill (1849–1909)." BlackPast, June 1, 2008. Accessed August 17, 2025. https://www.blackpast.org/african-american-history/councill-william-hooper-1849-1909/.

Bly, Antonio. "Literacy and Education of the Enslaved in Virginia." *Encyclopedia Virginia*, Virginia Humanities, December 7, 2020. https://encyclopediavirginia.org/entries/slave-literacy-and-education-in-virginia/.

Bogen, David S. "Precursors of Rosa Parks: Maryland Transportation Cases Between the Civil War and the Beginning of World War I." *Maryland Law Review* 63 (2004): 721–51. https://digitalcommons.law.umaryland.edu/fac_pubs/70/.

Bogen, David S. "Why the Supreme Court Lied in *Plessy*." *Villanova Law Review* 52, no. 3 (2007): 411–70.

Bollard, John K. *Protesting with Rosa Parks: From Stagecoaches to Driving While Black*. Athens, GA: NewSouth Books, 2025.

"Booker T. Washington and the 'Atlanta Compromise.'" National Museum of African American History and Culture, Smithsonian. Accessed August 14, 2025. https://nmaahc.si.edu/explore/stories/booker-t-washington-and-atlanta-compromise.

"Booker T. Washington Delivers the 1895 Atlanta Compromise Speech." History Matters: The U.S. Survey Course on the Web. Accessed August 14, 2025. https://historymatters.gmu.edu/d/39/.

Born in Slavery: Slave Narratives from the Federal Writers' Project, 1936 to 1938. Vol. 11, North Carolina, Pt.1 and Pt. 2. Library of Congress. https://www.loc.gov/collections/slave-narratives-from-the-federal-writers-project-1936-to-1938/?q=North+Carolina.

Bowman, Susan. "Sarah Louise Keys: An Unsung Hero in the Fight for Civil Rights." *Our Heritage*, February 2011.

Braden, Donna. "The Montgomery Bus Boycott in the News." *Past Forward: Activating the Henry Ford Archive of Innovation* (blog), The Henry Ford, February 17, 2021. Accessed August 17, 2025. https://www.thehenryford.org/explore/blog/the-montgomery-bus-boycott-in-the-news.

Branch, Paul, Jr. "Washington, N.C., Siege of." *NCpedia*, State Library of North Carolina, 2006. Accessed August 17, 2025. https://www.ncpedia.org/washington-nc-siege.

Branch, Taylor. *Parting the Waters: America in the King Years, 1954–63*. New York: Simon and Schuster, 1989.

Brooks, F. Eric. "Booker T. Washington." *Encyclopedia of Alabama*, updated August 29, 2023. Accessed August 17, 2025. https://encyclopediaofalabama.org/article/booker-t-washington/.

Broussard, Albert S. "Civil Rights, Racial Protest, and Anti-Slavery Activism in San Francisco, 1850–1865." Golden Gate National Recreation Area, National Park Service. Accessed August 14, 2025. https://www.nps.gov/goga/learn/historyculture/upload/Civil-Rights-Racial-Protest-Anti-Slavery-Activism-in-San-Francisco-1850-1865.pdf.

"*Browder v. Gayle*, 352 U.S. 903." Martin Luther King, Jr. Research and Education Institute, Stanford University. Accessed August 14, 2025. https://kinginstitute.stanford.edu/browder-v-gayle-352-us-903.

Bryant, James K., II. *The 36th Infantry United States Colored Troops in the Civil War: A History and Roster*. Jefferson, NC: McFarland, 2012.

Butterfield, G. K., Jr. "Sarah Keys Evans Plaza Ribbon Cutting Ceremony." *Congressional Record* 166, no. XX (July 31, 2020) at E714 (Extensions of Remarks).

"Butterfield, George Kenneth (G. K.), Jr." *Biographical Directory of the United States Congress*. Accessed August 14, 2025. https://bioguide.congress.gov/search/bio/B001251.

Caldwell, John T. "Chance, William Claudius, Sr." *NCpedia*, State Library of North Carolina (SLNC), 1979. Revised by SLNC Government and Heritage Library, November 2022. Accessed August 17, 2025. https://www.ncpedia.org/biography/chance-william-claudius.

Carbonneau, Rob. "Conflicting Images—Preaching to Catholics, Non-Catholics and 'Colored Catholics': The Sign and the Beginnings of the Passionist Presence in North Carolina in the 1920s." Passionist Historical Archives. Accessed August 14,2025. https://passionistarchives.org/conflicting-images-preaching-to-catholics-non-catholics-colored-catholics-the-sign-the-beginnings-of-the-passionist-presence-in-north-carolina-in-the-1920s/.

Cardona, Nina. "50 Years Before Rosa Parks, a Bold Nashville Streetcar Protest Defied Segregation." WPLN *News*, September 22, 2015. https://wpln.org/post/50-years-before-rosa-parks-a-bold-nashville-streetcar-protest-defied-segregation/.

Cassie, Ron. "And Service for All: Sixty Years Ago, Morgan State College Students Staged the First Successful Lunch-Counter Sit-Ins." *Baltimore Magazine*,

January 2015. https://www.baltimoremagazine.com/section/community/morgan-students-staged-reads-drugstore-sit-in-60-years-ago/.

Cecelski, David. "'As Long as a Star Can Be Seen': 1864 Plymouth Massacre." *Coastal Review*, May 28, 2024. Accessed August 17, 2025. https://coastalreview.org/2024/05/as-long-as-a-star-can-be-seen-1864-plymouth-massacre/.

Cecelski, David. "The Convict Labor Camp." David Cecelski: New Writing, Collected Essays, Latest Discoveries (website), February 16, 2020. https://davidcecelski.com/2020/02/16/the-convict-labor-camp/.

Cecelski, David S. *The Fire of Freedom: Abraham Galloway and the Slaves' Civil War*. Chapel Hill: University of North Carolina Press, 2012.

Cecelski, David S. *The Waterman's Song: Slavery and Freedom in Maritime North Carolina*. Chapel Hill: University of North Carolina Press, 2001.

Cecelski, David S., and Timothy B. Tyson, eds. *Democracy Betrayed: The Wilmington Race Riot of 1898 and Its Legacy*. Chapel Hill: University of North Carolina Press, 1998.

Census Reporter. "Washington, NC." Accessed August 13, 2025. https://censusreporter.org/profiles/16000US3771220-washington-nc/.

"Charles Evans Hughes Court (1930–1941)." Justia, US Supreme Court. Accessed August 17, 2025. https://supreme.justia.com/supreme-court-history/hughes-court/.

Childress, Greg. "Teacher Has Passion for Democracy, Historical Markers and Students." *NC Newsline*, September 15, 2023. https://ncnewsline.com/2023/09/15/teacher-has-passion-for-democracy-historical-markers-and-students/.

"Citizens Fight Bus Boycott: N. Carolina High Court Gets Dispute, State Says Buses Not Common Carriers." *Chicago Defender*, June 29, 1929. Available on ProQuest.

"Civic Life of Dr. Charlotte Hawkins Brown, The." North Carolina Historical Sites (Civic Life). Accessed October 11, 2025. https://historicsites.nc.gov/all-sites/charlotte-hawkins-brown-museum/history/dr-charlotte-hawkins-brown/civic-life

Clark, Alexis. "Returning From War, Returning to Racism." *New York Times*, September 8, 2020.

Clark, Kenneth B., and Mamie P. Clark. "Racial Identification and Preference in Negro Children." In *Readings in Social Psychology*, edited by Theodore M. Newcomb and Eugene L. Hartley, 169–78. New York: Henry Holt, 1947.

Clark, Robin White. *The Baton Rouge Bus Boycott: The Mark That Could Not Be Erased*. Baton Rouge, LA: Rhema Enterprises, 2020.

Coffey, Michael W. "African Americans Defend Washington, N.C., 1863." *NCpedia*, State Library of North Carolina, 2016. https://www.ncpedia.org/african-americans-defend-washington-nc-1863.

Colomb, Nayda Swonger, K. Todd Johnson, Benjamin R. Justesen, E. Michael Latta, Scott Matthews, and Jay Mazzocchi. "Public Education: Part 3: The First Graded Schools, the State Constitution of 1868, and Legal Segregation." *NCpedia*, State Library of North Carolina (SLNC), 2006. Revised by SLNC Government and Heritage Library, November 2022. https://www.ncpedia.org/public-education-part-3-first.

Colomb, Nayda Swonger, K. Todd Johnson, Benjamin R. Justesen, E. Michael Latta, Scott Matthews, and Jay Mazzocchi. "Public Education: Part 4: Expansion, Consolidation, and the School Machinery Act." *NCpedia*, State Library of North Carolina (SLNC), 2006. Revised by SLNC Government and Heritage Library, March 2022. https://www.ncpedia.org/public-education-part-4-expansion.

"Color of Freedom, The." Military Women's Memorial. Accessed August 14, 2025. https://womensmemorial.org/the-color-of-freedom/#traveling-exhibit.

"Commerce Clause." Legal Information Institute, Cornell Law School, last reviewed July 2022. https://www.law.cornell.edu/wex/Commerce_Clause.

"Common Law." Legal Information Institute, Cornell Law School, last reviewed May 2020. https://www.law.cornell.edu/wex/common_law.

Connor, R. D. W., and Clarence Hamilton Poe. *The Life and Speeches of Charles Brantley Aycock*. New York: Doubleday. https://docsouth.unc.edu/nc/connor/connor.html.

Craig, Lee A. *Josephus Daniels: His Life and Times*. Chapel Hill: University of North Carolina Press, 2013.

Crow, Jeffrey J., Amelia Dees-Killette, and Diane Huff. "Slavery." *NCpedia*, State Library of North Carolina (SLNC), 2006. Revised by SLNC Government and Heritage Library, December 2022. https://www.ncpedia.org/slavery.

Crow, Jeffrey J., Paul D. Escott, and Flora J. Hatley Wadelington. *A History of African Americans in North Carolina*. Chapel Hill: North Carolina Office of Archives and History, 2019.

Curtis, Clark. "The Story of Keysville." *Washington (NC) Daily News*, February 13, 2023.

Cutler, Kevin Scott. "Washington Museum Documents Underground Railroad Museum." *Washington (NC) Daily News*, February 24, 2017.

Daniels, Mrs. Josephus (Addie Worth Bagley). *Recollections of a Cabinet Minister's Wife, 1913–1921*. Raleigh, NC: Mitchell Printing Company, 1945. Facsimile, Literary Licensing, 2013.

DATA USA. "Roanoke Rapids, NC." Accessed August 14, 2025. https://datausa.io/profile/geo/roanoke-rapids-nc#demographics

Davis, Sarajanee. "Alone but Not Afraid: Sarah Keys v. Carolina Coach Company." ANCHOR, *NCpedia*, State Library of North Carolina, 2020. https://www.ncpedia.org/anchor/sarah-keys-carolina-coach-company.

Davis, Saranjee. "Wilmington Massacre November 1898." *NCpedia*, State Library of North Carolina, 2020. https://www.ncpedia.org/anchor/wilmington-massacre-correcting-the-record.

Dempsey, Paul Stephen. "The Rise and Fall of the Interstate Commerce Commission: The Tortuous Path from Regulation to Deregulation of America's Infrastructure." *Marquette Law Review* 95, no. 4 (2012): 1151–89. https://scholarship.law.marquette.edu/mulr/vol95/iss4/7/.

"Direct Action Campaign to Halt Jim Crow Streetcars: 1864." Washington Area Spark, Flickr, February 22, 2018. https://www.flickr.com/photos/washington_area_spark/40379768052.

Douglass, Frederick. *Ultimate Collection: Complete Autobiographies, Speeches and Letters*. Chicago: Musaicum Books, 2018. Kindle.

"Dr. Charlotte Hawkins Brown." North Carolina Historic Sites. Accessed August 14, 2025. https://historicsites.nc.gov/all-sites/charlotte-hawkins-brown-museum/history/dr-charlotte-hawkins-brown.

Du Bois, W. E. B. *Black Reconstruction in America, 1860–1880*. New York: Free Press, 1998. Originally published in 1935 by Harcourt Brace.

Du Bois, W. E. B., ed. *The Negro Artisan*. Atlanta: Atlanta University Press, 1902.

Du Bois, W. E. B. "On Being Black." *New Republic*, February 18, 1920.

Du Bois, W. E. B. "Race Relations in the United States, 1917–1947." *Phylon (1940–1956)* 9, no. 3 (1948): 234–47. https://doi.org/10.2307/271210.

Du Bois, W. E. B. *The Souls of Black Folk*. New Haven, CT: Yale University Press, 2015. First published by A. C. McClurg, 1903.

Elinson, Elaine. "San Francisco's Own Rosa Parks." *San Francisco Chronicle*, January 16, 2012.

Elinson, Elaine, and Stan Yogi. *Wherever There's a Fight: How Runaway Slaves, Suffragists, Immigrants, Strikers, and Poets Shaped Civil Liberties in California*. Berkeley: Heyday Books, 2009.

Elmore, John E. "Hyman, John Adams." *NCpedia*, State Library of North Carolina (SLNC), 1988. Revised by SLNC Government and Heritage Library, March 2023. https://www.ncpedia.org/biography/hyman-john-adams.

Engs, Robert Francis, and *Dictionary of Virginia Biography*. "Samuel Chapman Armstrong (1839–1893)." *Encyclopedia Virginia*, Virginia Humanities, December 7, 2020. https://encyclopediavirginia.org/entries/armstrong-samuel-chapman-1839-1893/.

Equal Justice Initiative. *Lynching in America: Confronting the Legacy of Racial Terror*. 3rd ed. Montgomery, AL: Equal Justice Initiative, 2017. https://lynchinginamerica.eji.org/report/.

"Excerpts from Bus Petition to I.C.C." *New York Times*, May 30, 1961.

Feiler, Andrew. *A Better Life for Their Children: Julius Rosenwald, Booker T. Washington, and the 4,978 Schools That Changed America*. Athens: University of Georgia Press, 2021.

Fenison, Jimmy. "Alexander T. Augusta (1825–1890)." BlackPast, March 29, 2009. https://www.blackpast.org/african-american-history/augusta-alexander-t-1825-1890/.

Fields, Karen E., and Barbara J. Fields. *Racecraft: The Soul of Inequality in American Life*. New York: Verso, 2012.

Fischer, Roger A. "A Pioneer Protest: The New Orleans Street-Car Controversy of 1867." *Journal of Negro History* 53, no. 3 (July 1968): 219–33.

Foner, Eric. *Reconstruction: America's Unfinished Revolution, 1863–1877*. New York: Harper and Row, 1988.

Foner, Eric. *The Second Founding: How the Civil War and Reconstruction Remade the Constitution*. New York: W. W. Norton, 2019.

Ford, David. "1920s Black-Owned Safe Bus: 'We Didn't Have to Ride in the Back.'" WUNC *News*, February 28, 2022. https://www.wunc.org/news/2022-02-28/1920s-black-owned-safe-bus-we-didnt-have-to-ride-in-the-back.

"Former I.C.C. Chairman Admits 'Indiscreet' Actions in Rail Case." *New York Times*, January 14, 1956.

Fox, Margalit. "Dovey Johnson Roundtree, Barrier-Breaking Lawyer, Dies at 104." *New York Times*, May 21, 2018.

Foy, Morgan. "How Woodrow Wilson's Racist Policies Eroded the Black Civil Service." University of California, Berkeley Haas School of Business, October 27, 2020. https://newsroom.haas.berkeley.edu/research/how-woodrow-wilsons-racist-segregation-order-eroded-the-black-civil-service/.

Franck, Julie. "Galloway, Abraham." *NCpedia*, State Library of North Carolina (SLNC), 2013. Revised by SLNC Government and Heritage Library, September 2022. https://www.ncpedia.org/biography/galloway-abraham.

Frank, John P. "The United States Supreme Court: 1946–47." *University of Chicago Law Review* 15, no. 1 (Autumn 1947): 1–50. https://www.repository.law.indiana.edu/facpub/1871.

Frankenberg, Erica, and Kendra Taylor. "ESEA and the Civil Rights Act: An Interbranch Approach to Furthering Desegregation." *RSF: The Russell Sage Foundation Journal of the Social Sciences* 1, no. 3 (December 2015): 32–49. Project MUSE. https://muse.jhu.edu/article/605399.

Franklin, John Hope. *The Free Negro in North Carolina, 1790–1860*. Chapel Hill: University of North Carolina Press, 1995.

"Freedom Rides." The Martin Luther King, Jr. Research and Education Institute, Stanford University. Accessed August 14, 2025. https://kinginstitute.stanford.edu/freedom-rides.

Gassiott, Kyle. "Civil Rights Icon Bruce Boynton Dies at 83." *All Things Considered*, NPR, November 24, 2020.

Gates, Henry Louis, Jr. "Was Jackie Robinson Court-Martialed?" PBS. Accessed August 14, 2025. https://www.pbs.org/wnet/african-americans-many-rivers-to-cross/history/was-jackie-robinson-court-martialed/.Originally posted on The Root.

George, Bernard. "The Legacy of St. Joseph's Church and School of New Bern." African American Heritage and Culture Center at St. Cyprian's Church, December 13, 2022. https://www.africanamericanheritageandculture.org/post/the-legacy-of-st-joseph-s-church-and-school-of-new-bern.

Gergel, Richard. *Unexampled Courage: The Blinding of Sgt. Isaac Woodard and the Awakening of America*. New York: Farrar, Straus and Giroux, 2019.

Gershenhorn, Jerry. "A Courageous Voice for Black Freedom: Louis Austin and the *Carolina Times* in Depression-Era North Carolina." *North Carolina Historical Review* 87, no. 1 (January 2010): 57–92. https://www.jstor.org/stable/23523683.

Gholson, A. W., Jr. "Constitutional Law—Public Utilities—Separate and Equal Accommodations in Motor Busses." *North Carolina Law Review* 8, no. 4 (1930): 455–57. http://scholarship.law.unc.edu/nclr/vol8/iss4/15.

Gilkes, Paul. "Gold Medal Bills Seeking Another Chance for Passage." Coin World, February 23, 2025. https://www.coinworld.com/news/us-coins/gold-medal-bills-seeking-another-chance-for-passage.

Gilmore, Glenda Elizabeth. *Defying Dixie: The Radical Roots of Civil Rights, 1919–1950*. New York: W. W. Norton, 2008.

Gilmore, Glenda Elizabeth. *Gender and Jim Crow: Women and the Politics of White Supremacy in North Carolina, 1896–1920*. Chapel Hill: University of North Carolina Press, 1996.

Girolimon, Mars. "Activist Joan Garner on Chronicling Her Family's Civil Rights Legacy." Southern New Hampshire University, November 2, 2023. https://www.snhu.edu/about-us/newsroom/community/activist-joan-garner-on-chronicling-her-familys-civil-rights-legacy.

Goldenberg, Richard. "African-American Troops Fought to Fight in World War I." U.S. Department of Defense, February 1, 2018. https://www.defense.gov/News/News-Stories/Article/Article/1429624/african-american-troops-fought-to-fight-in-world-war-i/.

"Great Thing, Says Victor in Bias Case: Ex-WAC Tells of Bus Episode." *New York Herald Tribune*, November 26, 1955.

Greenblatt, Alan. "The Racial History of the 'Grandfather Clause.'" *Code Switch*, NPR, October 22, 2013. https://www.npr.org/sections/codeswitch/2013/10/21/239081586/the-racial-history-of-the-grandfather-clause.

Greene, Jerry. "ICC Rule Puts Jim Crow off Trains, Buses." *New York Daily News*, November 26, 1955. Available on Newspapers by Ancestry.

Hand, Bill. "St. Joseph's—A New Bern 'First.'" *Sun Journal* (New Bern, NC), September 14, 2020. https://www.newbernsj.com/news/local/st-joseph-s-a-new-bern-first/article_31227ab6-6254-552a-af1b-7433a204ba01.html.

Harding, Archie Allen. "A Historical Account by Alumnus Archie Allen Harding: My Time. My Story." Elders Tell the Children, P. S. Jones Alumni Association. Accessed August 14, 2025. https://psjonesalumni.com/history.

Harris, Gloria G., and Hannah S. Cohen. *Women Trailblazers of California: Pioneers to the Present*. Charleston, SC: History Press, 2012.

Harris, Jennifer. "Barbara E. Pope (1854–1908)." *Legacy: A Journal of American Women Writers* 32, no. 2 (2015): 281–97. https://muse.jhu.edu/pub/17/article/605012/pdf.

Harris, Leslie M. *In the Shadow of Slavery: African Americans in New York City, 1626–1863*. Chicago: University of Chicago Press, 2003.

Harris, William C. "Black Codes." *NCpedia*, State Library of North Carolina, 2006. Accessed https://www.ncpedia.org/black-codes.

Harris, William C. "Caldwell, Tod Robinson." *NCpedia*, State Library of North Carolina, 1979. https://www.ncpedia.org/biography/caldwell-tod-robinson.

Harter, Allen Marcus. "Isaac Woodard: A Forgotten Story That Changed History." *Carolina News and Reporter*, February 19, 2019. https://carolinanewsandreporter.cic.sc.edu/isaac-woodard-a-forgotten-story-that-changed-history/.

Heggestad, Martin. "What Is Home Economics?" HEARTH—Home Economics Archive: Research, Tradition, History, Cornell University Library Digital Collections. Accessed August 24, 2025. https://digital.library.cornell.edu/collections/hearth/about.

Henry, Johnna Margot. "The 1961 Mississippi Freedom Riders' Mugshots: A Visual Intervention." *Panorama: Journal of the Association of Historians of American Art* 6, no. 1 (Spring 2020). https://doi.org/10.24926/24716839.9879.

Hewitt, John H. "The Search for Elizabeth Jennings, Heroine of a Sunday Afternoon in New York City." *New York History* 71, no. 4 (October 1990): 386–415.

Hill, Michael. "Journey of Reconciliation, 1947." *NCpedia*, State Library of New York, 2008. https://www.ncpedia.org/journey-reconciliation-1947.

Himmel, Charly. "NAACP Blasts Segregation in N.C. Schools." Courthouse News Service, September 1, 2015. https://www.courthousenews.com/naacp-blasts-segregation-in-n-c-schools/.

"Historical Marker B-59." North Carolina Highway Historical Marker Program, North Carolina Department of Cultural Resources. Accessed August 14, 2025. https://ncmarkers.com/Markers.aspx?MarkerId=B-59.

"History." City of Washington, North Carolina (website). Accessed August 14, 2025. https://www.washingtonnc.gov/residents/community_information/history.php.

"History of Home Economics." Home Economics and Household Management (Middlebury College student project website), January 29, 2016.https://sites.middlebury.edu/homeec/history-of-home-economics/.

Holm, Richard. "Library Holds Sarah Key Evans Program." *Daily Herald* (Roanoke Rapids, NC), February 19, 2020.

Holm, Richard. "Trailblazer Sarah Keys Evans Passes Away Thursday Morning." *Daily Herald (Roanoke Rapids, NC)*, updated December 25, 2023. https://www.rrdailyherald.com/news/local/trailblazer-sarah-keys-evans-passes-away-thursday-morning/article_9e6d5ab0-77d7-5b11-034-7b354425f23d.html.

Hoose, Phillip. *Claudette Colvin: Twice Toward Justice*. New York: Melanie Kroupa Books, 2009.

"Hotel Theresa." National Park Service. Accessed August 14, 2025. https://www.nps.gov/places/hotel-theresa.htm.

Houser, George, and Bayard Rustin. "We Challenged Jim Crow! A Report on the Journey of Reconciliation, April 9–23, 1947." Fellowship of Reconciliation—Congress of Racial Equality, 1947. Southern Sources: Exploring the Southern Historical Collection, UNC University Libraries. Accessed August 17, 2025. https://blogs.lib.unc.edu/shc/5168_jones_charles_001/.

Hudson, Caroline. "PS Jones Museum Honors Washington's Black History." *Washington (NC) Daily News*, October 27, 2017.

Hunt, James L. "Disfranchisement." *NCpedia*, State Library of North Carolina, 2006. https ://www.ncpedia.org/disfranchisement.

Hunt, James L. "Fusion of Republicans and Populists." *NCpedia*, State Library of North Carolina, 2006. https://www.ncpedia.org/fusion-republicans-and-populists.

Huston, Luther. "I.C.C. Orders End of Segregation on Trains, Buses." *New York Times*, November 26, 1955.

"ICC Ruling on Travel 'Frees' Brooklyn Girl." *New York Age Defender*, December 3, 1955.

"Interim Guidance: Get Your Mass Gatherings or Large Community Events Ready for Coronavirus Disease 2019 (COVID-19)." Centers for Disease Control and Prevention, March 15, 2020. https://stacks.cdc.gov/view/cdc/85893.

"Irene Morgan Kirkaldy (1917–2007)." Archives of Maryland (Biographical Series). Accessed August 14, 2025. https://msa.maryland.gov/megafile/msa/speccol/sc3500/sc3520/015200/015242/html/15242bio.html.

"Isadore I. Freidson, Retired ICC Law Judge." *Washington Post*, December 20, 1980. https://www.washingtonpost.com/archive/local/1980/12/20/isadore-i-freidson-retired-icc-law-judge/d13d1cd1-7094-4ba8-b018-7760ae1daa80/.

Itkin, Beth Kressel. "Creating 'What Might Have Been a Fuss': The Many Faces of Equal Public Rights in Reconstruction-Era Louisiana." *Louisiana History: The Journal of the Louisiana Historical Association* 56, no. 1 (Winter 2015): 42–74.

Jackson, Holly. "P. S. Jones Museum of African-American Education Opens in Washington." *Washington (NC) Daily News*, July 10, 2023.

Jacobs, Peter. "Take the Intentionally Confusing Reading Test That Was Given to Black Louisiana Voters in 1964." *Business Insider*, November 13, 2014. https://www.businessinsider.com/reading-test-given-to-black-louisiana-voters-in-1964-2014-11.

"Jeanes Teachers." Durham County Library. Accessed August 14, 2025. https://nccdigital.durhamcountylibrary.org/exhibits/durham-countys-rosenwald-schools-jeanes-teachers/jeanes-teachers.

"Jemison, Theodore Judson." Martin Luther King, Jr. Research and Education Institute, Stanford University. Accessed August 14, 2025. https://kinginstitute.stanford.edu/encyclopedia/jemison-theodore-judson.

Jenkins, Ruth. "Ex-WAC Recalls Historic Decision." *Dawn Magazine*, February 8, 1975.

"Jim Crow Laws: Tennessee, 1866–1955." *BlackPast*, January 3, 2011. https://www.blackpast.org/african-american-history/jim-crow-laws-tennessee-1866-1955/.

"Jo Ann Robinson: A Heroine of the Montgomery Bus Boycott." National Museum of African American History and Culture, Smithsonian Institution. Accessed August 14, 2025. https://nmaahc.si.edu/explore/stories/jo-ann-robinson-heroine-montgomery-bus-boycott.

Johnson, K. Todd. "Rosenwald Fund." *NCpedia*, State Library of North Carolina, 2006. https://www.ncpedia.org/rosenwald-fund.

Jones, Leesa. "Happy Birthday to a Hometown Hero." *Washington (NC) Daily News*, April 12, 2021.

Jones, Leesa. "A Local War Hero You Might Not Recognize." *Washington (NC) Daily News*, March 1, 2021.

Jones, Leesa. "The Underground Railroad Matriarch Earns Recognition." *Washington (NC) Daily News*, March 9, 2021.

Jones, Leesa. "Walking Tours Return Soon as Spring Beckons." *Washington (NC) Daily News*, March 17, 2021.

Jones, Leesa Payton. *Bright Ma: Day Clean—A Story About the Underground Railroad*. Washington, NC: Book Baby, 2020.

Jordan, Weymouth, Jr., and Gerald W. Thomas. "Massacre at Plymouth: April 20, 1864." *North Carolina Historical Review* 72, no. 2 (April 1995): 125–97.

"Judgment in Lola Houck Case, 1888." Records of Rights, National Archives. Accessed August 14, 2025. http://recordsofrights.org/records/44/judgment-in-lola-houck-case.

"Justice Stanley Reed." Justia: U.S. Supreme Court. Accessed August 14, 2025. https://supreme.justia.com/justices/stanley-reed/.

"Kate Brown Story, The." United States Senate. Accessed August 14, 2025. https://www.senate.gov/about/officers-staff/committee-office-staff/kate-brown-story.htm.

Keenan, Sister Michel. "Remembering Mother of Mercy School, Little Washington, North Carolina." Sisters, Servants of the Immaculate Heart of Mary, Scranton, PA, April 10, 2025. https://www.sistersofihm.org/2025/04/10/remembering-mother-of-mercy-school-little-washington-north-carolina/. Also published in *The Sisters, Servants of the Immaculate Heart of Mary, Scranton, Pennsylvania: 1919–1974*, Pittsburgh, PA: RoseDog Books, 2005.

Kelley, Blair LM. *Right to Ride: Streetcar Boycotts and African American Citizenship in the Era of "Plessy v. Ferguson."* Chapel Hill: University of North Carolina Press, 2010.

Kelley, Robin D. G. "'We Are Not What We Seem': Rethinking Black Working-Class Opposition in the Jim Crow South." *Journal of American History* 80, no. 1 (June 1993): 75–112.

Kelly, Jack. "The Rise and Fall of the Sleeping Car King." *Smithsonian Magazine*, January 11, 2019.

Knepler, Michael. "August 21, 1939: African Americans Arrested for Going to Public Library." Zinn Education Project. Accessed August 14, 2025. https://www.zinnedproject.org/news/tdih/alexandria-library-sit-in.

Korstad, Robert R., and James L. Leloudis. *To Right These Wrongs: The North Carolina Fund and the Battle to End Poverty and Inequality in 1960s America*. Chapel Hill: University of North Carolina Press, 2010.

Kousser, J. Morgan. *The Shaping of Southern Politics: Suffrage Restriction and the Establishment of the One-Party South, 1880–1910*. New Haven, CT: Yale University Press, 1974.

"Landmark: *Smith v. Allwright*." NAACP Legal Defense Fund. Accessed August 17, 2025. https://www.naacpldf.org/case-issue/landmark-smith-v-allwright/.

Lane, Charles. *The Day Freedom Died: The Colfax Massacre, the Supreme Court, and the Betrayal of Reconstruction*. New York: Henry Holt, 2008.

Legislative Papers, 1830–31. "Session of the General Assembly." *NCpedia*. State Library of NC. 2018. https://www.ncpedia.org/anchor/primary-source-bill-prevent.

Leland, John. "The 1963 March on Washington Changed America; Its Roots Were in Harlem." *New York Times*, August 26, 2023.

Leloudis, James. *Schooling the New South: Pedagogy, Self, and Society in North Carolina, 1880–1920*. Chapel Hill: University of North Carolina Press, 1996.

Leloudis, James L., and Robert R. Korstad. *Fragile Democracy: The Struggle over Race and Voting Rights in North Carolina*. Chapel Hill: University of North Carolina Press, 2020.

Lepore, Jill. *These Truths: A History of the United States*. New York: W. W. Norton, 2018.

Lerner, Max. "We Ride Together." *New York Post*, November 28, 1955.

"Letter from Frederick Douglass to John Marshall Harlan." *Brandeis and Harlan Watch* (blog), February 21, 2014. https://brandeiswatch.wordpress.com/2014/02/21/letter-from-frederick-douglass-to-john-marshall-harlan/.

Lewis, Danny. "The 1873 Colfax Massacre Crippled the Reconstruction Era." *Smithsonian Magazine*, April 13, 2016.

Lombroso, Linda. "Tale of a Hero Is Finally Told." *Journal News* (White Plains, NY), March 16, 2007.

"Louisiana Bars Change." *New York Times*, November 26, 1955.

Lovett, Bobby L., Linda T. Winn, and Caroline Eller. *Profiles of African Americans in Tennessee*. 2nd ed. Nashville: Annual Local Conference on Afro-American Culture and History, 2021.

Lowe, Turkiya. "Mary Ellen Pleasant (1814–1904)." BlackPast, January 30, 2007. http://www.blackpast.org/aaw/pleasant-mary-ellen-1814-1904.

Loy, Ursula Fogleman, and Pauline Marion Worthy, eds. *Washington and the Pamlico*. Washington, NC: Washington–Beaufort County Bicentennial Commission, 1976.

Luxenberg, Steve. "The Jim Crow Car: The North, the South and the Forgotten Origins of Racial Separation." *Washington Post Magazine*, February 20, 2019.

Luxenberg, Steve. *Separate: The Story of "Plessy v. Ferguson," and America's Journey from Slavery to Segregation*. New York: W. W. Norton, 2019.

MacLaury, Judson. "The Federal Government and Negro Workers Under President Woodrow Wilson." Paper delivered at the Annual Meeting of the Society for History in the Federal Government, Washington, DC, March 16, 2000. https://www.dol.gov/general/aboutdol/history/shfgpr00.

Mancini, Matthew J. "Convict Labor." *NCpedia*, State Library of North Carolina (SLNC), 2006. Revised by SLNC Government, and Heritage Library, January 2025. https://www.ncpedia.org/convict-labor.

Manumission Society of North Carolina. *An Address to the People of North Carolina, on the Evils of Slavery; By the Friends of Liberty and Equality*. Greensboro, NC: W. Swaim, 1830. https://docsouth.unc.edu/nc/manumiss/summary.html.

Marantos, Jeanette. "She Was the Rosa Parks of Her Day: So Why Was She in an Unmarked Grave for 129 Years?" *Los Angeles Times*, July 30, 2021.

"March on Washington for Jobs and Freedom." Martin Luther King, Jr. Research and Education Institute, Stanford University. Accessed August 14, 2025. https://kinginstitute.stanford.edu/march-washington-jobs-and-freedom.

Mariner, Cosmos. "African Americans Defend Washington." Historical Marker Database, February 27, 2018. Revised February 22, 2021. https://www.hmdb.org/m.asp?m=114466.

Mariner, Cosmos. "Hull Anderson." Historical Marker Database. Last revised March 6, 2025. https://www.hmdb.org/m.asp?m=224083.

Martin, Lance. "Bill Introduced Honoring Keys Evans with Congressional Gold Medal." *RRSpin*, November 15, 2021. https://rrspin.com/news/5078-bill-introduced-honoring-keys-evans-with-congressional-gold-medal.html.

Martin, Lance. "Committee Members Memorialize Keys at Plaza in Her Honor." *RRSpin*, November 30, 2023. https://www.rrspin.com/news/8170-committee-members-memorialize-keys-at-plaza-in-her-honor.html.

Martin, Lance. "Confederate Memorial to Be Removed from County Grounds." *RRSpin*, October 5, 2020. https://rrspin.com/news/3373-confederate-memorial-to-be-removed-from-county-grounds.html.

Martin, Lance. "Council Backs Location of Keys Art Project at MLK Park." *RRSpin*, April 17, 2019. https://www.rrspin.com/news/1079-council-backs-location-of-keys-art-project-at-mlk-park.html.

Martin, Lance. "Groups Support Push for Art Grant Honoring Sarah Keys." *RRSpin*, March 4, 2019. https://rrspin.com/news/901-groups-support-push-for-art-grant-honoring-sarah-keys.html.

Martin, Lance. "Highway Marker to Honor Enfield Native, Black Newspaper Publisher." *RRSpin*, December 20, 2018. https://www.rrspin.com/news/558-highway-marker-to-honor-enfield-native-black-newspaper-publisher.html.

Martin, Lance. "Keys-Evans Birthday Celebration Set at Plaza Honoring Her." *RRSpin*, April 14, 2021. https://www.rrspin.com/news/4169-keys-evans-birthday-celebration-set-at-plaza-honoring-her.html.

Martin, Lance. "Keys Plaza Committee Earns Governor's Medallion Award." *RRSpin*, April 22, 2022. https://www.rrspin.com/news/5826-keys-plaza-committee-earns-governor-s-medallion-award.html.

Martin, Lance. "Marker Honoring Keys Unveiled at Site Where She Was Arrested." *RRSpin*, January 15, 2022. https://www.rrspin.com/news/5345-marker-honoring-keys-unveiled-at-site-where-she-was-arrested.html.

Martin, Lance. "Saluting Sheer Bravery: Keys-Evans Honored." *RRSpin*, August 3, 2020. https://www.rrspin.com/news/3148-saluting-sheer-bravery-keys-evans-honored.html.

Martin, Lance. "Trailblazers Honored at Keys Evans Celebration." *RRSpin*, July 31, 2022. https://www.rrspin.com/news/6225-trailblazers-honored-at-keys-evans-celebration.html.

"Massachusetts Constitution of 1780." In *The Founders' Constitution*, vol. 5, doc. 6., edited by Philip B. Kurland and Ralph Lerner. Chicago: University of Chicago Press, 1986. https://press-pubs.uchicago.edu/founders/documents/bill_of_rightss6.html.

Massopust, Katherine. "Civil Rights Hero: Sarah Keys Evans." *Amboy Guardian*, March 3, 2017. https://www.amboyguardian.com/2017/03/03/civil-rights-hero-sarah-keys-evans.

Masur, Kate. *An Example for All the Land: Emancipation and the Struggle over Equality in Washington, D.C.* Chapel Hill: University of North Carolina Press, 2010.

Masur, Kate. "Winning the Right to Ride: How D.C.'s Streetcars Became an Early Battleground for Post-Emancipation Civil Rights." *Slate*, December 26, 2017. https://slate.com/human-interest/2017/12/black-activists-post-emancipation-battle-for-d-c-s-city-streetcars-one-of-the-first-civil-rights-victories-on-public-transportation.html.

Matthews, Steven, Jr. "What Is an HBCU? A Look at North Carolina's Historic Black Colleges and Universities." *News and Observer* (Raleigh, NC), updated August 18, 2023. https://www.newsobserver.com/news/local/education/article277662133.html.

Mazzocchi, Jay. "Roman Catholic Church." *NCpedia*, State Library of North Carolina (SLNC), 2006. Revised by SLNC Government and Heritage Library, November 2022. https://www.ncpedia.org/roman-catholic-church.

McBride, David. "Fourteenth Amendment Idealism: The New York State Civil Rights Law, 1873–1918." *New York History* 71, no. 2 (April 1990): 207–33.

McCabe, Katie. "She Had a Dream." *Washingtonian Magazine*, March 2002.

McCabe, Katie, and Dovey Johnson Roundtree. *Justice Older Than the Law: The Life of Dovey Johnson Roundtree*. Jackson: University of Mississippi Press, 2009.

McGregor, Susan E. "Sarah Keys Evans: Before the Boycott." *New York Amsterdam News*, December 7, 2005.

McLaughlin-Stonham, Hilary. *From Slavery to Civil Rights: On the Streetcars of New Orleans, 1830s–Present*. Liverpool: Liverpool University Press, 2020.

McWhorter, Diane. *A Dream of Freedom: The Civil Rights Movement from 1954 to 1968*. New York: Scholastic, 2004.

Medina, Eduardo. "A Civil Rights Pioneer Seeks to Have Her Record Cleared." *New York Times*, October 26, 2021.

Medley, Keith Weldon. *We as Freemen: Plessy v. Ferguson*. Gretna, LA: Pelican, 2003.

Medlin, Eric, and Alyssa Putt. "Rosenwald Schools in North Carolina." *NCpedia*, State Library of North Carolina, 2022. https://www.ncpedia.org/anchor/rosenwald-schools-north.

"Meet the Players: Freedom Riders." *American Experience*, PBS. Accessed August 14, 2025. https://www.pbs.org/wgbh/americanexperience/features/meet-players-freedom-riders/.

Meier, August, and Elliott Rudwick. *Along the Color Line: Explorations in the Black Experience*. Urbana: University of Illinois Press, 1976.

Meier, August, and Elliott Rudwick. "The Boycott Movement Against Jim Crow Streetcars in the South, 1900–1906." *Journal of American History* 55, no. 4 (March 1969): 756–75.

Meier, August, and Elliott Rudwick. *CORE: A Study in the Civil Rights Movement, 1942–1968*. New York: Oxford University Press, 1973.

Meier, August, and Elliott Rudwick. "Negro Boycotts of Segregated Streetcars in Virginia, 1904–1907." *Virginia Magazine of History and Biography* 81, no. 4 (October 1973): 479–87.

Melton, Christina. "We'll Keep Walking: The Baton Rouge Bus Boycott of 1953." *64 Parishes*, August 14, 2015. https://64parishes.org/baton-rouge-bus-boycott-of-1953.

Metrailer, Jamie. "Streetcar Segregation Act of 1903." *Encyclopedia of Arkansas*, updated August 23, 2023. https://encyclopediaofarkansas.net/entries/streetcar-segregation-act-of-1903-4346/.

Michals, Debra, ed. "Mary McLeod Bethune (1875–1955)." National Women's History Museum, 2015. https://www.womenshistory.org/education-resources/biographies/mary-mcleod-bethune.

Midgett, Ray. "Pamlico River's Past: Hull Anderson, Black Shipbuilder in 1800s Washington." *Washington (NC) Daily News*, February 21, 2013.

Midgett, Ray. "Pamlico's Past: The Burning of Washington." *Washington (NC) Daily News*, April 26, 2014.

Mikorenda, Jerry. *America's First Freedom Rider: Elizabeth Jennings, Chester A. Arthur, and the Early Fight for Civil Rights.* Guilford, CT: Lyons Press, 2020.

Miller, Mickey. "This Month in New Bern History—May 2020." New Bern Historical Society, May 19, 2020. https://newbernhistorical.org/this-month-in-new-bern-history-may-2020/.

Mills, Barbara. *"Got My Mind Set on Freedom": Maryland's Story of Black and White Activism, 1663–2000.* Bowie, MD: Heritage Books, 2007.

Milteer, Warren Eugene, Jr. *Beyond Slavery's Shadow: Free People of Color in the South.* Chapel Hill: University of North Carolina Press, 2021.

Milteer, Warren Eugene, Jr. *North Carolina's Free People of Color, 1715–1885.* Baton Rouge: Louisiana State University Press, 2020.

"Minutes of the Roanoke Rapids City Council." April 16, 2019. City Minutes Documents, Roanoke Rapids (NC). https://www.roanokerapidsnc.com/city-administration/city-minutes-documents.html?start=0.

Mitchell, Brian R., Barrington S. Edwards, and Nick Weldon. *Monumental: Oscar Dunn and His Radical Fight in Reconstruction Louisiana.* New Orleans: Historic New Orleans Collection, 2021.

"Montgomery Bus Boycott." Martin Luther King, Jr. Research and Education Institute, Stanford University. Accessed August 14, 2025. https://kinginstitute.stanford.edu/montgomery-bus-boycott.

"Mother of Mercy Catholic Church to Host Open House." *Washington (NC) Daily News*, March 26, 2019.

"Mother of Mercy Church to Celebrate Its History, Ties to Black Community." *Washington (NC) Daily News*, February 6, 2018.

Murray, Pauli. "Excerpt from Oral History Interview with Pauli Murray, February 13, 1976." Oral Histories of the American South. Accessed August 17, 2025. https://docsouth.unc.edu/sohp/G-0044/excerpts/excerpt_8639.html.

Murray, Pauli, ed. *States' Laws on Race and Color.* Athens: University of Georgia Press, 2016.

Nathan, Amy. *Count on Us: American Women in the Military.* Washington, DC: National Geographic Society, 2004.

Nathan, Amy. *Round and Round Together: Taking a Merry-Go-Round Ride into the Civil Rights Movement.* Philadelphia: Paul Dry Books, 2011.

Nathan, Amy. "Sarah Keys Evans." In *30 People Who Changed the World*, edited by Jean Reynolds, 49–52. Lake Forest, CA: Seagrass, 2017.

Nathan, Amy. *Take a Seat—Make a Stand: A Hero in the Family; The Story of Sarah Keys Evans, a Civil Rights Hero Who Would Not Be Moved.* Lincoln, NE: iUniverse, 2006.

Nathan, Amy. *Together: An Inspiring Response to the "Separate-but-Equal" Supreme Court Decision That Divided America*. 2nd ed. Philadelphia: Paul Dry Books, 2023.

Nathan, Amy, and Sarah Keys Evans. *Sarah Keys Evans: The Power of Quiet Courage*. Raleigh: North Carolina Office of Archives and History, 2025.

"Nathan Newbold 1871–1957 (H-127)." NC Department of Natural and Cultural Resources. Accessed November 21, 2025. https://www.dncr.nc.gov/blog/2024/06/27/nathan-newbold-1871-1957-h-127.

"N.C. Buses Must Carry Colored, Court Decides: Two-Year Fight Won by Interracial Commission; Common Carriers Separate but Equal Accommodations Ordered." *New Journal and Guide* (Norfolk, VA), February 22, 1930.

"New Bern." American Battlefield Trust. Accessed August 14, 2025. https://www.battlefields.org/learn/civil-war/battles/new-bern.

Nicholson, Lara. "Martha White, Who Helped Start the 1953 Baton Rouge Bus Boycotts, Dies at 99." *The Advocate*, June 7, 2021. https://www.theadvocate.com/baton_rouge/news/article_3d06587e-c7d6-11eb-ae53-d74c1e3811e9.html.

North Carolina General Assembly, "Slaves and Free Persons of Color. An Act Concerning Slaves and Free Persons of Color." North Carolina Revised Code No. 105, 1855. *Civil War Era NC*, accessed October 27, 2025, https://cwnc.omeka.chass.ncsu.edu/items/show/494.

"North Carolina's First Rosenwald School." NC Department of Natural and Cultural Resources (blog), October 8, 2016. https://www.dncr.nc.gov/blog/2016/10/08/north-carolinas-first-rosenwald-school.

Norwood, Arlisha R. "Maggie Lena Walker (1864–1934)." National Women's History Museum, 2017. https://www.womenshistory.org/education-resources/biographies/maggie-lena-walker.

Ortiz, Aimee. "Jackie Robinson: Hero on the Field and on the Battlefield." *Christian Science Monitor*, January 31, 2013.

Palmore, Joseph R. "The Not-So-Strange Career of Interstate Jim Crow: Race, Transportation, and the Dormant Commerce Clause, 1878–1946." *Virginia Law Review* 83, no. 8 (November 1997): 1773–1817.

Paschal, Richard A. *Jim Crow in North Carolina: The Legislative Program from 1865 to 1920*. Durham, NC: Carolina Academic Press, 2021.

Perkins, Kendric. "The Streetcar Protests of 1867." *First Draft* (blog), Historic New Orleans Collection, March 2, 2021. https://hnoc.org/publishing/first-draft/protests-politics-and-police-chase-fight-integrate-streetcars-1867.

"Pfc. Booker T. Spicely and the Dangers WWII Black Veterans Faced in Their Fight Against the Jim Crow South." Carolina K–12: Database of K–12 Resources, University of North Carolina at Chapel Hill. Accessed August 14,

2025. https://k12database.unc.edu/wp-content/uploads/sites/31/2023/09/BookerSpicelyLesson.pdf.

Pierce, Rodney D. "Marker Honoring Confederate General Should Be Removed." *RRSpin*, June 16, 2020. https://www.rrspin.com/opinion/2957-marker-honoring-confederate-general-should-be-removed.html.

Price, Jay. "In the Jim Crow Era, 'After-the-Fact Lynchings' Spread Racial Terror in Durham and Elsewhere." WUNC, September 24, 2018. https://www.wunc.org/military/2018-09-24/in-the-jim-crow-era-after-the-fact-lynchings-spread-racial-terror-in-durham-and-elsewhere.

Price, Jay. "A New Focus on the Women Who Helped End Discrimination on Interstate Buses." *Morning Edition*, NPR, November 17, 2021. https://www.npr.org/2021/11/17/1056397167/a-new-focus-on-the-women-who-helped-end-discrimination-on-interstate-buses.

"Prisoner Exchanges Halted—April 17, 1864." Richmond National Battlefield Park, National Park Service, updated November 30, 2023. https://www.nps.gov/rich/learn/historyculture/prisoner-exchanges-halted-april-17-1864.htm.

"Pullman Car Shops, The." Pullman National Historical Park, National Park Service. Updated January 8, 2023. https://www.nps.gov/pull/learn/historyculture/the-pullman-car-shops.htm.

Rabby, Glenda Alice. *The Pain and the Promise: The Struggle for Civil Rights in Tallahassee, Florida*. Athens: University of Georgia Press, 1999.

"Ram Albemarle." NC Department of Natural and Cultural Resources (blog), December 14, 2023. https://www.dncr.nc.gov/blog/2023/12/14/ram-albemarle-eee-1.

Raper, Horace W. "Holden, William Woods." *NCpedia*, State Library of North Carolina (SLNC), 1988. Revised by SLNC Government and Heritage Library, June 2023. Accessed August 17, 2025. https://www.ncpedia.org/biography/holden-william-woods.

"Rare Victory for Texas Woman, 1888, A." Records of Rights, National Archives. Accessed August 14, 2025. http://recordsofrights.org/events/57/a-rare-victory-for-texas-woman.

Rasmussen, Daniel. *American Uprising: The Untold Story of America's Largest Slave Revolt*. New York: Harper, 2011.

Rasmussen, Frederick N. "Edward Chance, 70, Civil Rights Activist Who Led 1963 Gwynn Oak Park Protest." *Baltimore Sun*, February 5, 2003.

Reaves, William M. *"Strength Through Struggle": The Chronological and Historical Record of the African-American Community in Wilmington, North Carolina, 1865–1950*. Edited by Beverly Tetterton. Wilmington, NC: New Hanover County Public Library, 1998.

"Reconstruction in North Carolina." ANCHOR, *NCpedia*, State Library of North Carolina, 2009. https://www.ncpedia.org/anchor/reconstruction-north.

Reid, Richard M. *Freedom for Themselves: North Carolina's Black Soldiers in the Civil War Era*. Chapel Hill: University of North Carolina Press, 2008.

"Rev. A. L. Davis; Founded Rights Unit with Dr. King in '57." *New York Times*, June 26, 1978.

"Revealing Experiment, A: Brown v. Board and 'the Doll Test.'" NAACP Legal Defense Fund. Accessed August 14, 2025. https://www.naacpldf.org/ldf-celebrates-60th-anniversary-brown-v-board-education/significance-doll-test/.

Rice, T. D. *Jim Crow, American: Selected Songs and Plays*. Edited by W. T. Lhamon. Cambridge, MA: Harvard University Press, 2009.

Richardson, Clem. "Like Parks, She Wouldn't Budge." *New York Daily News*, December 2, 2005. https://www.nydailynews.com/2005/12/02/like-parks-she-wouldnt-budge/.

"Richmond Streetcar Boycott, 1904." Shaping the Constitution: Resources from the Library of Virginia and the Library of Congress, Education @ Library of Virginia. Accessed August 14, 2025. https://edu.lva.virginia.gov/oc/stc/entries/richmond-streetcar-boycott-1904.

"Right of Colored People to Ride in the Street Cars Important Case, The." *New York Times*, June 30, 1864.

"Robert Kennedy Asks I.C.C. to End Bus Segregation." *New York Times*, May 30, 1961.

"Robert R. Taylor: First Black Student at MIT." MIT Black History, Massachusetts Institute of Technology. Accessed August 14, 2025. https://www.blackhistory.mit.edu/story/robert-r-taylor.

Rogers, Kim Lacy. *Righteous Lives: Narratives of the New Orleans Civil Rights Movement*. New York: New York University Press, 1993.

"Rosenwald Schools." State Historic Preservation Office, NC Natural and Cultural Resources. Accessed August 14, 2025. https://www.hpo.nc.gov/survey-and-national-register/rosenwald-schools.

Rothstein, Richard. *The Color of Law: A Forgotten History of How Our Government Segregated America*. New York: Liveright, 2017.

Roundtree, Dovey Johnson, and Katie McCabe. *Mighty Justice: My Life in Civil Rights*. Chapel Hill: Algonquin, 2019.

Roundtree, Dovey Johnson, and Katie McCabe. *Mighty Justice: The Untold Story of Civil Rights Trailblazer Dovey Johnson Roundtree*. Adapted by Jabari Asim. Young Readers' ed. New York: Roaring Brook, 2020.

Rowe, Jonathan. "Church Spotlights Long Heritage in Area." *Washington (NC) Daily News*, April 26, 2016.

"Ruling 'Means Nothing.'" *New York Times*, November 26, 1955.

Rumley, Vail Stewart. "Washington Native Ensures Leach Legacy." *Washington (NC) Daily News*, May 28, 2018.

"Safe Bus Company, The." North Carolina Transportation Museum. Accessed August 14, 2025. https://www.nctransportationmuseum.org/safe-bus-company/.

Salisbury, Stephan. "A Monument at Last for Octavius Catto, Who Changed Philadelphia." *Philadelphia Inquirer*, September 25, 2017.

"Sampling of Jim Crow Laws, A." ANCHOR, *NCpedia*, State Library of North Carolina, 2009. https://www.ncpedia.org/anchor/sampling-jim-crow-laws.

Sandifer, Alex, and Betty Dishong Renfer. "Schools for Freed Peoples." *Tarheel Junior Historian* 37, no. 1 (Fall 1997): 16–17. https://digital.ncdcr.gov/Documents/Detail/tar-heel-junior-historian-1997-fall-v.37-no.1/3700419?item=5368861.

Sarah Keys Evans Congressional Gold Medal Act. H.R. 5922, 117th Cong., introduced November 11, 2021. https://www.congress.gov/bill/117th-congress/house-bill/5922.

Sayblack, Philip. "College Named as Grant Recipient." *Daily Herald* (Roanoke Rapids, NC), June 6, 2019.

Schulz, Kathryn. "The Many Lives of Pauli Murray." *New Yorker*, April 10, 2017.

"Seek Ouster of Official Who Upheld Jim Crow." *JET*, October 14, 1954.

Seelye, Katharine Q. "Martha White, 99, Activist Who Sat in a 'White' Seat and Started a '53 Boycott." *New York Times*, June 17, 2021.

"Segregation by Design." Charlotte Urban Institute, May 3, 2023. https://ui.charlotte.edu/story/segregation-design/.

Sellars, Linda. "North Carolina Fund." *NCpedia*, State Library of North Carolina, 2006. https://www.ncpedia.org/north-carolina-fund.

"Sharecropping." Equal Justice Initiative, November 21, 2018. https://eji.org/news/history-racial-injustice-sharecropping/.

"Siege and Burning of Washington, April 1864, The." North Carolina Department of Natural and Cultural Resources (blog), April 30, 2016. https://www.dncr.nc.gov/blog/2016/04/30/siege-and-burning-washington-april-1864.

"Sign Magazine." *Passionist Historical Archives*. Accessed August 14, 2025. https://passionistarchives.org/category/publications/sign-magazine/.

Silva, Catherine. "Racial Restrictive Covenants History: Enforcing Neighborhood Segregation in Seattle." Seattle Civil Rights and Labor History Project, University of Washington, 2009. https://depts.washington.edu/civilr/covenants_report.htm.

Simpson, Bland. "Great Dismal Swamp." *NCpedia*, State Library of North Carolina (SLNC), 2006. Revised by SLNC Government and Heritage Library February 2022. https://www.ncpedia.org/great-dismal-swamp.

Smee, Matthew. "Take a Seat—Make a Stand: A Hero in the Family." Social Justice Books. Accessed August 17, 2025. https://socialjusticebooks.org/take-seat-make-stand-hero-family/?hilite=%27nathan%27.

Smith, C. Fraser. *Here Lies Jim Crow: Civil Rights in Maryland*. Baltimore: Johns Hopkins University Press, 2008.

Smith, Charles U., and Lewis M. Killian. *The Tallahassee Bus Protest*. New York: Anti-Defamation League of B'Nai Brith, 1958.

Smith, Harrison. "Bruce Carver Boynton, Who Helped Spark Freedom Rides, Dies at 83." *Washington Post*, November 26, 2020.

Smith, Sonia. "One Hundred Years of Greyhound." *Texas Monthly*, August 11, 2014.

"Southern Manifesto and 'Massive Resistance' to *Brown v. Board of Education*, The." NAACP Legal Defense Fund. Accessed August 14, 2025. https://www.naacpldf.org/brown-vs-board/southern-manifesto-massive-resistance-brown/.

Spangler, Ian. "The Rosenwald Schools: A Story of How Black Communities Across the American South Took Education into Their Own Hands." National Trust for Historic Preservation. Accessed August 14, 2025. https://www.arcgis.com/apps/Cascade/index.html?appid=7541c163fb20486598969c7acb559663.

Spurr, Kim Weaver. "Prison Camps and the Western North Carolina Railroad." UNC College of Arts and Sciences, October 10, 2022. https://college.unc.edu/2022/10/railroad-old-fort.

"State Historical Marker 'The Irene Morgan Story Begins' to Be Dedicated in Gloucester Co." Virginia Department of Historic Resources, January 28, 2020. https://www.dhr.virginia.gov/press_releases/state-historical-marker-the-irene-morgan-story-begins-to-be-dedicated-in-gloucester-co/.

Stewart, Alison. *First Class: The Legacy of Dunbar, America's First Black Public High School*. Chicago: Lawrence Hill Books, 2013.

Stitt, Chanel. "Learn About the Detroiter Who Fought for Black People to Ride the Boblo Boats." *Detroit Free Press*, July 26, 2020.

Stitt, Chanel. "She Was Kicked Off a Boblo Boat for Being Black. Now Her Home Is a Historic Site." *Detroit Free Press*, June 3, 2021.

Stoesen, Alexander R. "Greensboro Sit-Ins." *NCpedia*, State Library of North Carolina, 2006. https://www.ncpedia.org/greensboro-sit-ins.

Strauss, Valerie. "A New Story of School Segregation in North Carolina: A Private White-Flight Academy Is Turning Charter." *Washington Post*, March 11, 2019.

"Student Nonviolent Coordinating Committee (SNCC)." Martin Luther King, Jr. Research and Education Institute, Stanford University. Accessed August 14, 2025. https://kinginstitute.stanford.edu/student-nonviolent-coordinating-committee-sncc

Sturkey, William. "The Laws in Context." On the Books: Jim Crow and Algorithms of Resistance, UNC University Libraries. Accessed August 14, 2025. https://onthebooks.lib.unc.edu/laws/the-laws-in-context/.

"Supreme Court of the United States, Justices 1789 to Present." Supreme Court of the United States. Accessed August 28, 2025. https://www.supremecourt.gov/about/members_text.aspx.

Tabb, Kip. "For Some, Pamlico River Was Part of Underground Railroad." *Coastal Review*, February 22, 2022. https://coastalreview.org/2022/02/for-some-pamlico-river-was-part-of-underground-railroad/.

Tabor, Nick. "Dunbar High School." *Britannica*, October 11, 2023. https://www.britannica.com/topic/Dunbar-High-School-Washington-D-C.

"Tallahassee Bus Boycott 1956–57, The." Florida Memory: State Library and Archives of Florida. Accessed November 21, 2025. https://www.floridamemory.com/items/show/340068.

Taylor, David A. "The Rosa Parks of D.C." *Washington Post Magazine*, March 31, 2021.

Terry, Marshall. "When Cars Ran on Rails; Charlotte's Streetcar Past." WFAE, January 26, 2015. https://www.wfae.org/npr-arts-life/2015-01-26/when-cars-ran-on-rails-charlottes-streetcar-past.

Tester, Brandon. "Juneteenth Celebration Coming Soon." *Washington (NC) Daily News*, June 1, 2021.

Tester, Brandon. "A Walk Through History." *Washington (NC) Daily News*, May 18, 2021.

Thaggert, Miriam. *Riding Jane Crow: African American Women on the American Railroad*. Urbana: University of Illinois Press, 2022.

Theoharis, Jeanne. *The Rebellious Life of Mrs. Rosa Parks*. Boston: Beacon, 2013.

Thomas, Christopher. "Former Slaves Turned Soldiers in Historic Siege of Washington." Public Radio for Eastern North Carolina, May 1, 2017. https://www.publicradioeast.org/pre-news/2017-05-01/former-slaves-turned-soldiers-in-historic-seige-of-washington.

"Thomas Day Website Timeline." Historicsites.nc.gov. https://historicsites.nc.gov/all-sites/thomas-day-state-historic-site-future-site/history/timeline.

Thompson, Charles. "Plessy v. Ferguson: Harlan's Great Dissent." *Kentucky Humanities*, no. 1 (1996). https://louisville.edu/law/library/special-collections/the-john-marshall-harlan-collection/harlans-great-dissent.

Tippett, Rebecca. "Majority of NC-Born Adults Still Live Here." Carolina Demography, University of North Carolina at Chapel Hill, August 11, 2014. https://carolinademography.cpc.unc.edu/2014/08/11/majority-of-nc-born-adults-still-live-here/.

"To Fight Anti-Boycott Law." *New York Times*, October 20, 1903.

Tousignant, Marylou. "Book of the Week: Take a Seat—Make a Stand." *Washington Post*, February 10, 2008.

Towns, Edolphus. "A Tribute to Sarah Keys Evans." Speech in the US House of Representatives. *Congressional Record* 152, no. 30 (March 9, 2006) at E323 (Extensions of Remarks).

"Transportation Is for All." San Francisco Municipal Transportation Agency (SFMTA), February 11, 2020. https://www.sfmta.com/blog/transportation-all.

Tygiel, Jules. "The Court-Martial of Jackie Robinson." *American Heritage Magazine*, August/September 1984.

Umfleet, LeRae Sikes. *A Day of Blood: The 1898 Wilmington Race Riot*. Rev. ed. Raleigh: North Carolina Office of Archives and History, 2020.

Vaden, Ted. "The Case for Forced School Merger in Halifax County." *News and Observer*, updated October 11, 2015. https://www.newsobserver.com/opinion/op-ed/article38463999.html.

Vocci, Robert Blair. "Republican Party." *NCpedia*, State Library of North Carolina (SLNC), 2006. Revised by SLNC Government and Heritage Library, March 2022. https://www.ncpedia.org/republican-party.

Volk, Kyle G. *Moral Minorities and the Making of American Democracy*. New York: Oxford University Press, 2014.

Wadelington, Flora Hatley. "Segregation in the 1920s." *Tar Heel Junior Historian* 43, no. 2 (Spring 2004): 8–9. https://digital.ncdcr.gov/Documents/Detail/tar-heel-junior-historian-2004-spring-v.43-no.2/3700438?item=5369338.

Walsh, Margaret. "Tracing the Hound: The Minnesota Roots of the Greyhound Bus Corporation." *Minnesota History*, Winter 1985, 310–21.

Warner, James E. "Segregation's End on Buses, Trains Ordered by I.C.C." *New York Herald Tribune*, November 25, 1955.

Washington, Booker T. "An Address Before the National Educational Association" at Tuskegee Industrial School, Tuskegee, Alabama, July 11, 1900. Teaching American History. Accessed July 29, 2025. https://teachingamericanhistory.org/document/an-address-before-the-national-educational-association/.

Washington, Booker T. *Up from Slavery*. New York: Doubleday, Page, 1901.

"Washington High School." Beaufort County Schools, NC. Accessed August 14, 2025. https://whs.beaufort.k12.nc.us/.

"Washington Native Who Refused to Give Up Bus Seat Could Receive Congressional Gold Medal." WMBF *News*, November 11, 2021. https://www.wmbfnews.com/2021/11/11/washington-native-who-refused-give-up-bus-seat-could-receive-congressional-gold-medal/.

"Washington Waterfront Underground Railroad Museum." Visit North Carolina. Accessed August 20, 2025. https://www.visitnc.com/listing/72dc/washington-waterfront-underground-railroad-museum.

Waters, Rodney. "A Hero in the Family: Sarah Made History." *Catholic Review*, April 24, 2007.

Waxman, Olivia B. "Years Before Rosa Parks, Sarah Keys Refused to Give Up Her Seat on a Bus. Now She's Being Honored in the City Where She Was Arrested." *Time*, July 29, 2020.

Weise, Elizabeth. "'Not Out of the Woods': CDC Says Large Gatherings Are a High COVID-19 Risk, 'Strongly Encourages' Face Masks." *USA Today*, June 12, 2020.

Welke, Barbara Y. "When All the Women Were White, and All the Blacks Were Men: Gender, Class, Race, and the Road to *Plessy*, 1855–1914." *Law and History Review* 13, no. 2 (Autumn 1995): 261–316.

"'What Are We Fighting For?' Mary McLeod Bethune's Fight for Racial Equality in the Women's Army Corps." Roosevelt Institute for American Studies. Accessed August 14, 2025. https://www.roosevelt.nl/en/library/from-the-vaults/what-are-we-fighting-for-mary-mcleod-bethunes-fight-for-racial-equality-in-the-womens-army-corps/.

"Why Black Men Fought in World War I, 1919." History Resources, Gilder Lehrman Institute of American History. Accessed August 14, 2025. https://www.gilderlehrman.org/history-resources/spotlight-primary-source/why-black-men-fought-world-war-i-1919.

Wiegand, Wayne A., and Shirley A. Wiegand. *The Desegregation of Public Libraries in the Jim Crow South: Civil Rights and Local Activism*. Baton Rouge: Louisiana State University Press, 2018.

Williard, David C. "North Carolina in the Civil War." *NCpedia*, State Library of North Carolina, 2010. https://www.ncpedia.org/history/cw-1900/civil-war.

"Wilmington Coup, The." ANCHOR, *NCpedia*, State Library of North Carolina, 2009. https://www.ncpedia.org/anchor/wilmington-coup.

Wilson, Christopher. "The Moment When Four Students Sat Down to Take a Stand." *Smithsonian Magazine*, January 31, 2020.

Wiltz, Allison. "How Sharecropping Robbed Black Americans of Generational Wealth." *Medium* (AfroSapiophile), December 15, 2023. https://medium.com/afrosapiophile/how-sharecropping-robbed-black-americans-of-generational-wealth-cc143398264c.

"Winner Acclaims Decision by I.C.C." *New York Times*, November 27, 1955.

Wood, Sandra L., Linda Camp Keith, Drew Noble Lanier, and Ayo Ogundele. "The Supreme Court, 1888–1940: An Empirical Overview." *Social Science History* 22, no. 2 (Summer 1998): 201–24.

Wooten, Alan. "With Recounts Done, Pierce Can Prepare to Join General Assembly." *Center Square*, March 30, 2024. https://www.thecentersquare.com/north_carolina/article_3426e86e-eafa-11ee-9172-870b6d928cc6.html.

Wormser, Richard, and Bill Jersey, dirs. "Charlotte Hawkins Brown (1870–1924)." *The Rise and Fall of Jim Crow* (People), PBS Thirteen. Accessed August 14, 2025. https://www.thirteen.org/wnet/jimcrow/stories_people_brown.html.

Wormser, Richard, and Bill Jersey, dirs. "Ida B. Wells (1862–1931)." *The Rise and Fall of Jim Crow* (People), PBS Thirteen. Accessed August 14, 2025. https://www.thirteen.org/wnet/jimcrow/stories_people_wells.html.

Wormser, Richard, and Bill Jersey, dirs. "Wilmington Riot (1898)." Jim Crow Stories, *The Rise and Fall of Jim Crow* (Events), PBS Thirteen. Accessed August 14, 2025. https://www.thirteen.org/wnet/jimcrow/stories_events_riot.html.

Wynes, Charles E. *Race Relations in Virginia, 1870–1902*. Charlottesville: University of Virginia Press, 1961.

Wynn, Linda T. "Nashville's Streetcar Boycott (1905–1907)." In *Profiles of African Americans in Tennessee*, edited by Bobby L. Lovett and Linda T. Wynn, 87–99. Nashville, TN: Annual Local Conference on Afro-American Culture and History, 1996. https://ww2.tnstate.edu/library/digital/nashv.htm.

Yawn, Andrew J. "Seven Women Who Helped Change the Nation Through Freedom Rides." *Tennessean*, August 26, 2021. https://www.tennessean.com/story/news/american-south/2021/08/26/freedom-rides-7-women-who-helped-change-nation-civil-rights/5504845001/.

Zipf, Karin Lorene. "Sharecropping." *NCpedia*, State Library of North Carolina, 2006. https://www.ncpedia.org/sharecropping.

Z. Smith Reynolds Foundation. "Inclusive Public Art Initiative." Accessed August 14, 2025. https://zsr.org/grant/inclusive-public-art-initiative/.

Zucchino, David. *Wilmington's Lie: The Murderous Coup of 1898 and the Rise of White Supremacy*. New York: Atlantic Monthly Press, 2020.

Index

Note: Page numbers in *italics* refer to figures.

www.ingramcontent.com/pod-product-compliance
Lightning Source LLC
LaVergne TN
LVHW091112080826
845145LV00008B/1881